Elemer

Language Practice

with key

Michael Vince

with Kevin McNicholas

English Grammar and
Vocabulary

MACMILLAN

Macmillan Education
Between Towns Road, Oxford OX4 3PP
A division of Macmillan Publishers Limited
Companies and representatives throughout the world

ISBN 1 405 00763 X without key
ISBN 1 405 00764 8 with key

Text © Michael Vince 2003
Design and illustration © Macmillan Publishers Limited 2003

First published 1999
This edition published 2003

Designed by Mike Brain Graphic Design Limited
Layout and composition by eMC Design
Cover design by Oliver Design

Illustrated by:
Kathy Baxendale pp 45, 55, 62, 63, 89; eMC Design pp 124, 125;
Ruth Galloway pp 11, 13, 15, 31, 47, 58, 59, 61, 102, 115;
Julian Mosedale pp 46, 86, 94, 100, 185, 203, 208, 237, 241, 247;
Val Saunders pp 214, 216, 218, 222, 226, 232, 236, 239, 240;
Martin Shovel pp 18, 33, 39, 53, 72, 73, 74, 106, 133, 173, 178, 212;
Kingsley Wiggin pp 93, 99, 101, 107, 169, 224, 228, 230, 235.

Photographs by:
Eyewire, Photodisc and Andrew Oliver.

The author would like to thank the many schools and teachers
who have commented on these materials. Also special thanks
to Kevin McNicholas and Sarah Curtis.

Printed and bound in Italy by
G. Canale and C.S.p. A Borgaro T.se, Turin

2007 2006 2005 2004 2003
10 9 8 7 6 5 4 3 2 1

Contents

Grammar

Grammar 1	Present simple of *be*	8
Grammar 2	Present simple: affirmative; Frequency adverbs	10
Grammar 3	Present simple: negative and questions	12
Grammar 4	Present continuous: affirmative	14
Grammar 5	Present continuous: negative and questions	16
Grammar 6	Present continuous and present simple	18
Grammar 7	CONSOLIDATION 1	20
Grammar 8	Past simple: regular affirmative	22
Grammar 9	Past simple: regular negative and questions	24
Grammar 10	Past simple: irregular affirmative	26
Grammar 11	Past simple: irregular negative and questions	28
Grammar 12	Past simple of *be*	30
Grammar 13	Past continuous: affirmative, negative and questions	32
Grammar 14	CONSOLIDATION 2	34
Grammar 15	Past continuous and past simple	36
Grammar 16	Past habits: *used to*	38
Grammar 17	Present perfect: affirmative	42
Grammar 18	Present perfect: negative and questions	44
Grammar 19	Present perfect and past simple	46
Grammar 20	Present perfect and past simple: time expressions	48
Grammar 21	CONSOLIDATION 3	50

Grammar 22	Future plans and predictions	52
Grammar 23	Predictions: certainty and uncertainty	56
Grammar 24	Meetings, promises, decisions, refusing	58
Grammar 25	*will* and *going to*: problems	60
Grammar 26	Present continuous: future use	62
Grammar 27	Future time words: more contrasts	64
Grammar 28	CONSOLIDATION 4	66
Grammar 29	Conditional 1	68
Grammar 30	Conditional 2	70
Grammar 31	Conditionals 1 and 2	72
Grammar 32	Short answers	76
Grammar 33	*Wh-* questions; Subject and object questions	78
Grammar 34	Tag questions	80
Grammar 35	CONSOLIDATION 5	82
Grammar 36	Modals of ability and possibility	84
Grammar 37	Modals of obligation	86
Grammar 38	Modals of negative obligation	88
Grammar 39	Modals: past	90
Grammar 40	Modals: possibility, uncertainty, impossibility, certainty	92
Grammar 41	Modals: problems and contrasts	94
Grammar 42	CONSOLIDATION 6	96
Grammar 43	Plural nouns	98
Grammar 44	Countable and uncountable nouns: *a, an, some, any*	100
Grammar 45	Countable and uncountable nouns: problems	102

Grammar 46	Countable and uncountable nouns: *much, many*	104
Grammar 47	Countable and uncountable nouns: *much, many, enough*	106
Grammar 48	Numbers: cardinal, ordinal, fractions and decimals	110
Grammar 49	CONSOLIDATION 7	112
Grammar 50	Advice, agreeing/disagreeing, apologizing	114
Grammar 51	Descriptions, directions, excuses, greetings	116
Grammar 52	Asking for information, invitations, offers, permission	118
Grammar 53	Preferences, promises, reminders, requesting, suggesting, warning	120
Grammar 54	Calendar	122
Grammar 55	Time	124
Grammar 56	CONSOLIDATION 8	126
Grammar 57	Prepositions of place and position	128
Grammar 58	Prepositions and adverbials of place and position	132
Grammar 59	Articles 1	136
Grammar 60	Articles 2	138
Grammar 61	Pronouns 1	140
Grammar 62	Pronouns 2	142
Grammar 63	CONSOLIDATION 9	144
Grammar 64	Reported speech; Past perfect	146
Grammar 65	Passive 1	148
Grammar 66	Passive 2: agent	150
Grammar 67	Imperatives	152
Grammar 68	Gerunds	154
Grammar 69	Contractions	156

Grammar 70	CONSOLIDATION 10	158
Grammar 71	Possession 1	160
Grammar 72	Possession 2: apostrophe, *of*	162
Grammar 73	Adjectives, nationalities	164
Grammar 74	Order of adjectives; Problem adjectives	166
Grammar 75	Making comparisons 1: comparative adjectives	168
Grammar 76	Making comparisons 2: superlative adjectives	172
Grammar 77	CONSOLIDATION 11	174
Grammar 78	Adverbs: formation and position, irregular adverbs	176
Grammar 79	Subjects	178
Grammar 80	Problem verbs	180
Grammar 81	Problem verbs: phrasal verbs	182
Grammar 82	Verbs with prepositions, gerund or infinitive	184
Grammar 83	*Be* with adjectives and prepositions	188
Grammar 84	CONSOLIDATION 12	190
Grammar 85	Punctuation	192
Grammar 86	Spelling: rules, problems	196
Grammar 87	Same pronunciation, different spelling	198
Grammar 88	British and American spelling	200
Grammar 89	Prefixes, suffixes, phrasal verbs, compound words	202
Grammar 90	CONSOLIDATION 13	206

Vocabulary

Vocabulary 1	Personal details	210
Vocabulary 2	Family matters	212
Vocabulary 3	Free time	214
Vocabulary 4	Rooms	216
Vocabulary 5	Places	218
Vocabulary 6	Jobs	220
Vocabulary 7	Inside the house	222
Vocabulary 8	Food and drink	224
Vocabulary 9	Animals	226
Vocabulary 10	Clothes	228
Vocabulary 11	Weather	230
Vocabulary 12	The body	232
Vocabulary 13	Staying healthy	234
Vocabulary 14	The world around us	236
Vocabulary 15	Transport	238
Vocabulary 16	Useful things	240
Vocabulary 17	Other countries	242
Vocabulary 18	In the classroom	244
Vocabulary 19	Going out	246
Vocabulary 20	Shopping around	248
	Formation rules	250
	Irregular verbs	252
	Grammar index	254
	Grammar answers	257
	Vocabulary answers	283

Present simple of *be*

Explanations

Statements

I am	*he is*	*we are*
I'm	*he's*	*we're*
you are	*she is*	*they are*
you're	*she's*	*they're*
	it is	
	it's	

Negatives

I am not	*he is not*	*we are not*
I'm not	*he isn't*	*we aren't*
you are not	*she is not*	*they are not*
you aren't	*she isn't*	*they aren't*
	it is not	
	it isn't	

Yes/No **Questions**

Am I...?	*Is he...?*	*Is it...?*	*Are they...?*
Are you...?	*Is she...?*	*Are we...?*	

Examples

■ with ages
  *Carlos **is** fifteen.*   *Anna **is** fourteen.*

■ with nationality words
  *I'**m** Spanish.*   *She's Turkish.*

■ with jobs
  *Jim **is** a teacher.*   ***Are** you a student?*

■ with an adjective
  *You'**re** right.*   *I'**m** happy.*   *It's easy.*

■ with *this/that*
  *This **is** my bike.*   ***Is** that your seat?*

■ in questions
  ***Is** Jim here?*   ***Are** you fifteen?*   ***Are** they American?*
  ***Is** this your book?*   ***Is** it difficult?*

 SEE ALSO

Grammar 69: Contractions

Practice

1 **Put *am, is,* or *are* in each space.**

a) This .... *is* .... my family.

b) These .... my parents.

c) Lucy .... English.

d) We .... in the garden.

e) This .... her pen.

f) Maria and Anna .... students.

g) My dog .... happy.

h) I .... happy.

2 **Change the sentences into negative sentences.**

a) It's hot today. ..... *It isn't hot today.* ....

b) I'm at home. ....

c) My friends are here. ....

d) You're a teacher. ....

e) We're at the cinema. ....

f) This is difficult. ....

g) Katy is happy. ....

3 **Change the statements into questions.**

a) I'm late. ..... *Am I late?* ....

b) You're ill. ....

c) We're right. ....

d) He's fifteen. ....

e) It's cold. ....

f) The school is in this street. ....

g) My books are in your bag. ....

4 **Choose the most suitable answer to each question.**

a) What's your name?   1 No, I'm Brazilian.

b) Are you Portuguese?   2 I'm fifteen.

c) Are you at school?   3 My name is Carlos.

d) How old are you?   4 No, it's easy.

e) Is English difficult?   5 Yes, I'm a student.

Present simple: affirmative
Frequency adverbs

Explanations

Statements

We use the present simple to describe general facts, repeated actions and habits, things that are always true.

- general facts

  *I **like** milk.*   *They **speak** Turkish.*

  *Maria **plays** basketball.*   *We **live** in Australia.*

- repeated actions and habits

  *Harry often **arrives** late.*   *I usually **get up** at 7.30.*

  *I **walk** to school every day. My brother usually **walks** with me.*

- things that are always true

  *The sun **rises** in the east.*   *The earth **goes** round the sun.*

I walk	*we walk*
you walk	*they walk*
*BUT he walk**s***	*she walk**s*** *it walk**s***

Spelling

go	$\longrightarrow$	*goes*
miss	$\longrightarrow$	*misses*
watch	$\longrightarrow$	*watches*
wash	$\longrightarrow$	*washes*
relax	$\longrightarrow$	*relaxes*

always, usually, often, sometimes, never

always	*100%*	*Tim **always** wears jeans.*
usually	*80%*	*I **usually** go to bed at 9.30.*
often	*60%*	*Sue **often** goes to the cinema.*
sometimes	*40%*	*Sam **sometimes** walks to school.*
never	*0%*	*It **never** rains here in August.*

- The frequency adverb goes between subject and verb.

  *Monday **always** comes after Sunday.*

Practice

1 **Look at the pictures. Complete each sentence with a verb from the box.**

| arrive | ~~like~~ | live | rain | start | teach |

a) David ......*likes*...... chocolate.

b) It .... here in November.

c) Liz .... with her family in Italy.

d) George often .... late.

e) The lesson .... at 6.00.

f) Kate and Jim .... English in Spain.

2 **<u>Underline</u> the correct word in each sentence.**

a) Juan and Carmen <u>*live*</u>/*lives* in Madrid.

b) Harry *watch*/*watches* television every evening.

c) I usually *go*/*goes* to school by bus.

d) It never *snow*/*snows* in this city.

e) Sam *live*/*lives* in that house.

f) You never *clean*/*cleans* your teeth!

g) Carol *get*/*gets* up early every day.

h) All the buses *leave*/*leaves* from this bus-stop.

3 **Complete each sentence. Use the verb and frequency adverb in brackets.**

a) Tina (sometimes, miss) .....*sometimes misses*..... the bus to school.

b) I (never, get up) .... before 6.00.

c) We (usually, have) .... a holiday in August.

d) Jim and Helen (often, go) .... to the theatre.

e) I (often, sing) .... in the shower.

f) Pat (sometimes, play) .... football on Sunday.

g) You (never, finish) .... your homework!

h) Our teacher (always, wear) .... a tie.

Present simple: negative and questions

Explanations

Negatives

I **don't like** ice-cream.   She **doesn't eat** chocolate.

I do not walk.	He does not walk.	We do not walk.
I don't walk.	He doesn't walk.	We don't walk.
You do not walk.	She does not walk.	They do not walk.
You don't walk.	She doesn't walk.	They don't walk.
	It does not walk.	
	It doesn't walk.	

Examples

I **don't drink** coffee.   They **don't speak** Italian.
Tom **doesn't play** tennis.   We **don't live** in France.

Questions

Do you walk to school or **do you take** the bus?
I usually walk.

Do I walk?	Does he walk?	Do we walk?
Do you walk?	Does she walk?	Do they walk?
	Does it walk?	

Examples

Do you like ice-cream?   **Do they speak** Italian?
Does Ana play basketball?   **Do you live** in Australia?
Does Harry often **arrive** late?   **Do you** usually **get up** at 7.30?

Careful!

I walk, you walk, we walk	BUT	he walk<u>s</u>, she walk<u>s</u>, it walk<u>s</u>
He walk<u>s</u>.		Do<u>es</u> he walk?
I don't walk.	BUT	He do<u>es</u>n't walk. She do<u>es</u>n't walk.

Practice

1 **Complete each sentence. Put the words in brackets into the correct order.**

a) Our (smoke, not, teachers, do) ...... *teachers do not smoke* ...... at school.

b) Where (Helen, live, does) .... ?

c) (do, not, go, we) .... to the cinema on Friday.

d) (David, does, ride) .... a bike?

e) (play, do, you) .... football after school?

f) Kate (like, does, not) .... oranges.

g) I (lunch, usually, have) .... at 1.30.

2 **Complete each sentence. Use the words in brackets.**

a) Mary (like, not) .... *does not like* .... baseball.

b) (wash, Peter) .... his face every morning?

c) (watch, you) .... television every day?

d) I (eat, not, often) .... fruit.

e) (have, we) .... homework today?

f) My friends (live, not) .... near my house.

3 **Look at the pictures. Write a question or a negative sentence.**

Jack   Alice and Mike

a) Jack – get up at 7.00 ...... *Does Jack get up at 7.00* .... ?

b) Alice and Mike – walk to work .... ?

c) Jack – leave home at 8.00 .... ?

d) Alice and Mike – relax in the evening .... ?

e) Alice and Mike – not/like tennis ...... *Alice and Mike don't like tennis.* ......

f) Jack – not/wear school uniform ....

g) Alice and Mike – not/use computers ....

h) Jack – not/do his homework ....

Present continuous: affirmative

Explanations

We use the present continuous to talk about actions happening at the moment.

Statements

*I **am sitting** in my car. She's **watching** television.*

I am waiting.	*He is waiting.*	*We are waiting.*
I'm waiting.	*He's waiting.*	*We're waiting.*
You are waiting.	*She is waiting.*	*They are waiting.*
You're waiting.	*She's waiting.*	*They're waiting.*
	It is waiting.	
	It's waiting.	

Examples

*I'm **studying** English.*
*My brother's **talking** on the telephone now.*
*We're **swimming** in the sea.*
*Sue's **reading** a book at the moment.*

Spelling

Verbs with two vowels and ending in one consonant, add -*ing*.

wait   ⟶   *wait**ing***

Verbs ending in *e*, drop *e* and add -*ing*.

make   ⟶   *mak**ing***
decide   ⟶   *decid**ing***
write   ⟶   *writ**ing***

Verbs ending with one vowel and one consonant, double the consonant.

sit   ⟶   *sit**ting***
swim   ⟶   *swim**ming***
cut   ⟶   *cut**ting***

Verbs ending *ie*, change *ie* to *y*.

lie   ⟶   *l**y**ing*
tie   ⟶   *t**y**ing*
die   ⟶   *d**y**ing*

Verbs ending in a vowel and *y*, add -*ing*.

stay   ⟶   *stay**ing***
play   ⟶   *play**ing***
say   ⟶   *say**ing***

Practice

1 **Look at the pictures and write sentences.**

a) I/eat .... *I'm eating.* ....   b) They/listen ....

c) She/come ....   d) You/move ....

e) It/rain ....   f) We/sing ....

2 **Complete this letter. Put the verbs in brackets into the present continuous.**

Dear Jim,

We (1) (have) .... *are having* ..... a terrible holiday.

It (2) (rain) .... I (3) (sit) .... in the

hotel. I (4) (watch) .... television. Tom and Peter

(5) (play) .... computer games.

Alice (6) (read) .... a book. Susan (7) (make) ....

a cup of coffee. The baby (8) (cry) .... I want to go home.

All the best,

George

Present continuous: negative and questions

Explanations

Negatives

*I**'m not walking** to school today.*

I am not waiting. *I'm not waiting.* *You are not waiting.* *You aren't waiting.* *(You're not...)*	*He is not waiting.* *He isn't waiting.* *(He's not...)* *She is not waiting.* *She isn't waiting.* *(She's not...)* *It isn't waiting.* *It is not waiting.* *(It's not waiting.)*	*We are not waiting.* *We aren't waiting.* *(We're not...)* *They are not waiting.* *They aren't waiting.* *(They're not...)*

Examples

*I**'m not drinking** milk, I'm drinking cola.*
*They are**n't playing** football. They're playing rugby.*

Questions

***Are you walking** to school today?*

Am I waiting? *Are you waiting?*	*Is he waiting?* *Is she waiting?* *Is it waiting?*	*Are we waiting?* *Are they waiting?*

Examples

*What **are you doing?***   ***Are you reading?***
*I**'m fixing** my bike.*   *No, I**'m not reading**.*

Careful!

*With **I, you, he, she, it, they** and **we**, it is better to use the contractions in statements and negatives.*

Practice

1 **Change the statements into questions.**

a) I'm making a lot of noise.   *Am I making a lot of noise?*

b) Clare is reading.   ....

c) You are watching the news.   ....

d) It is snowing.   ....

e) We are waiting in the right place.   ....

f) You are sitting here.   ....

g) David is enjoying the film.   ....

h) The bus is stopping.   ....

2 **Change the statements into negative sentences.**

a) You're listening to me.   *You aren't listening to me.*

b) Tim is studying.   ....

c) We're talking.   ....

d) You are writing.   ....

e) Katherine is lying.   ....

f) They are waiting for us.   ....

g) Anna's having a good time.   ....

h) I'm reading at the moment.   ....

3 **Correct each sentence or question.**

a) I playing tennis with my best friend.
        I'm playing tennis with my best friend.

b) You're coming to the cinema tonight?
        ....

c) John and Mandy don't going to the beach.
        ....

d) Is Emma and Katy flying to America?
        ....

e) My sister is walk on the beach now.
        ....

f) We not studying French at school this year.
        ....

g) What's that noise? The dog is outside?
        ....

h) I aren't watching the TV. Turn it off.
        ....

i) Fred are eating a sandwich for his lunch.
        ....

j) Are waiting they for a bus?
        ....

Present continuous and present simple

Explanations

Present continuous

To talk about things happening at the moment, use the present continuous.

> *Jim **is watching** television at the moment.*

Present simple

To talk about habits and routines use the present simple.

- Things we do often, every day, every week, etc.
- Things that always happen.

> *I **arrive** at school at 8.30.*
> *The first lesson **starts** at 8.45.*
> *The lesson **finishes** at 9.30.*

Jim is watching TV.

Careful!

> *Joe **lives** in New York. New York is his home. He lives there all the time.*
> *We **are living** near the station at the moment. We want to move to another house soon.*

- Verbs usually used with the present simple:

cost	*This bike costs £200.*
like	*Anna likes rap music.*
know	*Do you know the answer?*
understand	*I don't understand this.*
believe	*Do you believe me?*

- Some verbs have one meaning in the simple form, but a different meaning in the continuous form.

  > ***Do you have** a bike?* = Do you own a bike?   (in general)
  > ***I'm having** a great time!* = It's a great party!   (at the moment)

  > ***I think** this film is great!* = I like this film a lot.   (in general)
  > *Quiet! **I'm thinking**.* = I'm doing a difficult exercise.   (at the moment)

Practice

1 **Choose the most suitable sentence or question.**

a) 1 I wash my hair.

2 I'm washing my hair. ✔

b) 1 Do you know the answer?

2 Are you knowing the answer?

c) 1 Do you wait for the school bus? You're in the wrong place!

2 Are you waiting for the school bus? You're in the wrong place!

d) 1 That bike costs £350.

2 That bike is costing £350.

e) 1 Do you understand?

2 Are you understanding?

f) 1 I do my homework.

2 I'm doing my homework.

2 **Complete each sentence. Use the words in brackets. Use present simple or present continuous.**

a) Richard (always, get up) ....*always gets up*.............. before 7.00.

b) Hurry up! The bus (wait) .... for us!

c) Where (we, go) .... ? This is the wrong road!

d) My friends (not believe) .... my story.

e) Please be quiet! I (read) .... a very interesting book.

f) (like, Susan) .... horror films?

3 **Choose the most suitable word or phrase for each space.**

a) 'Someone ..*B*.. for you outside.' 'Who is it?'

A) waits   B) is waiting   C) waiting

b) 'What ..... of this book?' 'I think it's fantastic!'

A) do you think   B) is you think   C) you do think

c) ..... in ghosts?

A) Are you believe   B) Are you believing   C) Do you believe

d) Kate is busy. She ..... for a test.

A) is study   B) is studying   C) is studies

e) ..... a great time at the moment!

A) We are have   B) We're have   C) We're having

f) Tina usually ..... at 7.00.

A) get up   B) is getting up   C) gets up

Consolidation 1

1 **Correct each sentence or question.**

a) I doesn't likes this film. .... *don't like* ....

b) What do you wants? ....

c) Jim walk sometimes to school. ....

d) When the lesson begins? ....

e) I don't gets up early on Saturdays. ....

f) Tina not like computer games. ....

g) Figen watchs television every night. ....

2 **Put one word in each space. Contractions are one word.**

a) What ....*do*....... you usually eat for lunch?

b) George and Terry .... speak Portuguese. They speak English.

c) It's 9.30 and the children .... sitting at their desks.

d) Ken .... like tea. In fact, he hates it.

e) When it rains, ... you take an umbrella?

f) What .... it say on the board? I can't see from here.

3 **Choose the most suitable word or phrase for each space.**

a) What time ...*C*... to bed?

A) usually do you go   B) do usually you go   C) do you usually go

b) Every day, Frank ..... to work.

A) goes   B) is going   C) go

c) Stop it! ..... it!

A) I'm not liking   B) I don't like   C) I not like

d) What ..... ? Is it an orange?

A) you are eating   B) are you eating   C) do you eat

e) Yumiko feels ill, so she ..... basketball.

A) doesn't play   B) isn't play   C) isn't playing

f) Pay attention, Philip! ..... ?

A) Do you listen   B) Is it listening   C) Are you listening

g) Excuse me. ..... to Manchester?

A) This road goes   B) Does this road go   C) Is this road go

4 **Change each sentence. Use the words in brackets.**

   a) Jo goes to school by bus. (usually) *Jo usually goes to school by bus.*

   b) I'm working hard. (not) ....

   c) Sara likes sport. (not) ....

   d) I get up at 6.30. (always) ....

   e) We speak German. (not) ....

   f) Pierre goes to the beach. (often) ....

   g) George drinks beer. (never) ....

   h) We're having a good time. (not) ....

5 **Present simple or present continuous? Change the verb if it is wrong.**

   a) Are you having a motorbike?
   Do you have a motorbike? ....

   b) I'm staying in a hotel near the sea.
   ....

   c) I'd like to buy this coat. How much is it costing?
   ....

   d) What you doing?
   ....

   e) I'm usually getting up at 6.00.
   ....

   f) This book is difficult. I'm not understanding it.
   ....

   g) I watch a lot of TV every night.
   ....

   h) Excuse me. Are you knowing the way to the museum?
   ....

Think about grammar! Are the sentences true or false?

   a) When you talk about a habit or a routine, you use the present simple.

   b) The present continuous is for actions that do not finish.

   c) When the subject of the sentence is *he, she* or *it*, add -s or -es.

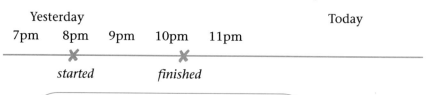

Past simple: regular affirmative

Explanations

- We use the past simple to describe finished events in the past.

Yesterday   Today

7pm   8pm   9pm   10pm   11pm

        ✗   ✗

      started   *finished*

> *Yesterday I **watched** a great film on TV.*
> *It **started** at 8pm and **finished** at 10.15pm.*

- Regular verbs | *watch + ed   start + ed* |

Statements

*John **played** football last week.*
*My grandparents **moved** to Scotland last year.*

I started	he started	we started
you started	she started	they started
	it started	

Examples

*The bus **arrived** at 9.30.*
*In 1998 I **decided** to move to Australia.*
*Kate **stayed** in Turkey last summer.*
*Yesterday I **walked** to school.*

Spelling

fit	⟶	fit**ted**
stop	⟶	stop**ped**
cry	⟶	cr**ied**
try	⟶	tr**ied**

Careful!

Two syllable verbs with the stress on the first syllable do NOT double the final consonant.

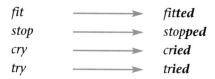

| ad<u>mit</u> | ⟶ | admi<u>tted</u> |
| <u>an</u>swer | ⟶ | answer<u>ed</u> |

Other regular verbs

answer	listen	start
arrive	live	stop
decide	marry	turn
like	open	watch

Task

Make your own list of regular verbs.

Elem. Lang Practice M Vince Macmillan

Practice

1 **Change the verbs in brackets into the past simple.**

My day yesterday

a) My mother (call) .... *called* .... me at 7.00.

b) I (wash) .... and (dress) .... very quickly.

c) I (walk) .... to school.

d) After school I (watch) .... television.

e) Then I (play) .... basketball with my friends.

f) At 8.30 we (finish) .... the game.

g) Before bedtime I (telephone) .... my friend.

2 **Complete the paragraph in the past simple. Use verbs from the box.**

~~arrive~~	continue	finish	listen	play	start	talk	work

My first day at school

I remember my first day at school in 1995! I (1) ..*arrived*.. at 8.30 and

(2) .... lessons at 9.00. We (3) .... from 9.00 to 12.00. The

teachers (4) .... to us a lot! Then we (5) .... football for an hour.

In the afternoon we (6) .... the lessons and (7) .... to the teacher

carefully. Then at 3.30 the lessons (8) .... It was a long and tiring day!

3 **Change the sentences into past simple sentences.**

a) Tom looks out of the window.

   .... *Tom looked out of the window.* ....

b) We arrive at 6.30.

   ....

c) Laura watches television all afternoon.

   ....

d) The bus stops at the end of the street.

   ....

e) I visit an old castle this week.

   ....

f) Sue waits for her friends for more than an hour.

   ....

g) They decide to come to my party.

   ....

Past simple: regular negative and questions

Explanations

Negatives

*I did**n't start** learning English last year. I started this year.*

I did not start *I didn't start*	*he did not start* *he didn't start*	*we did not start* *we didn't start*
you did not start *you didn't start*	*she did not start* *she didn't start*	*they did not start* *they didn't start*
	it did not start *it didn't start*	

Yes/No Questions

***Did** you **start** learning English last year?*

Did I start? *Did you start?*	*Did he start?* *Did she start?* *Did it start?*	*Did we start?* *Did they start?*

Wh- questions

*When **did** you **start** learning English?*
*When **did** you **finish** your homework?*

Examples

***Did** they **arrive** yesterday? No, they **didn't arrive** yesterday.*
*They **arrived** on Monday.*

***Did** you **finish** your homework? No, I **didn't finish** my homework.*
It was very difficult.

*When **did** you **start** school? I **started** school in 1993.*

Careful!

The order of the words is different in questions and statements.

Practice

1 **Change the sentences into negative sentences.**

a) Our bus arrived on time.
   Our bus didn't arrive on time.

b) Sue phoned last night.

c) Maria finished work early yesterday.

d) The train stopped at Harry's station.

e) I wanted to go to bed early.

f) Carlos answered my letter.

g) John invited lots of people to his party.

h) The shops opened on Sunday.

i) Peter liked his new shoes.

2 **Change the statements into questions.**

a) Tim arrived at 2.00.
   Did Tim arrive at 2.00?

b) Sam phoned home.

c) Helen wanted to make a phone call.

d) Paul visited the doctor.

e) Bill missed the bus.

f) George walked to school.

g) Jim opened the window.

h) Emma helped the teacher.

i) Alice washed her hair.

10 Past simple: irregular affirmative

Explanations

Irregular verbs do not have *-ed* endings for the past simple. Each verb has its own form and we have to learn these forms.

go	⟶	*went*	*eat*	⟶	*ate*
come	⟶	*came*	*do*	⟶	*did*
have	⟶	*had*	*get*	⟶	*got*
take	⟶	*took*	*bring*	⟶	*brought*

Statements

*Last week we **went** to the cinema.*
*Pedro **ate** 10 cakes yesterday.*

<u>go</u>	<u>eat</u>
I went	I ate
you went	you ate
he went	he ate
she went	she ate
it went	it ate
we went	we ate
they went	they ate

Examples

*Yesterday I **drank** Japanese beer.*
*Harry always **came** late.*
*We **made** dinner last night.*

Task

Complete the list. Use the words from the box.

sent	got	did	knew	began	flew	brought	took	went	had
came	told	gave	stood	met	made	found	wore	drank	ran

<u>Verb</u>	<u>Past simple</u>	<u>Verb</u>	<u>Past simple</u>
begin	*began*	have	....
bring	....	know	....
come	....	make	....
do	....	meet	....
drink	....	run	....
find	....	send	....
fly	....	stand	....
get	....	take	....
give	....	tell	....
go	....	wear	....

Now check your answers. Look at the list of irregular verbs on page 252.

Practice

1 **Change the verbs in brackets into the past simple.**

a) The last lesson (begin) ......*began*............... at 2.30.

b) Joe (feel) .... ill after lunch.

c) Suddenly a bird (fly) .... in the window!

d) I think you (do) .... the wrong thing.

e) Jane (get) .... ready very quickly.

f) We (know) .... the answer.

g) The students (stand) .... up when the teacher arrived.

h) It was cold, but I (wear) .... two pullovers.

i) Anna (eat) .... two plates of spaghetti.

j) Rick (tell) .... us the time.

2 **Choose the correct words to complete this article about Sally Green.**

A day in the life of Sally Green

Yesterday was a normal day for Sally Green, the writer. She (1) .C. up at 6.00.
She (2) ..... to the bathroom, and then she (3) ..... her clothes. After that she
(4) ..... breakfast and (5) ..... the newspaper. Then she (6) ..... her bed. From 7.00 to
10.00 she (7) ..... in the living-room and (8) ..... television. Then she (9) .....
shopping. At 1.00 she (10) ..... home and (11) ..... her lunch. After lunch she
(12) ..... work. She (13) ..... from 2.00 to 9.00. She (14) ..... a lot of tea. Then she
(15) ..... her friends at a nightclub.

1)	**A** get	**B** gets	**C** got
2)	**A** went	**B** goed	**C** goes
3)	**A** put on	**B** putted on	**C** puts on
4)	**A** eat	**B** have	**C** ate
5)	**A** read	**B** saw	**C** readed
6)	**A** made	**B** make	**C** making
7)	**A** sat	**B** sit	**C** was
8)	**A** watches	**B** watched	**C** wached
9)	**A** does	**B** went	**C** did
10)	**A** comed	**B** come	**C** came
11)	**A** has	**B** had	**C** have
12)	**A** begin	**B** beginned	**C** began
13)	**A** writes	**B** write	**C** wrote
14)	**A** drinks	**B** drunk	**C** drank
15)	**A** meets	**B** met	**C** meet

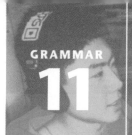

Past simple: irregular negative and questions

Explanations

Negatives

go   ⟶   *went*

eat   ⟶   *ate*

We **didn't go** to school last week.

Katy **didn't eat** an ice-cream yesterday.

I did not go	*he did not go*	*we did not go*
I didn't go	*he didn't go*	*we didn't go*
you did not go	*she did not go*	*they did not go*
you didn't go	*she didn't go*	*they didn't go*
	it did not go	
	it didn't go	

Examples

They **didn't give** Jack a present.

I **didn't have** breakfast.

Questions

Did you **go** to the cinema last night?

Did I go?	*Did he go?*	*Did we go?*
Did you go?	*Did she go?*	*Did they go?*
	Did it go?	

Examples

Did you **send** me a letter last week?

Where **did** you **go** yesterday?

What **did** you **do**?

Careful!

When **did** is in a question, the main verb is not in the past.

Practice

1 **Read the answers. Write a question for each answer.**

a) *Did Nick fly to the USA?* .... Yes, Nick flew to the USA.

b) .... Yes, Ana went to Italy.

c) .... Yes, Jack found the money.

d) .... Yes, Helen knew the answer.

e) .... Yes, Alex gave Sue a present.

f) .... Yes, Pat brought the flowers.

g) .... Yes, Kate sent Mike a letter.

h) .... Yes, Alan made the cake.

i) .... Yes, Tina wore a hat.

j) .... Yes, Rick felt ill.

2 **Change the statements into negative sentences.**

a) Tom and Anna had breakfast. *Tom and Anna didn't have breakfast.*

b) Mike took the bus. ....

c) Maria and Carlos did the homework. ....

....

d) Catherine got a prize. ....

e) Peter knew the teacher. ....

f) Sam went to university. ....

g) Paula ate a sandwich. ....

h) Murat and Soraya ran fast. ....

i) Joe made mistakes. ....

j) Carla came early. ....

3 **Change the verbs in brackets into the past simple.**

a) When (you, come) *did you come* to this country?

b) Jack (not, wear) .... his raincoat.

c) Pat (leave) .... his coat in the hall.

d) How many pages (you, write) .... ?

e) What (the teacher, say) .... ?

f) (you, not, tell) .... us your name.

g) (you, go) .... to the basketball match yesterday?

h) Ann (not, know) .... the other girl's name.

i) Which books (you, take) .... to school?

j) (Jane, not, get) .... any letters.

29

Past simple of *be*

Explanations

Statements

*At 8.00 last night I **was** at home.*

I was	*he was*	*we were*
you were	*she was*	*they were*
	it was	

Examples

*Dave and Sue **were** at the cinema last night.*
*It **was** very cold yesterday.*
*I **was** ill last week.*

Negatives

*I **wasn't** here yesterday.*

I was not	*he was not*	*we were not*
I wasn't	*he wasn't*	*we weren't*
you were not	*she was not*	*they were not*
you weren't	*she wasn't*	*they weren't*
	it was not	
	it wasn't	

Examples

*Kate **wasn't** happy at work last year.*
*We **weren't** at home last night.*
*I **was** late yesterday.*

Questions

***Was** it cold yesterday?*

Was I?	*Was he?*	*Were we?*
Were you?	*Was she?*	*Were they?*
	Was it?	

***Were** you at home at 6.00 last night?*
***Was** Harry in London yesterday?*
***Were** you at school on Tuesday?*

Careful!

*When the main verb is **be**, do not use **did**.*

Practice

1 Look at the pictures and complete the questions and answers.

at the cinema

at work

at home

at school

a) .... *Was Helen* .... at home yesterday?

Helen .... *wasn't at home* .... She .... *was at the cinema* ....

b) .... at school yesterday?

Yannis and Emma ....

They ....

c) .... at home yesterday?

Nick .... He ....

d) .... at the cinema yesterday?

Liz and Jane ....

They ....

2 Use the prompts to make questions and negative sentences.

a) Jim/at home/last night ..... *Was Jim at home last night* .... ?

b) you/at school/on Monday .... ?

c) the cinema/open/on Sunday .... ?

d) all your friends/at your party .... ?

e) Kevin and Mel/at my party ..... *Kevin and Mel weren't at my party* .... .

f) Nick/in class yesterday ....

g) It/warm yesterday ....

h) We/at the match yesterday ....

31

Past continuous: affirmative, negative and questions

Explanations

We use the past continuous to describe a continuing situation in the past. We often interrupt a continuing situation with a sudden event.

6.30pm	7pm	7.30pm	8pm	8.30pm

having a bath   phone rang   Now

*Nadia phoned me at 7.30. I **was having** a bath.*

Statements

*Last month I **was working** in Brazil.*

I was sitting.	*He was sitting.*	*We were sitting.*
You were sitting.	*She was sitting.*	*They were sitting.*
	It was sitting.	

Negatives

*The teacher **was talking**, but Harry **wasn't listening**.*

was not = wasn't   were not = weren't

I wasn't sitting.	*He wasn't sitting.*	*We weren't sitting.*
You weren't sitting.	*She wasn't sitting.*	*They weren't sitting.*
	It wasn't sitting.	

Yes/No Questions

***Were** they **working** in the office?*

Was I sitting?	*Was he sitting?*	*Were we sitting?*
Were you sitting?	*Was she sitting?*	*Were they sitting?*
	Was it sitting?	

Wh- questions

*What **were** you **doing** at 6.00?   Who **was** he **talking** to?*

Examples

*Steve **was eating** in the restaurant when the fire started.*
*Carmen **wasn't teaching** in 1990, she **was studying**.*
***Were** you **eating** dinner when I phoned?*

Practice

1 Look at the picture of a classroom at 2.00 yesterday. Complete each sentence about it using a verb from the box.

| play football | read a book | listen to music | write on the board |
| draw pictures | look out of the window | | |

a) Anna *was reading a book* ....

b) Paula and Jim ....

c) Tim ....

d) Kate and Bill ....

e) Sam ....

f) Ed and Lisa ....

2 Correct each sentence.

a) Anna was drawing pictures. ...... *Anna wasn't drawing pictures.* ......

b) Paula and Jim were looking out of the window. ....

c) Tim was reading a book. ....

d) Kate and Bill were writing on the board. ....

e) Sam was playing football. ....

f) Ed and Lisa were listening to music. ....

3 Use the prompts to make questions.

a) Tim/draw pictures ...... *Was Tim drawing pictures?* ....

b) Kate and Bill/look out of the window ....

c) Ed and Lisa/read a book ....

d) Paula and Jim/write on the board ....

e) Anna/play football ....

f) Sam/listen to music ....

1 **Change the verbs in brackets into the past simple.**

a) Tom (look) ....*looked*.............. out of the window.

b) We (take) .... the bus from the airport to the city centre.

c) Laura (read) .... the book all afternoon.

d) Kate (close) .... all the windows and doors.

e) An old friend (come) .... to see me yesterday.

f) I (see) .... an interesting film last week.

2 **Choose the most suitable answer (1–7) for each question (a–g).**

a) What were you doing when you saw the accident? ....4........

b) Did you go to Italy last summer? ....

c) What did you do last weekend? ....

d) What did you do when you saw the two men? ....

e) Did you go to school yesterday? ....

f) Did you have a good time at the party? ....

g) When did you find the money? ....

1 Yes, I really enjoyed myself.

2 I called the police.

3 Yes, I spent three weeks there.

4 I was standing at the bus-stop.

5 While I was cleaning the floor.

6 I met my friends, and spent time with my family.

7 No, I was ill. I stayed at home.

3 **Rewrite each sentence using a negative form of a verb from the box. Do not change the meaning.**

close	forget	get up	like	~~miss~~	sit down	go out	win

a) David caught the train. ....*David didn't miss the train.*..........

b) Cristina remembered her book. ....

c) They stayed at home. ....

d) John opened the door. ....

e) Terry stayed in bed. ....

f) Karen hated Chinese food. ....

g) Chris's team lost the match. ....

h) I stood up on the bus all the way home. ....

4 **Correct each sentence or question.**

a) Where did you went last night? ...... *Where did you go last night?* ......

b) I didn't knew the answer. ....

c) Harry maked a lot of noise. ....

d) I didn't liked my new teacher. ....

e) Took you your medicine? ....

f) Helen comed home late last night. ....

g) I didn't got up early this morning. ....

h) What did you saw at the cinema? ....

5 **Read the answers. Write a question for each answer.**

a) Were ...... *you working last night?* ....

Last night? No, I wasn't working last night.

b) Was ....

Yes, that's right. Tim was waiting at the bus-stop.

c) Was ....

No, Mary wasn't talking.

d) Was ....

Yes, that's right. Kate was wearing jeans.

e) Were ....

Yes, Ali and Mehmet were playing football.

f) Was ....

Raining? Yes, it was.

6 **Change the verbs in brackets into the past continuous.**

a) (you, play) ...... *Were you playing* .... tennis with Paolo yesterday?

b) (Mary, have) .... lunch at 1 o'clock.

c) (we, watch) .... basketball all day.

d) Who (you, dance) .... with at the party last night?

e) (Some of the boys, look) .... out of the window.

f) (I, walk) .... home in the rain.

Think about grammar! Are the sentences true or false?

a) When actions in the past are completed, use the past simple.

b) When actions in the past are not completed, use the past continuous.

c) *Did* is for negative sentences only.

Past continuous and past simple

Explanations

We often contrast a continuing situation with a sudden event.

Statements

*I **was writing** a letter when Paul **phoned**.*
(continuing situation)   (sudden event)

6.20pm	7pm	7.30pm	8pm	8.30pm

writing a letter   telephone rang   Now

*I **started** the letter at 7.00.*
*Paul **phoned** at 8.00.*

*I **was writing** a letter when Paul **phoned**.*
*While I **was writing** a letter, Paul **phoned**.*

*While I **was waiting** for the bus, I **saw** the accident.*
(continuing situation)   (sudden event)

10am	11am

waiting   saw accident

I started waiting for the bus at 10.00.
I saw the accident at 10.30.
*I **saw** the accident when I **was waiting** for the bus.*

*I **saw** the accident while I **was waiting** for the bus.*
*I **was waiting** for the bus when I **saw** the accident.*
*When I **saw** the accident, I **was waiting** for the bus.*

Questions

*What **were you doing** when I phoned?*
*I **was writing** a letter when you **phoned**.*

*When **did you see** the accident?*
*I **saw** the accident while I **was waiting** for the bus.*

- You can use **when** with both past simple and continuous, but **while** is only used with the continuous.

Practice

1 Underline the correct verb form in each sentence.

a) While I _was doing_ /did my homework, I had a good idea.

b) Jim _was breaking/broke_ his leg when he was playing golf.

c) When I arrived, I _was going/went_ into the kitchen.

d) We _were finding/found_ an old box while we were digging in the garden.

e) I _was seeing/saw_ an old friend while I was waiting for the train.

f) While I _had/was having_ a bath, the phone rang.

2 Complete each sentence. Use the verbs in brackets. Use past simple or past continuous.

a) Chris (eat) .... _ate_ .... spaghetti every day last week.

b) When I (come) .... into the room, two boys
   (play) .... football.

c) Peter (turn on) .... the TV, but nothing
   (happen) ....

d) While we (run) .... in the park, Mary
   (fall over) ....

e) While I (listen) .... to music, I (hear) ....
   the doorbell.

f) I (break) .... my pen while I (do) .... my
   homework.

3 Read the paragraph. Choose the most suitable word for each space.

Last week my friend Sandy and I (1) .A. to go to the beach on the bus. While we
(2) ..... for the bus, it suddenly (3) ..... to rain. We (4) ..... summer clothes, and we
(5) ..... an umbrella. While we (6) ..... there in the rain, Sandy's mother (7) .....
past, so we (8) ..... to her. Luckily, she (9) ..... us, and (10) ..... us home in the car.

1)	A decided	B was deciding	C were deciding
2)	A were waiting	B waiting	C was waiting
3)	A start	B was starting	C started
4)	A was wearing	B wore	C were wearing
5)	A weren't having	B had	C didn't have
6)	A stood	B were standing	C standed
7)	A drived	B driving	C drove
8)	A were waving	B waved	C was waving
9)	A noticing	B noticed	C didn't notice
10)	A took	B take	C taked

Past habits: *used to*

Explanations

We use *used to* when we describe a state or habit in the past.

Statements

*I **used to play** tennis.*

| *I used to play* | *he used to play* | *we used to play, etc.* |

Negatives

*Sheila **didn't use to play** basketball.*

| *I didn't use to play* | *she didn't use to play* | *we didn't use to play, etc.* |

Questions

***Did** they **use to play** football?*

| *Did he use to play?* | *Did you use to play?* | *Did they use to play? etc.* |

■ We often use *used to* to contrast a past habit with what we do now.
   *I **used to have** a motorbike when I was younger.* (past state)
   *I **used to drink** coffee, but now I drink tea.* (past habit)

■ There is no present form of *used to*.
   *I **used to work** in London, but now I work in Manchester.*

■ The past simple is also possible in these examples, but *used to* is more common.
   *I **had** a motorbike when I was younger.*
   *I **played** tennis, but now I play football.*

Practice

1 **Look at the pictures and complete the sentences.**

The past / Now
a) David

The past / Now
b) Anna

The past / Now
c) Nick

The past / Now
d) Kate

The past / Now
e) Carol

The past / Now
f) Jack

a) like ice-cream/hate it *David used to like ice-cream, but now he hates it.*

b) live in the country/in the city ....

c) walk to school/ride a bike ....

d) get up late/early ....

e) have short hair/long hair ....

f) be short/tall ....

2 Look at the table below. Write sentences about the past. Use *used to* and *didn't use to*.

	200 years ago
ride horses	✔
drive cars	✗
read books	✔
go to the cinema	✗
wash their clothes by hand	✔
watch TV	✗
look after animals	✔
use computers	✗

Two hundred years ago ...

a) people (ride) .... *used to ride* .... horses.

b) they (drive) .... cars.

c) they (read) .... books.

d) they (go to) .... the cinema.

e) they (wash) .... their clothes by hand.

f) they (watch) .... TV.

g) they (look after) .... animals.

h) they (use) .... computers.

3 Make statements, negatives or questions with *used to*.

a) Susan/have/a dog? (question)

.... *Did Susan use to have a dog?* ....

b) people/use/mobile phones (negative)

....

c) he/go/swimming (statement)

....

d) they/like/jazz music? (question)

....

e) Ewa's family/live/in Moscow (statement)

....

f) we/drink/coffee (negative)

....

g) my sister/watch/television (negative)

....

h) Tony/work/in a bank? (question)

....

4 **Rewrite each sentence or question with *used to*. Do not change the meaning.**

a) I was in the school tennis team.

   I used to be in the school tennis team.

b) Sophie had long hair when she was at school.

   ....

c) Mary didn't listen when her teachers were speaking.

   ....

d) Ricardo got up at 6.00 when he was training for the Olympics.

   ....

e) What did you usually do on Saturday evenings?

   ....

f) Becky was afraid of dogs when she was a girl.

   ....

g) We always gave our teachers presents at the end of term.

   ....

h) Did you live next door to Mrs Harrison?

   ....

i) My brother wore glasses when he was small.

   ....

j) Did Marcin learn German at school?

   ....

5 **Complete the sentences with your personal details.**

a) I used to eat .... , but now I don't.

b) I used to hate .... , but now I love it.

c) I didn't use to drink .... , but now I do.

d) I used to read .... , but now I don't.

e) I didn't use to watch .... , on television, but now I do.

f) I used to get up at .... , on Saturdays, but now I don't.

g) I used to play .... , but now I play ....

h) I didn't use to have .... , for breakfast, but now I do.

6 **What did your grandparents and parents use to do?**

   My grandfather used to live in _____ , but my dad

   ....

   ....

   ....

   ....

   ....

Present perfect: affirmative

Explanations

- We often explain a present situation by saying what happened before it. We do not mention an exact time.

  Why are you walking home?
  *I've **broken** my bike.*

  The past action (breaking the bike) has a result in the present (I'm walking home).

  Why are you late?
  *I've **lost** my watch.*

  The past action (losing the watch) has a result in the present (I'm late).

- We use the present perfect when we talk about our experiences in the past and do not mention an exact time.

  *I've **lived** in fifteen different countries.*

Regular verbs

Forming the present perfect: | *have/has* + past participle |

  *The film **has started**.*
  *I've **finished** my homework.*

With regular verbs, the past participle is the same as the past simple.

Statements

I have started	*he has started*	*we have started*
I've started	*he's started*	*we've started*
you have started	*she has started*	*they have started*
you've started	*she's started*	*they've started*
	it has started	
	it's started	

Irregular verbs

Each irregular verb has its own past participle. Sometimes the participle is the same as the past simple, sometimes it has a different form.

Verb	Past simple	Past participle
eat	*ate*	*eaten*
leave	*left*	*left*
drink	*drank*	*drunk*

- There is a list of irregular verbs on page 252.

Practice

1 **Complete each sentence with *has/have* and a participle from the box.**

broken	bought	~~eaten~~	finished	found	happened
left	lost	taken	written		

a) My dog ....*has eaten*.......... my sandwich!

b) Helen .... her bag.

c) I'm sorry. I .... your pen.

d) Where's my dictionary? Someone .... it!

e) We're too late. The programme ....

f) Tina isn't here. She ....

g) There is water on the floor! What .... ?

h) I .... your book! Here it is!

i) Jack .... five letters.

j) I .... some new shoes. Do you like them?

2 **Change the verbs in brackets into the present perfect.**

a) Harry (do) ....*has done*........ the housework.

b) Kate and Bill (find) .... a new flat.

c) Nick (send) .... an email.

d) I (try) .... to learn Japanese.

e) Sam and Dave (eat) .... all the sandwiches.

f) Carlos (buy) .... a dog.

g) Maria and Helen (start) .... at a new school.

h) Frances (break) .... her cup.

i) I (lose) .... my umbrella.

j) Max (take) .... the dog for a walk.

3 **Complete each sentence with the present perfect form of a verb from the box.**

arrive	copy	have	make	~~miss~~	phone	read	see	spend	wash

a) Oh no! That's the last bus, and we ....*have missed*........ it.

b) (you) .... any James Bond books? They're really good.

c) I haven't got any more money. I .... all of it!

d) I .... an idea! Let's go to Big Burger's!

e) I won't lose this information now. I .... the disk.

f) Your hair looks terrible! (you) .... it?

g) Hurry up, Carol. Your taxi .... It's waiting outside.

h) I'm sorry I (not) .... the travel agent. I've been very busy.

i) (you) .... *Harry Potter*? It's my favourite film.

j) Read this again. You .... some mistakes.

Present perfect: negative and questions

Explanations

Negatives

*I **haven't visited** China before.*
This is the first time.
*I **have not found** my car keys.*
I'm still looking for them.

have not = haven't   has not = hasn't

Regular		Irregular	
I haven't started	*we haven't started*	*I haven't eaten*	*we haven't eaten*
you haven't started	*they haven't started*	*you haven't eaten*	*they haven't eaten*
he hasn't started		*he hasn't eaten*	
she hasn't started		*she hasn't eaten*	
it hasn't started		*it hasn't eaten*	

Questions

***Have** you **started** your homework?*   *I've **finished** it!*
***Have** you ever **visited** Cairo?*   *Yes, I've **been** there twice.*

Regular		Irregular	
Have I started?	*Have we started?*	*Have I eaten?*	*Have we eaten?*
Have you started?	*Have they started?*	*Have you eaten?*	*Have they eaten?*
Has he started?		*Has he eaten?*	
Has she started?		*Has she eaten?*	
Has it started?		*Has it eaten?*	

 SEE ALSO

Grammar 20: Present perfect and past simple: time expressions

Practice

Read Nick's list of 'Things to Do' for his holiday.

Book hotel	✓
Check the timetable	✓
Invite Tim	✗
Borrow a guide book	✓
Look at the map	✓
Buy a ticket	✗
Pack my suitcase	✗
Choose my clothes	✗

1 Read Nick's list. Write questions about it. Use the words in brackets.

a) (hotel) *Has he booked the hotel?* ....

b) (Tim) ....

c) (map) ....

d) (suitcase) ....

e) (timetable) ....

f) (guide book) ....

g) (ticket) ....

h) (clothes) ....

2 Read Nick's list. Write statements and negative sentences.

a) (hotel) *He's booked the hotel.* ....

b) (Tim) ....

c) (map) ....

d) (suitcase) ....

e) (timetable) ....

f) (guide book) ....

g) (ticket) ....

h) (clothes) ....

3 Complete this letter. Use the correct verb form of the words in brackets.

Dear Mum and Dad,

We (1) *have enjoyed* (enjoy) our holiday so far. We

(2) .... (not do) any sightseeing. We

(3) .... (spend) a lot of time on the beach. Luckily, it

(4) .... (not rain). Tim (5) .... (learn)

wind-surfing. I (6) .... (not try) it. I think it's dangerous!

(7) .... (you receive) my other postcards?

Love, Nick

Present perfect and past simple

Explanations

Contrast

*Sorry, he isn't here. He's **left**.*
*Sorry, he isn't here. He **left** at 8.00.*

*Ronaldo **has scored** a goal!*
We are interested that he has scored! We are not interested in when he did this.

*Ronaldo **scored** a goal in the second minute of the match.*
We are interested in the time when he scored.

*I've **broken** my pen. Now I can't write my essay!*
This explains why we can't do something now.

*I **broke** my pen at school in the maths test.*
This explains what happened, where it happened and when it happened.

***Have** you **been** to China? Yes.*
*When **did** you **go** to China? I went in 1998.*

been and *gone*

*Kate has **been** to school. She's at home now.*
*Kate has **gone** to school. She's not at home now. She's at school.*

Practice

1 **Choose the best sentence (a–f) for each picture (1–6).**

1

2

3

4

5

6

a) I lived there for ten years. ....3.........

b) I have lived here for ten years. ....

c) Pat has gone shopping. ....

d) Pat has been shopping. ....

e) We've missed the bus. ....

f) We missed the bus. ....

2 <u>Underline</u> **the correct verb form in each sentence.**

a) Can I have another book? I'*ve read*/*read* this one.

b) I'm not ready. I *didn't finish/haven't finished* my homework.

c) I can't find my wallet. I think I'*ve lost/lost* it.

d) *Did you eat/Have you eaten* spaghetti last night?

e) Harry *left/has left* at 10.30.

f) Hurry up, Jim! You *didn't start/haven't started*!

g) *Did you see/Have you seen* this film last year?

3 **Change the verbs in brackets into the past simple or present perfect.**

a) Where (you go) ....*did you go*......... for your holidays last year?

b) I can't play any more. I (just hurt) .... my foot.

c) Jane is a famous writer, and (write) .... over fifty books.

d) Sorry, I (not finish) .... my letters yet.

e) 'We had a great party last week.' 'Who (you, invite) .... ?'

f) Where (you, meet) .... Sam? Was it at the sports centre?

g) Peter (not play) .... basketball for a month.

Present perfect and past simple: time expressions

Explanations

We use the present perfect with:

- *ever, never*   *(any time/not any time)*
  ***Have you ever** seen a lion?*   *I've **never** seen a lion.*

- *just*   (a short time ago)
  *Is Peter here? No, he's **just gone** out. There he is!*

- *yet*   (not finished – with negatives and questions)
  I haven't finished yet.
  ***Have** you **finished** your homework **yet**?*   *No, I'm still doing it.*

- *already*   (finished – with statements)
  Have a sandwich!
  *No thanks, I've **already eaten**. I had lunch at 12.00.*

- *since* (from the start)

  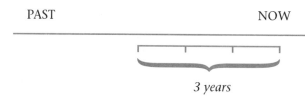

  | 1997 | **1998** | NOW |

  started

  *I've **lived** in this town **since** 1998. I live here now.*
  (1998 <u>is the time I started</u> living here.)

We can use the present perfect or the past simple with:

- *for*   (a period of time)
  *I've **lived** in this house **for three years**. I live in it now.*
  *I **lived** in that flat **for two years**, but I don't live there now.*

  | PAST | NOW |

  3 years

  *I've **lived** in this town **for three years**. I live here now.*
  (Three years is <u>the period of time</u> I've lived here.)

  Compare with *since*.

We use the past simple with:

- *ago*
  *I **started** learning English a year **ago**.*

Practice

1 **Match each sentence (a–g) with a sentence of a similar meaning (1–7).**

a) Jim has just written a book.   ....4....

b) Has Jim written a book yet?   ....

c) Jim has already written a book.   ....

d) Jim wrote a book a year ago.   ....

e) Jim has never written a book.   ....

f) Has Jim ever written a book?   ....

g) Jim has written two books since 1996.   ....

1   This is not his first book.

2   Does Jim write books?

3   He finished his book last year.

4   He finished a few days ago.

5   Jim started writing in 1996 and has written two books between then and now.

6   Jim doesn't write books.

7   Has he finished a book?

2 <u>Underline</u> **the correct word in each sentence.**

a) Have you *ever/yet* visited Slovenia?

b) Tim has *for/just* come back from the USA.

c) I'm not hungry. I've *already/since* eaten.

d) Jane lived in Greece *since/for* fifteen years.

e) Brian and Claire got married *ten years ago/since ten years*.

f) I can't come out. I haven't done my homework *already/yet*.

g) Mark has worked in Turkey *ago/since* 1998.

3 **Complete each sentence with a time word from the box.**

already	ever	~~for~~	just	never	since	yet

a) Sue has been on the beach ......*for*...... an hour, but she hasn't had a swim yet.

b) I don't want to see this film. I've .... seen it.

c) Have you .... been to the Greek islands?

d) Can you wait a moment? I haven't finished ....

e) Ouch! An insect has .... bitten me!

f) George has .... eaten Chinese food, so this is the first time for him!

g) Rick has lived in Japan .... 1998.

1 **Correct each sentence. Use the past continuous or the past simple.**

a) When I <u>was arriving</u> at Dan's house, he was waiting
   outside. ....*arrived*.................

b) While we were doing a maths test, the head teacher
   was coming into the room. ....

c) While we swam, it started to rain. ....

d) While I was having a bath, the lights were going out. ....

e) Debra watched television when the storm began. ....

f) While I was walking to the shop I was losing my bag! ....

g) What were you doing when I was seeing you yesterday? ....

h) I was walking up the stairs when I was hearing the
   phone. ....

2 **Complete each sentence. Use one word in each space.**

a) Kate has ....*taken*.... twenty photos of the children so far.

b) Have you ever .... this book? It's really good.

c) Have you ever .... to Egypt?

d) The dog's not hungry. It hasn't .... its dinner.

e) I'm going to bed. I think I've .... a cold.

f) Oh no! I've .... my bag on the bus.

g) Jim has just .... a new mountain bike. It was very expensive.

h) The washing machine doesn't work. I think I've .... it.

3 **Change the verbs in brackets into the past simple or the present perfect simple.**

a) Tina isn't here. She (just go) .....*has just gone*..... to school.

b) What time (you get up) .... this morning?

c) Paul (have) .... a bad car accident three years ago.

d) I (live) .... in the same house since 1995.

e) What (you do) .... last night?

f) Brian (not finish) .... his work yet.

g) Tina (arrive) .... here in 2001.

h) (you see) .... 'Men in Black'? It's a great film.

4 Complete each sentence or question with a time expression.

a) Sam has worked for the same company ....*for*............ three years.

b) Karen hasn't finished her project ....

c) A: What's Madrid like?

B: I don't know. I have .... been there.

d) I waited at the bus-stop .... two hours.

e) I've .... had a phone call from my brother in Canada.

f) Helen has lived here .... 1998.

g) Have you .... eaten Chinese food?

5 Rewrite each sentence using the words in **bold**. Do not change the meaning.

a) I last went to the cinema a long time ago.   **haven't**

I ......*haven't been to the cinema*...... for a long time.

b) Jane rode a bike to school.   **ride**

Jane .... to school.

c) Peter is at school.   **has**

Peter .... to school.

d) Tim and Sue played in the garden every day.   **used**

Tim and Sue ....

e) How long were you in Turkey?   **stay**

.... in Turkey?

f) Joe started living here three years ago.   **for**

Joe .... three years.

g) Is this your first visit to Scotland?   **have**

.... before?

6 Correct each sentence or question.

a) When <u>have you arrived</u> here?   *did you arrive*

b) What you were doing when I phoned you?   ....

c) I didn't do the shopping yet.   ....

d) When I was young I was wearing glasses.   ....

e) Dan arrived late because he was missing the bus.   ....

f) Peter, this is Mary. Did you meet before?   ....

g) I use to get up early every morning.   ....

Think about grammar! Are the sentences **true** or **false**?

a) The present perfect simple connects the past with the present.

b) In the present perfect, all irregular verbs end with -en.

c) *Used to* is for things that happened a long time ago.

Future plans and predictions

Explanations

Plans or intentions

When you decide to do something in the future you make a plan or have an intention. Plans can change, so it is not 100% certain.

> *Carol has bought her train ticket and booked her course.*
> *She **is going to study** in France next month.* (This is her plan or intention.)

Predictions from the situation

Sometimes we can see that something is going to happen.

> *Look out! Those books **are going to fall** on your head.*

Statements

*He's **going to cook** dinner.*

I'm going to cook	*he's going to cook*	*we're going to cook*
you're going to cook	*she's going to cook*	*they're going to cook*
	it's going to cook	

Negatives

*Clare **isn't going to cook** dinner.*

I'm not going to cook	*he isn't going to cook*	*we aren't going to cook*
you aren't going to cook	*she isn't going to cook*	*they aren't going to cook*
	it isn't going to cook	

Yes/No Questions

***Are** you **going to cook** dinner?*

Am I going to cook?	*Is he going to cook?*	*Are we going to cook?*
Are you going to cook?	*Is she going to cook?*	*Are they going to cook?*
	Is it going to cook?	

Wh- questions

*What **are you going to do** in the summer?*
*When **are you going to phone** me?*

Examples

*Is it **going to rain**?*
*Mike's **going to run** in the Marathon in April.*
*Linda **is going to learn** Chinese.*

Careful!

- We do not use *gonna* in writing.

 SEE ALSO

Grammar 5: Present continuous: negative and questions
Grammar 26: Present continuous: future use

Practice

1   Look at the pictures. Complete each sentence with a verb from the box.

| crash | ~~fall~~ | hit | miss | rain |

a)

Careful! You <u>are going to fall</u> !

b)

I think it ....

....

c)

Look out! You ....

.... the tree!

d)

Oh dear, I think he ....

....

e)

Hurry up, we ....

.... the bus.

2 **Complete each sentence. Use *going to* and the verb in brackets.**

a) (you, buy) .... *Are you going to buy* .... a new bike?

b) Tom (not be) .... a doctor.

c) I (buy) .... some new shoes.

d) (Helen, catch) .... the train?

e) Who (carry) .... the shopping for me?

f) Jim and Dinah (not get) .... married.

g) Sam (take) .... a holiday.

h) What time (you, phone) .... me?

i) Where (we, eat) .... tonight?

j) I (not give) .... Dave a birthday present!

3 **Rewrite each sentence or question with *going to*.**

a) Joe plans to buy a new computer next year.
   Joe is going to buy a new computer next year.

b) We don't plan to play tennis this weekend.

   ....

c) Does Nick plan to join the sports club?

   ....

d) What are your plans for next summer?

   ....

e) Look! That tree is about to fall over!

   ....

f) Do you plan to work hard this year?

   ....

g) I don't intend to get a new car.

   ....

h) The forecast for tomorrow is rain.

   ....

i) Do Mike and Pat plan to make sandwiches for the party?

   ....

j) I think it's about to snow.

   ....

4 Read Tom's plans for his holiday. Complete the sentences.

Saturday	Wednesday
arrive at 4.00pm	see the museum
Sunday	**Thursday**
walk around the village	climb the mountain
Monday	**Friday**
visit the castle	buy presents at the market
Tuesday	**NOTES**
sit on the beach	

a) On Saturday *he's going to arrive at 4.00pm* .

b) .... on Sunday.

c) On Monday ....

d) .... on Tuesday.

e) On Wednesday ....

f) .... on Thursday.

g) On Friday ....

5 What are your plans for next summer? Write sentences.

Next summer I'm going to have a really good time. I'm going to....

....

....

....

....

....

....

....

....

....

....

....

....

Explanations

A prediction is what you think will happen.

> Jim **will pass** all his exams.   It **will rain** tomorrow.
> I**'ll be** late tonight.   He **will come** to the party.

Sometimes we emphasise that we are not certain. We can use *perhaps, probably, think* or *expect.*

> Jim **will probably pass** all his exams.   I **expect** it **will rain** tomorrow.
> **Perhaps** I'**ll be** late tonight.   I **think** he **will come** to the party.

Statements

They'**ll leave** tomorrow.

I will leave	he will leave	we will leave
you will leave	she will leave	they will leave
	it will leave	

don't know	perhaps	think	probably	expect	sure
0					10

Negatives

I won't be at school on Friday.

won't = will not

I won't leave	he won't leave	we won't leave
you won't leave	she won't leave	they won't leave
	it won't leave	

Questions

Will the shop **be** open tomorrow?

Will I leave?	Will he leave?	Will we leave?
Will you leave?	Will she leave?	Will they leave?
	Will it leave?	

Examples

I'**ll fly** to Scotland next week.
It **won't rain** tomorrow.
Will the train **be** late?

I **expect** it **will rain**.	I **don't expect** it **will rain**.
I **think** it **will rain**.	I **don't think** it **will rain**.
I'**m sure** it **will rain**.	I'**m sure** it **won't rain**.

 SEE ALSO

Grammar 52: Asking for information, invitations, offers, permission
Grammar 53: Preferences, promises, reminding, requesting, suggesting, warning

Practice

1 **Complete each sentence or question. Use *will* or *won't* and the verb in brackets.**

a) I (choose) ......*will choose*...... the team next week.

b) You (not have) .... a lot of time to answer the questions.

c) Mr Jones (be) .... back at about 7.30.

d) Dimitri (not know) .... the answer.

e) I'm sure Jane (like) .... her birthday present.

f) (you give) .... us any homework on Friday?

g) There (not be) .... any lessons tomorrow.

h) (we see) .... you tomorrow evening?

i) Lots of people (read) .... Michael White's new book.

j) I think our team (win) .... the match.

2 **Rewrite each sentence using the words in bold.**

a) It'll be cold tomorrow. **I'm sure**
...... *I'm sure it will be cold tomorrow.* ......

b) We'll win. **I expect**
....

c) I'll leave now. **I think**
....

d) Jim won't be late. **I'm sure**
....

e) It won't take long. **I expect**
....

f) You won't have any problems. **I'm sure**
....

g) You'll enjoy the party. **I think**
....

h) They won't decide anything yet. **I imagine**
....

i) The train won't be late. **I don't expect**
....

j) Jane will have cooked dinner. **I imagine**
....

Meetings, promises, decisions, refusing

Explanations

We use *will* and *won't* when we make promises, decisions of the moment and when we refuse to do things.

■ Meetings and appointments

I'll see you outside the cinema at 7.30.

■ Decisions of the moment

Waiter: *What would you like?*
Customer: *I'll have chicken, please.*

■ Promises

I'll give you the money tomorrow.

■ Refusing

'*Come here!*'   '*No, I won't!*'

→ SEE ALSO

Grammar 50: Advice, agreeing, disagreeing, apologizing
Grammar 51: Descriptions, directions, excuses, greetings
Grammar 52: Asking for information, invitations, offers, permission
Grammar 53: preferences, promises, reminding, requesting, suggesting, warning

Practice

1 **Choose the most suitable reply (1–6) for each statement or question (a–f).**

a) Bye for now!

b) Give me that piece of cake!

c) Where's your homework?

d) What would you like to eat?

e) Where are we going to meet?

f) Please remember to call me.

1 Don't worry, I won't forget.

2 I'll bring it tomorrow, I promise!

3 No, I won't! It's mine.

4 I'll have a sandwich, please.

5 Bye, I'll see you later.

6 I'll see you outside the cinema.

2 **Look at the pictures and make sentences with *will* or *won't*.**

a) Decide to have the giant pizza.

   I'll have the giant pizza.
   ....

b) Promise to be home before midnight.

   ....
   ....

c) Arrange to meet tomorrow at 6.30.

   ....
   ....

d) Decide to take the red pair.

   ....
   ....

e) Refuse to do this!

   ....
   ....

f) Promise to pay your friend back at the end of the week.

   ....
   ....

59

will and *going to*: problems

Explanations

It is difficult to decide when to use *will* and when to use *going to*.

Study these examples.

■ Plan

> *Do you want to go to the cinema this evening?*
> *No, **I'm going to do** lots of work this evening.*

■ Intention

> ***Are you going to play** basketball tonight?*
> *No, I don't think so.*

■ Promise

> *You haven't done your homework. Where is it?*
> ***I'll do** lots of work this evening.*

■ Formal Prediction

> *Here is the weather forecast; tomorrow **it will rain** in the afternoon.*

■ Prediction from clues

> *What do you think about the weather?*
> ***It's going to rain** this afternoon.*

■ Refusing

> ***Will you wash** the floor?*
> *No, **I won't**! You made it dirty!*

Practice

1 Tick (✔) the most suitable sentence or question for each picture.

a)

1 That tree is going to fall! ✔
2 That tree will fall!

b)

1 I'll be back!
2 I'm going to be back!

c)

1 Are you going to play?
2 Will you play?

d)

1 I'm not going to eat it.
2 I won't eat it.

e)

1 The King will arrive at 6.00.
2 The King is going to
   arrive at 6.00.

f)

1 I won't be late tomorrow.
2 I'm not going to be late tomorrow.

2 Choose each sentence with the correct form of the verb in brackets.

a) Jane (have) ....*is going to have*.. a baby in the summer.

b) Bye for now. Perhaps I (see) .... you later.

c) Next summer I (stay) .... with my relatives in New York.

d) I don't know my plans for the weekend. What (do you) .... ?

e) Jim's tired, so he (go) .... to bed early.

f) Helen (move) .... to London next year.

Explanations

We can use the present continuous when we talk about arrangements for the future. Arrangements are plans, but we are sure they will happen. We often write them in our diaries.

- *My parents **are buying** me a bike for my birthday.* (I'm sure about this.)
- *I**'m going** to the doctor's on Friday.* (It's fixed. I have an appointment.)

> *Doctor Goodwell*
> *Nightingale Surgery, Old Town Road, Hadlow, Suffolk IP20 3AA*
> *Telephone 01229 054001*
>
> *Appointment,*
> *Friday 6th 9.30am*

- *'**Are** you **doing** anything on Saturday?'*   *'I**'m having** a party.'*
  (It's fixed. I've invited my friends.)

- *What **are** you **doing** tomorrow?*   *I**'m staying** at home and **studying**.*

- *come* and *go*
  *My brother **is coming** to stay.*
  *I**'m going** to Prague <u>tomorrow</u>.*

- *going to* or present continuous?

*I**'m having** a party.*	Fixed arrangement
*I**'m going to have** a party.*	Plan/Intention

*Jean **is going to get** her hair cut.*	Plan/Intention

  (She doesn't know when exactly.)

*Jean **is getting** her hair cut <u>next week</u>.*	Fixed arrangement

  (She has an appointment at the hairdresser's.)

Practice

1   **Look at the diary. Write a sentence for each day. Use the verb in brackets.**

Saturday	Dentist 4.30
Sunday	Stay at home
Monday	Basketball 3 p.m.
Tuesday	Do some shopping in afternoon
Wednesday	London
Thursday	Party
Friday	Jim and Carol – lunch

a) (see)   *I'm seeing the dentist at 4.30 on Saturday.* ....

b) (stay) ....

c) (play) ....

d) (do) ....

e) (go) ....

f) (have) ....

g) (come) ....

2   **Change the verbs in brackets into the present continuous.**

a) What (you do) ...... *are you doing* .... this evening?

b) I (not come) .... to school tomorrow.

c) Tina (go) .... to Italy next week.

d) (you have) .... a party this week?

e) We (not go) .... home on the bus after school.

f) (Mrs Simpson teach) .... us this afternoon?

g) Catherine and George (not arrive) .... tomorrow.

h) (Joaquim go) .... to the football match tomorrow?

i) Ann (not work) .... on Friday.

j) (you leave) .... this afternoon?

63

Explanations

Here are some examples of time words we use when we are talking about the future:

- *tomorrow*
  *I'm leaving for France **tomorrow**.*

- *next week*
  *I'll see you at the meeting **next week**.*

- *soon*
  *Goodbye! I'll see you **soon**.*

- *later, after*
  *I'll phone you **later**.*   (no object)
  I'll phone you after <u>the film</u>.   (object)

- *in a moment*, etc.
  *I'll be back **in a moment**.*
  *I'll see you **in two weeks**.*

- *at* (+ the time)
  *I'll be back **at** 6.00.*

More contrasts

*In the year 2100, people **will live** on the moon.*   Prediction
*Our school trip starts tomorrow. **We're leaving** at six.* Fixed arrangement

I've forgotten my keys and we can't get in the house.
*What **are we going to do** now?*   Plan/Intention

Practice

1 **Choose the most suitable ending to complete each conversation.**

a) Are you free tomorrow night? ....*1*........

   1 Sorry, I'm going to the cinema with Peter.

   2 Sorry, I'll go to the cinema with Peter.

   3 Sorry, I'm go to the cinema with Peter.

b) What are your plans for the holidays? ....

   1 I have a good rest!

   2 I'll to have a good rest!

   3 I'm going to have a good rest!

c) What are the arrangements for the school trip tomorrow? ....

   1 We're meeting outside the front entrance at 8.30.

   2 We'll meet outside the front entrance at 8.30.

   3 We've met outside the front entrance at 8.30.

d) Where are you going? I want to talk to you. ....

   1 I'll be back in a moment.

   2 I'm going to be back in a moment.

   3 I'm being back in a moment.

e) Are you going to be here on Thursday? ....

   1 No, I leaving on Wednesday afternoon.

   2 No, I'm leave on Wednesday afternoon.

   3 No, I'm leaving on Wednesday afternoon.

f) Does your leg still hurt? ....

   1 Yes, I've gone to the doctor's tomorrow.

   2 Yes, I'm going to the doctor's tomorrow.

   3 Yes, I went to the doctor's tomorrow.

2 **Complete each sentence with words from the box.**

later	a minute	~~tomorrow~~	after	at	in	next year

a) What are you doing the day after ....*tomorrow*........ ?

b) Kate is going to start learning French ....

c) Thomas is leaving .... the morning.

d) Rita will be back ....

e) The new school will open .... 8.30.

f) I'm just going to the library. I'll see you in ....

g) Jorge won't be long. He'll be back .... lunch.

Consolidation 4

1 **Choose the most suitable word or phrase for each space.**

a) 'Do you have any plans for your birthday?' 'Yes, _B_ a party.'

    A) I'll have   B) I'm having

b) 'I need some help with the shopping tomorrow.' 'Don't worry, ...'

    A) I'll help   B) I'm helping

c) What ..... when you go on holiday?

    A) will you do   B) are you going to do

d) 'Do you want to come to a football match on Saturday?' 'Which teams ..... ?'

    A) are playing   B) are going to play

e) Don't carry all those heavy books. Some of the children ..... you.

    A) will help   B) are going to help

f) The doctor is on his way. He ..... in fifteen minutes.

    A) will be here   B) is being

g) Good news. Ann ..... a baby.

    A) will have   B) is going to have

h) I'm sorry I can't come to the lesson tomorrow. ..... my dad in hospital.

    A) I'll visit   B) I'm visiting

2 **Complete each sentence with the present continuous form of the verb in brackets. Then tick (✔) the sentences which refer to the future.**

a) Next summer Kate (spend) ...... _is spending_ ...... a month in France.   ✔

b) Hurry up, Mehmet. Everyone (wait) .... for you.

c) (you do) .... anything on Friday? Do you want to come to a party?

d) Helen (read) .... in bed at the moment.

e) We (go) .... to the cinema this evening.

f) I can't answer the phone. I (have) .... a bath.

g) What (you do) .... later? **Do** you want to come for a walk?

h) David (leave) .... tomorrow. Have you said goodbye to him?

3 **Correct each sentence or question.**

a) We'll go to the cinema this evening. Do you want to come?
We're going to the cinema this evening. Do you want to come?

b) Look out! That car will crash!
....

c) Bye for now! I'm going to see you tomorrow.
....

d) Sorry I can't meet you. I will go to the doctor's.
....

e) Have you heard the weather forecast? It's raining tomorrow.
....

f) I've bought my ticket. I'll leave tomorrow.
....

4 **Complete each sentence with a word from the box. More than one answer may be possible.**

at	in	later	on	this	tomorrow	~~tonight~~

a) I'll be late *tonight* but I'll be home before midnight.

b) Can you wait, please? I'll be ready .... a minute.

c) Don't worry, I'll be here .... 7.00.

d) I've finished now. I'll be back .... afternoon.

e) It's cold today, but it'll be warmer ....

f) Bye for now. I'll see you ....

g) There won't be any lessons .... Monday.

5 <u>Underline</u> **the correct word in each sentence.**

a) Tina will definitely be here <u>at</u>/*on* 6.00.

b) Our new sports centre will be ready *next year/the next year*.

c) Hurry up! The bus will be here *later/soon*.

d) I'll see you *after/later* the lesson.

e) Are you doing anything *at night/tonight*?

f) I won't be long. I'll be ready *after/in* a minute.

g) Everything will be different *at/in* the year 3500!

Think about grammar! Are the sentences true or false?

a) There are two ways of talking about the future in English.

b) The present continuous is for fixed arrangements.

c) *Won't* means *will not*.

Explanations

If sentences

Some *if* sentences describe what always or usually happens; or give instructions.

- Things that usually or always happen.
  In this type of sentence we use the present simple in both clauses.

clause 1	clause 2
If + present simple,	present simple

If I **have** a cold, I (usually/always) **stay at home.**

- Instructions in situations.
  In this type of sentence we use the present simple after *if* ..., and an imperative in the other clause.

clause 1	clause 2
If + present simple,	imperative

If you feel tired, have a rest.

Conditional 1: real situations

Conditional sentences describe possible situations and their results. In 'real situations' we are certain that something will happen if someone does something. We call these 'real situations' in contrast to 'imaginary situations'.

We use the present simple after *if* ..., and *will* in the other clause. When the *if* clause is true, the speaker is certain about the information in the other clause.

clause 1	clause 2
If + present simple,	*will*

Examples of conditional 1

*If we **miss** the bus, we'**ll be** late.*
*If we **don't catch** the bus, we'**ll be** late.*
*If we **catch** the bus, we **won't be** late.*
*If we **don't miss** the bus, we **won't be** late.*

Warnings

*If you **ride** your bike like that, you'**ll fall off!***
*If you **touch** that, you'**ll burn** yourself!*

Reversing the clauses

The clauses in *if* sentences and conditional sentences can be reversed.
Note the use of commas.

*If you **miss** the bus, your teacher **will be** angry.*   (comma used)
*Your teacher **will be** angry if you **miss** the bus.*   (no comma)

 SEE ALSO

Grammar 30: Conditional 2
Grammar 67: Imperatives

Practice

1 **Complete each sentence. Use the correct form of the verbs in brackets.**

a) If Jack (not leave) *doesn't leave* now, he (miss) ....*will miss*.... his bus.

b) If Helen (work) .... hard, she (pass) .... her exams.

c) If it (rain) ...., we (go) .... into a shop.

d) If Mary (not practise) .... her French, she (not improve) ....

e) If it (rain) .... tomorrow, we (not go) .... swimming.

f) If George (come) .... late, the teacher (be) .... angry.

g) If I (see) .... Joe tomorrow, I (tell) .... him your news.

2 <u>Underline</u> **the correct word(s) in each sentence.**

a) If you *press/will press* that button, a bell rings.

b) If you wear your coat tomorrow, you *aren't/won't be* cold.

c) If I *feel/will feel* tired, I go to bed early.

d) If you *will come/come* back next week, David will be here.

e) If it *rains/will rain* tomorrow, we'll stay at home.

f) If I go to university when I am older, I*'ll work/work* very hard.

3 **Read the situation, then complete each sentence.**

a) A friend wants you to play basketball in the classroom. You are worried about breaking the window. You say:

If we *play basketball in the classroom, we'll break the window.*

b) You want to leave the party now, because you are worried about missing the last bus. You say:

If we ....

c) Your dog bites people. A friend wants to touch the dog, so you say:

If you ....

d) It's raining. You want to stand under a tree, because you are worried about getting wet. You say:

If we ....

e) You want to take the bus to the city centre. Your friend wants to walk. You are worried about getting tired. You say:

If we ....

f) You are walking to school with a friend. You don't want to be late. You suggest hurrying. You say:

If we don't ....

Explanations

**Conditional 2:
Imaginary
conditions**

Conditional sentences describe possible situations and their results. In 'imaginary situations' we imagine what the future would be like, if the present were different.

In this type of sentence, we use the past simple after *if* ..., and *would/wouldn't* in the other clause.

clause 1	clause 2
If + past simple,	*would* + verb

If I **knew** the answer, I **would tell** you.
In this situation, I do not know the answer.

Note: the past simple here <u>does not</u> describe past time. It imagines a different present time.

**Examples of
conditional 2**

If I **had** a helicopter, I'**d fly** to school.
If I **landed** my helicopter at school, my teacher **wouldn't like** it!

If I were ...   (in written/formal English)
If I **were** a rock star, I'**d live** in New York.
If I **were** the head teacher, I'**d give** the class a holiday!

If I was ...   (possible in informal speech)
If I **was** a rock star, I'**d live** in New York.
If I **was** rich, I'**d buy** you a drink!

Giving advice

If I were you, ...
A: *I've got a terrible headache!*
B: **If I were you**, I'**d take** an aspirin.

A: *I feel really tired.*
B: **If I were you**, I **wouldn't go** to bed late!

Practice

1 **Change the verbs in brackets into the past simple or use *would*.**

a) If I (have) .... *had* .... the time, I (go) ...... *would go* ...... to the cinema
    more often.

b) If I (find) .... some money, I (take) .... it to the police.

c) If I (have) .... a dog, I (take) .... it for a walk every day.

d) If I (meet) .... an alien, I (try) .... to talk to it.

e) If everyone (speak) .... Spanish, nobody (learn) ....
    English!

f) If I (see) .... a snake, I (run) .... away.

2 **Complete each sentence with a verb from the box.**

> ~~met~~   robbed   saw   slept   were   won   ~~would ask~~   would be
> would buy   would catch   would fly   would visit

a) If I .... *met* .... a famous person, I ... *would ask* ... them some questions.

b) If I .... a helicopter, I .... to school.

c) If I .... a bank, the police .... me.

d) If I .... a lot of money, I .... presents for my family.

e) If I .... in the classroom, my teacher .... very angry!

f) If I .... an astronaut, I .... other planets.

3 **Read the situations. Complete the advice. Use the verb in brackets.**

a) Your friend has bad toothache.
    If ...... *I were you, I would go to the* .... dentist's. (go)

b) Your friend can't decide whether to go to the cinema, or stay at home.
    If .... cinema. (go)

c) Your friend wants to buy a new bike, but hasn't got any money.
    If .... your parents. (ask)

d) Your friend is having problems studying.
    If .... teacher. (talk to)

e) Your friend always feels tired in class, and sometimes falls asleep!
    If .... bed early. (go)

f) Your friend wants to take more exercise and be fit.
    If .... a sports club. (join)

Explanations

Situation 1

Conditional 1

We are on the roof of a block of flats. You are standing very near the edge. This is dangerous! I say:

*If you **fall**, you'll **hurt** yourself.*

Conditional 1   *Conditional 2*

Conditional 2

We are on the roof of a block of flats. You are not near the edge. There is no danger. I imagine a dangerous situation and say:

*If you **fell**, you'd **hurt** yourself!*

Situation 2

Conditional 1

It is a cold day in winter. We are going to leave the house. I have got a coat for you. I say:

*If you **wear** this coat, you **won't be** cold.*

Conditional 1   *Conditional 2*

Conditional 2

It is a cold day in winter. We are outside. I am wearing a coat. I am warm. You are not wearing a coat. You are cold. I say:

*If you **wore** a coat, you **wouldn't be** cold!*

Practice

1   **Tick (✔) the best sentence for each picture.**

a)

    1 If we miss the bus we'll be late for school.   ✔

    2 If we missed the bus, we would be late for school.

b)

    1 If I have a helicopter, I'll fly to work.

    2 If I had a helicopter, I'd fly to work.

c)

    1 If we live at the North Pole, we'll feel cool.

    2 If we lived at the North Pole, we'd feel cool.

d)

    1 If you drop that, it'll break!

    2 If you dropped that, it would break.

e)

1 If he eats all that ice cream, he'll be sick.

2 If he ate all that ice cream, he'd be sick.

f)

1 If I'm taller, I'll be in the team.

2 If I were taller, I'd be in the team.

2 **Complete each sentence. Use either Conditional 1 or Conditional 2.**

a) Sue doesn't ride a bike to school, because she doesn't have one.

If Sue .....*had a bike, she would ride it to school.*.....

b) Chris will pass his exams, but he has to work hard.

If Chris ....

c) John isn't fat, because he doesn't eat a lot.

If John ....

d) Ellen doesn't have a car, so she walks to work.

If Ellen ....

e) Ali's English will improve, but he has to practise.

If Ali ....

f) Pat won't be late but she has to hurry.

If Pat..

g) Rita doesn't like swimming so she doesn't go to the beach.

If Rita ....

h) Paulo will get better, but he has to take his medicine.

If Paulo ....

i) David doesn't get up early because he lives near the school.

If David ....

j) Carol will catch the bus but she has to leave now.

If Carol ....

3 Choose the most suitable word or phrase for each space.

a) If I were you, I *B* on holiday and relax.
   A) will go   B) would go   C) go

b) If you don't have any money, ... a job!
   A) get   B) you would get   C) you will get

c) If I ..... a car, I wouldn't walk to work.
   A) did own   B) owned   C) own

d) If he weren't tired, he ..... go to the party.
   A) would   B) will   C) did

e) If you ..... the door, the cat won't escape.
   A) close   B) closed   C) will close

f) If we ..... by plane, we'd get there much quicker.
   A) go   B) will go   C) went

g) If Sue ..... now, she will miss the bus.
   A) didn't leave   B) won't leave   C) doesn't leave

h) If my brother had an expensive car, he ..... really happy.
   A) would be   B) will be   C) was

i) If I ..... a pop star, I would buy an enormous house.
   A) be   B) was   C) will be

j) If it rains, the children usually ..... inside.
   A) played   B) will play   C) play

4 Complete these conditional sentences. Use *will* or *would* and the present simple or past simple.

a) We're going to the beach after school. If you (want) ....*want*........ to come with us, I ....*will ask*........ my mum if it is OK.

b) I always ride my bicycle to work. If I (win) .... the lottery, I (get) .... a taxi every day instead!

c) It's amazing! Everyone in the class passed the exam! If I (be) .... the teacher, I (be) .... really pleased.

d) It is a very easy machine to use. If you (place) .... the fruit in the top, the juice (appear) .... at the bottom ready to drink.

e) We've been waiting for almost an hour now. If they (not come) .... soon, we (not see) .... the start of the concert.

f) Look at the sky! If it (start) .... raining, the race (finish) .... early.

Short answers

Explanations

Yes/No questions

Present simple	*Do you like swimming?*
Present continuous	*Are you reading this?*
Present perfect	*Have you ever been to Italy?*
Past simple	*Did you post my letter?*
Past continuous	*Were you working?*
will	*Will it rain tomorrow?*
going to	*Are you going to pay me?*
be (present)	*Are you American?*
be (past)	*Was that your money?*

Short answers

Did I pass the test?	*Yes, you did.*	*No, you didn't.*
Are you waiting?	*Yes, I am.*	*No, I'm not.*
Does Jim like swimming?	*Yes, he does.*	*No, he doesn't.*
Is Maria reading this?	*Yes, she is.*	*No, she isn't.*
Was it working?	*Yes, it was.*	*No, it wasn't.*
Have we won?	*Yes, we have.*	*No, we haven't.*
Have they finished?	*Yes, they have.*	*No, they haven't.*

Careful!

The verbs *be, do* and *have* are sometimes the main verb in a sentence, and sometimes used as auxiliary verbs.

What <u>are</u> you doing?	*are* is the auxiliary, *do* is the main verb
<u>Do</u> you <u>have</u> any milk?	*do* is the auxiliary, *have* is the main verb
<u>Have</u> you <u>done</u> your homework?	*have* is the auxiliary, *do* is the main verb

Practice

1   **Choose the correct responses (1–8) for the questions (a–h).**

a) Was Ann driving?   1   Yes, I do.

b) Did you see Tom yesterday?   2   No, he isn't.

c) Do you know the answer?   3   No, I haven't.

d) Have you seen this film?   4   Yes, I was.

e) Are you reading this?   5   No, she wasn't.

f) Were you sitting here?   6   No, she hasn't.

g) Is George leaving?   7   Yes, I did.

h) Has Helen finished yet?   8   No, I'm not.

2   **Use the prompts and the verb forms in brackets to write questions.**

a) they/work hard   (past continuous)

Were they working hard?
....

b) Jim/eat yet   (present perfect)

....

c) you/read a lot   (present simple)

....

d) Tom/writing a letter   (present continuous)

....

e) Tina/leave yesterday   (past simple)

....

f) we/meet before   (present perfect)

....

g) Sam/watch TV   (past continuous)

....

3   **Write a short answer for each question.**

a) Have you seen my wallet?   No, ...*I haven't*...... .

b) Is David studying French?   Yes, ...

c) Did it rain yesterday?   No, ...

d) Do you like Indian food?   Yes, ...

e) Have you ever been to Prague?   Yes, ...

f) Are you having a good time?   No, ...

g) Does Mary work here?   No, ...

h) Was Tom bothering you?   No, ...

Wh- questions;
Subject and object questions

Explanations

Wh- questions

We use:

who with people	*Who is that? It's Jack.*
what with things	*What are you looking for? A pen.*
when with time	*When are you leaving? At 6.00.*
where with places	*Where do you live? In that house.*

Present simple	***When*** *do you usually get up?*
Present continuous	***What*** *are you doing?*
Present perfect	***Why*** *have you stopped?*
Past simple	***How*** *did you feel?*
Past continuous	***Where*** *were you going?*
Future	***Who*** *are you going to meet?*
	When *will you come home?*
	Why *are you leaving?*

Short answers

When *do you usually get up?*	*At 7.30.*
What *are you doing?*	*Writing a letter.*
Why *have you come?*	*To give you a present.*
How *did you feel?*	*Terrible.*
Where *were you going?*	*Home.*

Subject and Object questions

We use *What* and *Who* to ask questions about the subject or the object. Questions about the subject do not use the auxiliary *do* (*does, did*).

Subject	Verb	Object
Cats	*eat*	*fish*

Subject question:	**What** eats fish?	**Cats** eat fish.
Object question:	**What** do cats eat?	Cats eat **fish.**

Examples

■ Subject questions

What *makes people happy?*	***Love*** *makes people happy!/**Love** does.*
Who *sits in this seat?*	***Helen*** *sits in this seat./**Helen** does.*

■ Object questions.

What *do you wear in winter?*	*I wear **an overcoat**./An overcoat.*
What *are you reading?*	*I'm reading '**Oliver Twist**'./'Oliver Twist'.*

Careful!

When the main verb is *be*, or the tense is past continuous or present continuous, *do* is not used.

Practice

1 Use the prompts and the verb forms in brackets to write questions.

a) Why/you cry?   (present continuous)
    Why are you crying?

b) How/you get here   (past simple)

c) What/Jack usually do/on Saturdays   (present simple)

d) How long/you live here   (present perfect)

e) Where/David/go   (past continuous)

f) Who/you talk to   (present continuous)

g) What/you do   (past continuous)

2 Complete each question.

a) 'What *makes you tired* ?' 'Running makes me tired.'

b) 'Who .... ?' 'I talked to the manager.'

c) 'What .... ?' 'I read a newspaper.'

d) 'Who .... ?' 'Kate brought the ice-cream.'

e) 'What .... ?' 'Joe decided to take the job.'

f) 'Who .... ?' 'I answer most of the questions.'

g) 'Which .... ?' 'This house is mine.'

h) 'Who .... ?' 'Pat looks after the children.'

3 Change the answers in brackets into short answers.

a) 'What are you eating?' (I'm eating a sandwich.)   *A sandwich.*

b) 'Who helps you?' (My teacher helps me.)

c) 'What do you watch?' (I watch cartoons.)

d) 'Who do you write to?' (I write to my penfriend.)

e) 'What makes you laugh?' (You make me laugh!)

f) 'Who loves you?' (Somebody loves me!)

Explanations

- We can put tag questions at the end of statements and make the statements into questions.
- The tag is made of the auxiliary + pronoun. When there is no auxiliary, use *do/does/did*.
- Positive questions have a positive verb + negative tag.
- Negative questions have a negative verb + positive tag.

Examples

statement	*You like chips.*
with a tag question	*You **like** chips, **don't you?***

Present simple	*You **like** chips, **don't you?***
	*You **don't like** chips, **do you?***

Present continuous	*We're arriving soon, aren't we?*
	We aren't leaving, are we?

Present perfect	*She's finished, hasn't she?*
	She hasn't arrived yet, has she?

Past simple	*You bought some milk, didn't you?*
	You didn't buy any bread, did you?

Past continuous	*Tina was running quickly, wasn't she?*
	Tina wasn't wearing running shoes, was she?

will	*You won't be late, will you?*
	You'll be careful, won't you?

going to	*You're going to have a party, aren't you?*
	We aren't going to be late, are we?

be	*Tom is good fun, isn't he?*
	You weren't late, were you?

have got	*You've got a brother, haven't you?*
	You haven't got a sister, have you?

Intonation and meaning

- Real questions (I'm not sure of the answer)

    *You **like** swimming, **don't you?***

    *You **don't like** swimming, **do you?***

- Checking (I think I know the answer)

    *You **like** swimming, **don't you?***

    *You **don't like** swimming, **do you?***

Practice

1 <u>Underline</u> the correct tag in each sentence.

a) Jim got lost, *did he/<u>didn't he</u>*?

b) You don't know the answer, *do you/don't you*?

c) The children were making a lot of noise, *wasn't it/weren't they*?

d) Harry doesn't feel well, *isn't it/does he*?

e) George didn't complain, *did he/didn't he*?

f) Something has gone wrong, *has it/hasn't it*?

g) You aren't sitting here, *isn't it/ are you*?

h) You will read this, *will you/won't you*?

i) Paul likes Jill, *isn't it/doesn't he*?

j) You're waiting for Sue, *isn't it/aren't you*?

2 Complete the questions. Choose the correct tag (1–10) for the statements (a–j).

a) Ann catches the bus,   1   wasn't she?

b) Jan is leaving in the morning,   2   is she?

c) Sally won't be back,   3   didn't she?

d) Helen has left,   4   doesn't she?

e) Kate finished the book,   5   will she?

f) Sue hasn't got a bike,   6   did she?

g) Tina isn't a French teacher,   7   does she?

h) Paula didn't say a lot,   8   hasn't she?

i) Mary was sitting next to you,   9   has she?

j) Pam doesn't like classical music, 10   isn't she?

3 Write a tag for each sentence.

a) Harry has been helping you, ...*hasn't he*........... ?

b) You don't eat meat, ... ?

c) Paul was sleeping, ... ?

d) I missed a good film, ... ?

e) Jane is leaving in the morning, ... ?

f) We are going to win, ... ?

g) Jack hasn't done his homework, ... ?

h) You weren't having dinner, ... ?

i) David and Kate aren't coming to the party, ... ?

j) Sue didn't leave early, ... ?

1 **Complete these conditional sentences. Use *will* or *would* and the present simple or past simple.**

a) Look at that sky! It's going to rain. If I (get)............*get*............wet, I'm sure I (catch) ....*will catch*.............. a cold.

b) I'm not your teacher so I don't know the answer. If I (be) .... your teacher, I (tell) .... you to look in your dictionary!

c) I often imagine being on a desert island. If I (live) .... on a desert island, I (spend) .... all day fishing and sunbathing!

d) Yes, I often see Helen. If I (see) .... her tomorrow, I (tell) .... her to call you.

e) Come on, hurry up. If we (hurry) ...., we (get) .... to the cinema before the beginning of the film.

f) Sorry, but I haven't got a pencil sharpener. If I (have) .... one, I (lend) .... it to you, but I haven't got one!

g) Let's go now. If we (not get) .... there before 7.00, there (not be) .... any tickets left for the rock concert.

h) I don't believe in aliens. Anyway, if aliens (land) .... on Earth, I think they (soon decide) .... to return to their planet!

2 **Rewrite each sentence beginning as shown. Do not change the meaning.**

a) I advise you to go to the doctor's.
If .....*I were you, I would go to the doctor's.*..................... .

b) I'm sure your name isn't Jim.
Your .... it?

c) I think you've forgotten your homework!
You .... you!

d) If you don't hurry, we'll be late.
If .... won't ....

e) I hope our team isn't going to lose.
Our team .... it?

f) Why don't you go to bed early?
If ....

g) I'm sure you weren't at school yesterday.
You .... you?

h) You feel hungry because you don't eat breakfast.
.... wouldn't ....

3 **Complete the questions.**

a) Who ....*do*................. you ....*sit next to*................. in class?

I sit next to Jim.

b) .... to India?

No, I haven't. I've never been to India.

c) What .... ?

Tomorrow? I'm going to have a rest, I think!

d) What .... ?

Being with my friends makes me happy.

e) Why .... ?

I'm not looking at you, actually!

f) .... swimming?

Yes, I do. I like swimming very much.

g) Who .... there?

In that house? Mark lives there, I think.

4 **Write a tag for each sentence.**

a) You like ice-cream, ...*don't you*..... ?

b) Your name's Ewa, ... ?

c) We're not late, ... ?

d) You're waiting for Jack, ... ?

e) Roberto hasn't got a brother, ... ?

f) They'll be here soon, ... ?

g) You weren't writing, ... ?

5 **Correct each sentence or question.**

a) What <u>you are</u> doing this evening? ....*are you*.......

b) Who does live here? ....

c) If I am rich, I am buying a big car! ....

d) You haven't got a pen, got you? ....

e) What means this? ....

f) You're Helen, isn't it? ....

Think about grammar! Are the sentences true or false?

a) Conditional 2 sentences are about the past.

b) Never use *do* in subject questions.

c) Tag questions are not real questions.

Modals of ability and possibility

Explanations

can

Statements	Negatives	Questions
I can swim.	*I can't swim.*	*Can I swim?*
You can swim.	*You can't swim.*	*Can you swim?*
He can swim.	*He can't swim.*	*Can he swim?*
She can swim.	*She can't swim.*	*Can she swim?*
It can swim.	*It can't swim.*	*Can it swim?*
We can swim.	*We can't swim.*	*Can we swim?*
They can swim.	*They can't swim.*	*Can they swim?*

cannot

I cannot swim.   In formal writing and speech.

Short answers

Can *you see it?*
Yes, I **can.**
No, I **can't.**

Tag questions

You **can** *see it,* **can't you?**
You **can't** *see it,* **can you?**

Examples

Can *you* **ride** *a bike?*
Sorry, but I **can't come** *to your party on Friday.*
I **can't lift** *this table.*

Careful!

For the past, *could* is used. For the future, *be able to.*

Practice

1 **Read the form and write sentences about Nicola.**

What can you do?	
Name: *Nicola Schiffon*	
walk?	✔
run?	✗
dance?	✔
smile?	✔
speak English?	✗
ride a bicycle?	✗

a) *She can walk.* ....

b) ....

c) ....

d) ....

e) ....

f) ....

2 **Rewrite each sentence using *can* or *can't*. Do not change the meaning.**

a) I'm not able to come to your party.
   I can't come to your party. ....

b) Is it possible for you to play basketball tonight?
   ....

c) Do you know how to use a computer?
   ....

d) It isn't possible for you to borrow my bike.
   ....

e) It's impossible for us to answer this question.
   ....

f) It's not possible for me to help you.
   ....

g) I don't know how to play this game.
   ....

h) Is it possible for you to help me?
   ....

Explanations

must

Situations for *must*:

We usually use *must* when we talk about necessary or important actions.

> I **must leave** now. I don't want to be late.
> We **must remember** to take our passports.

Children must obey their parents.

I must leave.	We must leave.
You must leave.	They must leave.
He must leave.	It must leave.
She must leave.	

We can also use *have to* in these situations.

have to

Situations for *have to*:

We use *have to* when we talk about a rule made for us by somebody else.

> We **have to wear** a uniform at my school.　(a rule)
> When the lights are red, you **have to stop**.　(a rule)

I have to leave.	Do I have to leave?
You have to leave.	Do you have to leave?
He has to leave.	Does he have to leave?
She has to leave.	Does she have to leave?
It has to leave.	Does it have to leave?
We have to leave.	Do we have to leave?
They have to leave.	Do they have to leave?

We don't usually use *must* in these situations.

> I **must leave** at 6.00.　Do I **have to leave** at 6.00?
> I **have to leave** at 6.00.　Do I **have to leave** at 6.00?

should

Situations for *should*:

Should gives the speaker's opinion of what is a good thing to do.

> You **should check** your work at the end of the lesson.
> You **should eat** fruit every day.
> (This means: It's a good idea for you to do this.)

Practice

1   **Rewrite each imperative with *must*.**

a) Do it again!   *You must do it again!*

b) Work faster! ....

c) Turn to page 50! ....

d) Hurry up! ....

e) Stop talking! ....

f) Listen to me! ....

g) Give me your homework! ....

h) Sit down! ....

2   **Change the statements into questions and the questions into statements.**

   Life at school

a) We have to wear a uniform.   *Do you have to wear a uniform?*

b) Do you have to do homework? ....

c) I must sit in the same place ....

d) He has to arrive before 8.00. ....

e) Does she have to eat lunch at school? ....

f) I have to change classrooms. ....

g) They must do gym. ....

h) Do you have to learn German? ....

3   **Complete each sentence with *should*.**

a) If I were you, I'd go to the doctor's.

   I think   *you should go to the doctor's.*

b) It's a good idea to wear a warm coat.

   You ....

c) My advice is to leave early.

   I think you ....

d) It's a good idea to take more exercise.

   You ....

e) In my opinion, it's a good idea for you to read a lot.

   I think ....

f) It's a good idea to do that.

   You ....

g) My advice is for you to ride a bike.

   I think ....

h) If I were you, I would buy a dog.

   I think ....

Explanations

mustn't

must not = mustn't

I mustn't do that.	He mustn't do that.	We mustn't do that.
You mustn't do that.	She mustn't do that.	They mustn't do that.
	It mustn't do that.	

You **mustn't shout!**   (These actions are not allowed.)
Students **must not eat** or **drink** in the classroom.

Must not is more formal and is used in written English.

don't have to

do not = don't   does not = doesn't

I don't have to	he doesn't have to	we don't have to
you don't have to	she doesn't have to	they don't have to
	it doesn't have to	

We **don't have to go** to school tomorrow.   (These actions are not necessary.)
Jim **doesn't have to get up** early tomorrow.

shouldn't

should not = shouldn't
Shouldn't gives the speaker's opinion of what is a bad thing to do.

You **shouldn't watch** television all day. (In my opinion this is a bad idea.)
Kate **shouldn't eat** so much chocolate.

Careful!

The first 't' in *mustn't* is silent.

Practice

1 Look at the notices and say what is not allowed.

a)

NO TALKING

b)

c)

DO NOT OPEN THE WINDOW

d)

e)

P

f)

a) ....*You mustn't talk.*...........   b) ....

c) ....   d) ....

e) ....   f) ....

2 Use the prompts to write sentences with *should* and *shouldn't*.

Information for Olympic athletes

a) smoke ✗ ....*You shouldn't smoke.*...............................

b) keep fit ✔ ....

c) eat healthy food ✔ ....

d) drink alcohol ✗ ....

e) go to the gym ✔ ....

f) take drugs ✗ ....

3 Use the verbs in brackets to make negative sentences with *have to*.

a) Kate (take) ....*doesn't have to take*...... an exam tomorrow.

b) Jim (get up) .... early.

c) I (make) .... a phone call.

d) George (do) .... the shopping.

e) You (sit) .... here.

f) Helen (do) .... her homework.

39 Modals: past

Explanations

Past ability

■ *could*

I could hear.	*He could hear.*	*We could hear.*
You could hear.	*She could hear.*	*They could hear.*
	It could hear.	

Jane **could swim** when she was six. (She knew how to swim.)

■ *couldn't*
could not = couldn't

I couldn't hear.	*He couldn't hear.*	*We couldn't hear.*
You couldn't hear.	*She couldn't hear.*	*They couldn't hear.*
	It couldn't hear.	

I looked for my wallet but I **couldn't find** it.

Past obligation

■ *had to* (*must* does not have a past form – use *had to*)

I had to go.	*He had to go.*	*We had to go.*
You had to go.	*She had to go.*	*They had to go.*
	I had to go.	

I **had to do** a lot of homework yesterday.

■ *didn't have to*
did not = didn't

I didn't have to go.	*He didn't have to go.*	*We didn't have to go.*
You didn't have to go.	*She didn't have to go.*	*They didn't have to go.*
	I didn't have to go.	

Tom **didn't have to go** to school today.

Practice

1 **Complete each sentence (a–f) with an ending (1–6).**

a) I didn't light a fire because ....*3*........

b) I didn't do my homework because ....

c) I didn't use the computer because ....

d) I didn't do the shopping because ....

e) I didn't go to the doctor's because ....

f) I didn't go to the party because ....

1 I couldn't make an appointment.

2 I couldn't understand the instructions.

3 I couldn't find the matches.

4 I couldn't remember the exercise.

5 I couldn't get ready in time.

6 I couldn't go to the supermarket.

2 **Write what you *had to do* or *didn't have to do* yesterday.**

a) wash the dishes ....*I didn't have to wash the dishes.*.......

b) cook dinner ....

c) do homework ....

d) go shopping ....

e) go to school ....

f) write a letter ....

3 **Rewrite each sentence using *could/couldn't* or *had to/didn't have to*. Do not change the meaning.**

a) It was impossible for Sarah to get home before 7.00.

Sarah ....*couldn't get home before 7.00.*........................

b) It was necessary for Paul to leave at 6.00 to catch his plane.

Paul ....

c) It was impossible for us to believe our luck!

We ....

d) It wasn't necessary for Mike to wait long for the bus.

Mike ....

e) Ann's friend knew how to speak five languages.

Ann's friend ....

f) Sorry I didn't phone, but it was impossible to find your number.

Sorry I didn't phone, but I ....

....

Modals: possibility, uncertainty, impossibility, certainty

Explanations

- Uncertainty – future time

    *Our team **might** win the basketball match.*
    *I **may/might** see you next week.*
    *I **may/might** not have time to finish tonight.*

- Possibility – present time

    *The cat **could** be in the kitchen.*
    *The baby **may/might** be crying because he's tired.*

- Impossibility or certainty – present time

    *It **can't** be Tuesday today! It was Tuesday yesterday!*

*He **must** be at home.*	(I'm sure he is at home.)
*She **can't** be in Spain! I saw her today!*	(I'm sure she isn't in Spain.)

- We cannot use *can't* and *must* for impossibility or certainty in future time.

Careful!	We can't say:
	It can be Tuesday! ✗
	It mustn't be Tuesday. ✗

Practice

1 **Rewrite each sentence using *might, can't* or *must*. Do not change the meaning.**

a) Perhaps it will rain. *It might rain.* ....

b) I'm sure this is right. ....

c) Perhaps I'll see you tomorrow. ....

d) I'm sure that isn't the answer. ....

e) I'm sure this is the place. ....

f) Perhaps I won't come to your party. ....

g) I'm sure you're not serious! ....

h) I'm sure we are early. ....

2 **Look at the pictures. Choose the most suitable sentence (a–f) for each picture (1–6).**

1	2	3

4	5	6

a) Try room 4. She might be teaching.   ....6....

b) I think he must be a tourist.   ....

c) This can't be the right house!   ....

d) I think your watch must be wrong.   ....

e) This can't be right!   ....

f) Careful! You might fall off!   ....

Modals: problems and contrasts

Explanations

- Modals do not have third person -*s* endings.

  I can swim.   *Helen can swim.*

- Modals have more than one meaning. This depends on the context.

*You **must** pay before 21st January.*	(Obligation)
*I think Carol **must** be very happy.*	(Certainty)
***Can** you use a computer?*	(Ability)
***Can** you open the window?*	(Informal request)
*Nick **can't** dance. He's never learned.*	(Inability – not able to do it)
*It **can't** be Tuesday!*	(Impossibility)

- Some modals have the same meanings in the same context.

  I have to go. = I must go.

The negative forms have different meanings.

I don't have to go.	(It's not necessary.)
I mustn't go.	(It's not allowed.)

- Some modals have only small differences of meaning.

I have to wear a suit and tie.	(This is the rule.)
I should wear a suit and tie.	(This is not a rule but people expect me to do it. I can choose not to do it!)

*Alan **has to** study for his exam, but he **can't** concentrate.*

 SEE ALSO

Grammar 37: Modals of obligation
Grammar 38: Modals of negative obligation

Practice

1 **Underline the correct words in each sentence.**

a) We *mustn't/<u>don't have to</u>* go to school on Tuesday. It's a holiday.

b) In this country, you *have to/should* have an identity card.

c) Sorry I'm late. I *must/had to* go to the doctor's.

d) You *don't have to/shouldn't* eat so much chocolate. It's bad for you!

e) I'm sorry, but I*'m not able to/don't have to* meet you tomorrow.

f) You *mustn't/don't have to* leave the room without permission.

g) Where *did you have to/must you* go yesterday?

h) I don't think you *must/should* go out today.

i) Sorry, I don't understand. I *can't/mustn't* speak German.

2 **Rewrite each sentence using the words in bold. Do not change the meaning.**

a) It wasn't necessary for me to go to school yesterday.   **have**
   I didn't have to go to school yesterday.

b) I'm sure this isn't right.   **can't**

c) Tina knew how to play the piano at an early age.   **could**

d) Perhaps I'll see you tomorrow.   **may**

e) Harry managed to repair the radio.   **able**

f) It was necessary for Bill to return his library book.   **had**

g) It's possible that Carol will phone tonight.   **might**

3 **Complete the sentences. Write one word for each space.**

a) Jack ......*has*...... to be home before 10.00.

b) Emma .... swim very well for a child of her age.

c) Students .... not leave coats in this room.

d) We .... to get up before 6.00 tomorrow.

e) I think we .... go home now.

f) Jenny .... to leave early in the morning.

g) You don't .... to do this if you don't want to.

h) Tim .... to do all his homework again.

Consolidation 6

1 **Underline** the correct words in each sentence.

a) Sorry I'm late. I _had to go_ /may go to the library.

b) My brother *could walk/might walk* before he started talking.

c) You've worked very hard. You *could be/must be* tired.

d) George *didn't have to wait/hadn't to wait* long for the bus.

e) Don't wait for me. I *could be/had to be* late.

f) Helen *mustn't do/couldn't do* her homework, because she was ill.

g) This bus *had to go/might go* to the centre. Shall I ask the driver?

h) Sam dropped the three glasses, but *was able to catch/might catch* one!

2 **Complete the sentences. Write one word for each space.**

a) That was a long walk! You ....*must*.... be tired.

b) Sorry I was away yesterday. I .... to go to the hospital.

c) Will you be .... to give me some help tomorrow?

d) Do you .... to go now?

e) Peter .... ride a bike when he was seven.

f) Mary .... be in her bedroom. The light is on.

g) Students .... not leave their bicycles near this door. It is forbidden.

h) We .... to try very hard, but we succeeded in the end.

3 **Rewrite each sentence beginning as shown. Do not change the meaning.**

a) I'm sure that bag isn't yours.
   That ....*can't be*.. your bag.

b) My advice is to talk to your teacher about it.
   I think you ....

c) It's not necessary for you to be here before 8.00.
   You ....

d) I'm sure that Sam knows the answer.
   Sam .... the answer.

e) I'm sorry I'm late. It was necessary for me to go to the doctor's.
   I'm sorry I'm late. I ....

f) Perhaps Cathy is at the library.
   Cathy .... at the library.

g) What is your advice?
   What do you think .... do?

4 **Rewrite each sentence using the words in bold. Do not change the meaning.**

a) It's very important for you to be here at 6.00.   **must**

You must be here at 6.00.
....

b) It's impossible for me to see you tomorrow.   **can't**

....

c) It's necessary to press the button twice.   **to**

....

d) It's not a good idea to eat lots of sweets.   **shouldn't**

....

e) It's not possible for Jean to come to the party.   **able**

....

f) It's not necessary for you to pay now.   **don't**

....

g) Parking here is forbidden.   **mustn't**

....

h) It's necessary for you to work harder.   **should**

....

5 **Complete the sentences. Write one word for each space.** *Can't, couldn't* **etc. are**
one word.

a) You're only wearing a t-shirt and shorts. You ..... *must* ..... feel cold!

b) I .... not be at school tomorrow. I feel ill.

c) Tina searched the swimming pool, but wasn't .... to find her ring.

d) Perhaps you left your wallet on the bus, or it .... be at home.

e) The exam was long, and I .... finish all the questions.

f) Brian didn't .... to do any homework, so he went to the cinema.

g) This .... be the house. It's the wrong number. Let's try down there.

h) Ann .... run much faster than her friends.

i) This bill .... be right. There's a mistake in it somewhere.

j) Sorry I was out. I .... to go to the shops.

Think about grammar! Are the sentences true or false?

a) *Mustn't* is the same as *don't have to*.

b) There is very little difference between *must* and *have to*.

c) *Should* is used when you think something is a good idea.

Explanations

- Spelling rules for regular noun plurals
  One vowel, one consonant

  | *cat* | ⟶ | *cats* | *bed* | ⟶ | *beds* |

  Words ending in *ss, sh*

  | *glass* | ⟶ | *glasses* | *dish* | ⟶ | *dishes* |

  Words ending in *ch*

  | *match* | ⟶ | *matches* | *watch* | ⟶ | *watches* |

  Words ending in *x*

  | *box* | ⟶ | *boxes* | *fax* | ⟶ | *faxes* |

  Words ending in *o*

  | *potato* | ⟶ | *potatoes* | *tomato* | ⟶ | *tomatoes* |

  Words ending in consonant and *y*

  | *family* | ⟶ | *families* |

  Words ending in vowel and *y*

  | *donkey* | ⟶ | *donkeys* |

  Words with final consonant *f*

  | *knife* | ⟶ | *knives* | *life* | ⟶ | *lives* |
  | *leaf* | ⟶ | *leaves* | *thief* | ⟶ | *thieves* |

- Irregular noun plurals
  Some nouns have irregular plurals or do not change.

man	⟶	*men*
woman	⟶	*women*
child	⟶	*children*
tooth	⟶	*teeth*
mouse	⟶	*mice*
foot	⟶	*feet*

- No change
  Some words have the same singular and plural.

  | *sheep* | ⟶ | *sheep* |
  | *fish* | ⟶ | *fish* |

  Some words are always plural.

  | *scissors* | *a pair of scissors* |
  | *trousers/jeans/shorts* | *a pair of trousers/jeans/shorts* |

Practice

1 **What are they?**

a)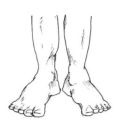

b)

c)

d)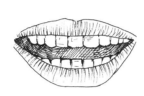

e)

f)

a) ....._feet_.......   b) ....   c) ....

d) ....   e) ....   f) ....

2 **Write the plural of each word in brackets.**

a) Can you go to the shops? We need some (potato) ...._potatoes_........ .

b) Most (family) .... enjoy going on holiday together.

c) Jack decided to make some (bookshelf) .... for his bedroom.

d) Do you think you could help me wash the (dish) .... ?

e) Sue bought three (box) .... of chocolates.

f) In the afternoon we went to the zoo and fed the (monkey) ....

3 **Complete the words.**

a) In the autumn, the l_eaves_............. on the trees change colour, and then fall off.

b) In the library there were lots of s........................ full of books.

c) We wanted to light a fire so we bought a box of m........................ .

d) Kate has got two c........................ a son and a daughter.

e) Nowadays w........................ want to do the same jobs as men.

f) My eyes ache when I read. I think I need new g........................ .

Countable and uncountable nouns: *a, an, some, any*

Explanations

Countable nouns

We can count countable nouns.

a bottle   **two bottles**   **three** *bottles*

Countable nouns – singular   *a/an*
We use *an* before words beginning with a vowel.

*I've got **an** umbrella.*   **Have you got a** *chair?*

Some words are irregular because the sound is different.

***an** hour (the h is silent)*   ***a** university*

Countable nouns – plural   *some, any, not any*
We use *some* for statements.
*There are **some** chairs in the other room.*

We use *any* for questions.
*Are there **any** chairs in the other room?*

We use *not ... any* for negatives.
*There **aren't any** chairs in the other room.*

Uncountable (mass) nouns

We cannot count uncountable nouns.

some coffee   *some milk*   *some rice*

All uncountable/mass nouns   *some, any, not any*
*We bought **some** tea.*
*Did you buy **any** tea?*
*We didn't buy **any** tea.*

■ *Could you buy me **some** tea?*   (I expect you to say 'Yes'.)
*Are there **some** sandwiches for me?*

*There **isn't any** food left.*

Practice

1 **Choose *a* or *some*.**

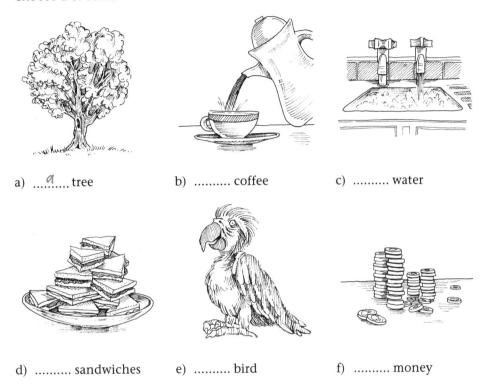

a) ...*a*... tree b) .... coffee c) .... water

d) .... sandwiches e) .... bird f) .... money

2 <u>Underline</u> **the correct word in each sentence.**

a) Jack hasn't got <u>a</u>/*any* brother.

b) There weren't *some/any* letters for me this morning.

c) Could I have *a/some* water, please?

d) I went to the supermarket because I didn't have *a/any* milk.

e) There isn't *a/any* railway station in this town.

f) Sorry, we don't have *some/any* boxes left.

g) Have you got *a/any* pen that I can borrow?

3 **Choose *some* or *any* for each space.**

a) There aren't ......*any*...... good restaurants in this town.

b) Don't worry about lunch. I've brought .... sandwiches.

c) You need .... scissors to cut the paper.

d) Have you got .... brothers and sisters?

e) I think you owe me .... money.

f) We'd like to stay longer, but we don't have .... time.

g) Could you give me .... information please?

Countable and uncountable nouns: problems

Explanations

Some nouns are countable with one meaning and uncountable with another meaning.

Change of meaning

a fish		some fish	
a coffee		some coffee	
a paper	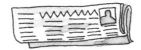	some paper	
a wood		some wood	
an iron		some iron	
a glass		some glass	

Uncountables with no s plural

advice	*Can I have **some** advice?*
spaghetti	*I'd like **some** spaghetti.*
English (language)	*Your English **is** good!*
hair	*Your hair **is** beautiful!*
furniture	*This furniture **is** very modern.*
information	*Could you give me **some** information?*
weather	*The weather **is** awful!*
money	*The money **is** on the table.*
luggage	*My luggage **is** in the taxi.*

Other problems

people	*There **are some people** in the garden.*
	*There **is** a person in the garden.*
bread	*Could you buy **a loaf of** bread?*
	*(We cannot say **a** bread.)*
fish	*One fish, two **fish**, etc.*
police	*The police **are** coming!* (singular form, plural verb)
news	*The news **is** on TV.* (plural form, singular verb)

Practice

*Eth lang
Practice
M. Vince.
Macmillan*

1 **Complete the sentences. Choose *a, an* or *no article* for each space.**

a) The old bridge was made of ....—........ iron.

b) Shall we have .... fish? This restaurant is famous for it.

c) Could you bring me .... glass, please?

d) They make these towels from .... recycled paper.

e) That was silly of me. Now there's .... coffee all over the table.

f) My shirt is dry now. Have you got .... iron?

g) One wall is .... glass, so there is lots of light in the room.

h) Can you buy me .... paper? I want to check the football results.

2 **Choose the most suitable word or phrase for each space.**

a) I'll post your letters. Have you got ..*B*..?

A) a stamp   B) any stamps   C) any stamp

b) The streets were empty. There weren't ..... there.

A) peoples   B) some people   C) any people

c) Have you got .....? I can help you.

A) a luggage   B) some luggages   C) any luggage

d) Do you like .....? No, I don't.

A) hot milk   B) a hot milk   C) some hot milk

e) We've just moved into our house, and we haven't got ..... .

A) a furniture   B) any furniture   C) some furniture

f) There wasn't any wood, so we used ..... .

A) plastic   B) any plastic   C) a plastic

g) Can you help me? I'd like ..... .

A) an advice   B) some advice   C) advices

3 **Choose *is* or *are* for each space.**

a) Helen's hair ....*is*..........very long.

b) The weather .... really good at the moment.

c) Don't worry. The police here .... very friendly.

d) Can you turn on the television? The news .... on.

e) Women .... usually better listeners than men.

f) Where .... the money that I gave you yesterday?

g) Your glasses .... on the table.

h) David's French .... good. He's been taking lessons.

Countable and uncountable nouns: *much, many*

Explanations

much and *many* –
questions and
negatives

*There isn't **much** time.*   countable
*Is there **much** time?*

*There aren't **many** seats.*   uncountable
*Are there **many** seats?*

In informal statements, we use *lots of*.
   *There is **lots of** time.*
   *There are **lots of** seats.*

In formal statements, we use *many*.
   ***Many** people believe in ghosts.*
   *Mr Harrison visited Argentina **many** years ago.*

How much...? uncountables

How much *homework have you got?*   *Lots!*
How much *time have we got?*   *We've got fifteen minutes.*
How much *milk do you want?*   *Not much.*

How many...? countables

How many *pages do you have to read?*   *Ten.*
How many *brothers and sisters have you got?* *Two brothers.*
How many *people are there here?*   *A hundred.*

How many *players are there?*   *Not very **many**.*

Practice

1 <u>Underline</u> the correct word in each sentence.

a) There isn't *many/<u>much</u>* food in the fridge, I'm afraid.

b) Have you read *many/much* books in German?

c) We don't have *many/much* rain in the summer.

d) There isn't *many/much* coffee left.

e) You haven't made *many/much* mistakes.

f) Have you got *many/much* friends in this town?

g) Hurry up. We haven't got *many/much* time.

h) Do *many/much* cars park in this street?

2 Complete the questions with *How much* or *How many*.

a) ....*How much*........ money have you got?

b) .... students are in the class?

c) .... words do we have to write?

d) .... paper do you need?

e) .... pages are there in this book?

f) .... time have we got left?

g) .... water do you drink in a day?

h) .... times have you been to London?

3 Write one word in each space.

a) I'll try to call you tonight, but I don't have ......*much*...... time.

b) How .... times do you brush your teeth every day?

c) Shall I make some more tea? I didn't make ....

d) Kate only ate a sandwich because she didn't have .... money.

e) There weren't .... seats so some of us had to stand up.

f) Have you got .... work, or do you want to come to the cinema?

g) We invited lots of people to our party, but not .... turned up.

h) You'll have to share, because there aren't .... books.

4 Read the answers. Write a question for each answer. Use *How much* or *How many*.

a) ......*How many brothers have you got?*...... I've got two brothers.

b) .... It costs £2.00.

c) .... There are ten people.

d) .... I need two bicycles.

e) .... I'd like a lot of rice.

f) .... He has got three children.

g) .... I haven't got any money.

Countable and uncountable nouns: *much, many, enough*

Explanations

too much –
uncountables

*I've put **too much** sugar in my tea.*   (more than I wanted)
*I've got **too much** work.*   (more than is possible to complete)

too many –
countables

*There are **too many** students in this class.*   (It's very crowded.)
*I've got **too many** books. I need some new shelves!*   (The shelves are full.)

enough – **countable**
and uncountable

*Are there **enough** chairs? No. There are twenty people and fifteen chairs.*
*Is there **enough** time? Yes. We can have lunch and then catch the bus.*

*There **aren't enough** chairs.*
*There **isn't enough** time.*

*There are **too many** students in the classroom. There **aren't enough** chairs.*

Practice

1 Choose the most suitable sentence (a–f) for each picture (1–6).

1

2

3

4

5

6

a) There is too much noise. ...... *5* ......

b) There are too many people. ....

c) There isn't enough water. ....

d) I haven't got enough money. ....

e) There aren't enough chairs. ....

f) I put too much pepper in it. ....

2   <u>Underline</u> the correct sentence.

a) Sorry, but I can't pay the bill.

   1   I've got too much money.   2   <u>I haven't got enough money</u>.

b) I cooked spaghetti for ten, but only two people came.

   1   I've got too much **spaghetti**.   2   I've got too many spaghetti.

c) Jim is very lonely.

   1   He has got too many friends.   2   He hasn't got enough friends.

d) You can't take ten suitcases on the plane!

   1   You've got too much luggage.   2   You haven't got enough luggage.

e) Please share the books, one between two.

   1   There are too many books.   2   There aren't enough books.

f) Eight people can't go in one taxi.

   1   There is too much room.   2   There isn't enough room.

g) We didn't enjoy our holiday.

   1   There was too much rain.   2   There wasn't enough rain.

h) Please write this again.

   1   There are too many mistakes.   2   There aren't enough mistakes.

i) I'm too tired to get out!

   1   I've had too much sleep.   2   I haven't had enough sleep.

j) This bread tastes horrible!

   1   There is too much salt in it.   2   There are too many salt in it.

3   Choose the best ending (1–10) for each sentence (a–j).

a) I can't play tennis now.   1   There isn't enough light.

b) I feel a bit sick.   2   There's too much noise.

c) I can't drive you home.   3   I haven't got enough sugar.

d) I can't have a bath.   4   I've got too many clothes.

e) There is no room in my wardrobe.   5   I haven't got enough petrol.

f) I can't sleep in this room.   6   I've got too much homework.

g) I can't read here.   7   I haven't got much money.

h) I can't eat this soup.   8   I've eaten too many apples.

i) I can't make a cake.   9   There's too much salt in it.

j) I can't buy a new bike.   10   There isn't enough hot water.

4   **Choose the most suitable word or phrase for each space.**

a) There is no room on the bus. There are ..A.. people.

    A) too many   B) too much   C) not enough

b) I'm still very hungry. There was ..... food.

    A) too much   B) not enough   C) enough

c) Have we got ..... drinks for the party?

    A) enough   B) too many   C) not enough

d) John didn't buy the CD. It cost ..... money.

    A) too many   B) enough   C) too much

e) We can't go to the library today. There is ..... time.

    A) too many   B) enough   C) not enough

f) Yuk! This sandwich is disgusting. There's ..... salt in it.

    A) too much   B) enough   C) too many

g) My homework is very difficult. There are ..... new words to learn.

    A) not enough   B) too many   C) enough

h) Katy has ..... money to buy a car. She's lucky!

    A) too much   B) enough   C) too many

i) We can't all sleep in here. There ..... beds.

    A) not enough   B) too many   C) enough

j) Clare is very happy. She had ..... friends at her party.

    A) too much   B) enough   C) not enough

5   **Rewrite each sentence using *too much* or *too many* and the words in bold. Do not change the meaning.**

a) This room is very crowded.   **people**

    There are too many people.

b) I can't hear anything you say!   **noise**

    ....

c) I'm very busy, so I can't come out.   **things to do**

    ....

d) There is a traffic jam in the city centre.   **cars**

    ....

e) My coffee is very sweet! I can't drink it!   **sugar**

    ....

f) I can't find room on the shelves for all my books!   **books**

    ....

Explanations

Cardinal numbers

1	*one*	11	*eleven*	21	*twenty-one*
2	*two*	12	*twelve*	22	*twenty-two, etc.*
3	*three*	13	*thirteen*	30	*thirty*
4	*four*	14	*fourteen*	40	*forty*
5	*five*	15	*fifteen*	50	*fifty*
6	*six*	16	*sixteen*	60	*sixty*
7	*seven*	17	*seventeen*	70	*seventy*
8	*eight*	18	*eighteen*	80	*eighty*
9	*nine*	19	*nineteen*	90	*ninety*
10	*ten*	20	*twenty*	100	*a hundred/one hundred*

0 = *nought* or *zero*. In telephone numbers we say it like the letter 'O'. In football we say *nil*. In tennis we say *love*.

101	*a hundred <u>and</u> one*
200	*two hundred* (*hundred* is not plural)
300	*three hundred*
999	*nine hundred <u>and</u> ninety-nine*
1,000	*a thousand/one thousand*
1,001	*a thousand and one*
2,250	*two thousand, two hundred <u>and</u> fifty* (*thousand* is not plural)
999,999	*nine hundred <u>and</u> ninety-nine thousand, nine hundred <u>and</u> ninety-nine*
1,000,000	*a million/one million*
5,000,000	*five million* (*million* is not plural)

Ordinal numbers

1st	*first*	9th	*ninth*	17th	*seventeenth*	25th	*twenty-fifth*
2nd	*second*	10th	*tenth*	18th	*eighteenth*	26th	*twenty-sixth*
3rd	*third*	11th	*eleventh*	19th	*nineteenth*	27th	*twenty-seventh*
4th	*fourth*	12th	*twelfth*	20th	*twentieth*	28th	*twenty-eighth*
5th	*fifth*	13th	*thirteenth*	21st	*twenty-first*	29th	*twenty-ninth*
6th	*sixth*	14th	*fourteenth*	22nd	*twenty-second*	30th	*thirtieth*
7th	*seventh*	15th	*fifteenth*	23rd	*twenty-third*	31st	*thirty-first*
8th	*eighth*	16th	*sixteenth*	24th	*twenty-fourth*		

Other examples

Fractions and decimals

½ = *a half*	1½ = *one and a half*	1.5 = *one point five*
¼ = *a quarter*	2¼ = *two and a quarter*	2.25 = *two point two five*
¾ = *three quarters*	5¾ = *five and three quarters*	5.75 = *five point seven five*

Practice

1 **Write the words as cardinal numbers.**

a) a hundred and nine .... *109* ....

b) eighty-seven ....

c) two hundred and fifty-five ....

d) three hundred and thirty-two ....

e) two thousand and one ....

f) two million ....

g) two hundred thousand ....

h) fifty one thousand, two hundred and ten ....

2 **Write the cardinal numbers as words.**

a) 18 .... *eighteen* ....   e) 64 ....

b) 90 ....   f) 97 ....

c) 49 ....   g) 23 ....

d) 71 ....   h) 14 ....

3 **Write the ordinal numbers as words.**

a) 3rd .... *third* ....   e) 5th ....

b) 9th ....   f) 2nd ....

c) 21st ....   g) 43rd ....

d) 30th ....   h) 1st ....

4 <u>Underline</u> **the correct answer.**

a) 296   =   1 two thousand, nine hundred and sixty

                             2 <u>two hundred and ninety-six</u>

b) 5,695   =   1 five thousand, six hundred and ninety-five

                             2 fifty six hundred and nine and five

c) 10,000,000   =   1 ten hundred thousand

                             2 ten million

d) 5.75   =   1 five point seven five

                             2 five comma seventy-five

e) ¾   =   1 four thirds

                             2 three quarters

f) 1½   =   1 a one and half

                             2 one and a half

g) 200,000   =   1 two hundred thousand

                             2 two hundred thousands

1 <u>Underline</u> the correct word in each sentence.

a) Are there *a/<u>any</u>* people at the bus stop?

b) Sorry, I haven't got *some/any* time to talk now.

c) Look at this shirt! Can I borrow *an/some* iron?

d) Could I have *some/any* stamps, please?

e) I can't pay the bill! Can you lend me *a/some* money?

f) Did you buy *a/some* paper? I want to read the news.

g) Could you buy *a/some* bread at the supermarket?

2 Write one word in each space.

a) How ....*much*.... does this cost?

b) Jane has got too .... luggage.

c) Sorry, we haven't got .... cakes left, not a single one.

d) If you haven't got .... money, I can lend you some.

e) There are too .... people in this room. It's crowded.

f) How .... books have you got at home?

g) Are there .... cinemas in this town?

3 Choose *is* or *are* for each space.

a) Your trousers ....*are*.......... on the chair.

b) The mice .... under your bed!

c) The news .... on at 10.00.

d) Don't worry! The police .... coming.

e) People .... worried about you!

f) My tooth .... broken.

g) Your advice .... exactly right!

4 Complete each sentence with *much* or *many*.

a) I can't come to the cinema. I've got too ...*much*... homework.

b) We can't all have baths. There isn't .... hot water.

c) Some students don't have .... opportunities to speak in English.

d) We can't stop for a meal now. We haven't got .... time.

e) Paul felt lonely. He didn't have .... friends.

f) Not everyone can sit down. There are too .... people.

g) I couldn't sleep last night. There was too .... noise in the street.

5 Rewrite each sentence beginning as shown. Do not change the meaning.

a) I can't afford to go on holiday this year.

I haven't got ...... *enough money* ...... to go on holiday this year.

b) Paula has got long hair.

Paula's hair .... long.

c) My suitcases are over there.

My luggage .... over there.

d) We are short of paper. Can you borrow some?

We haven't got .... paper. Can you borrow some?

e) I'm in a hurry!

I .... much time.

f) There are very few good restaurants in this city.

There aren't .... good restaurants in this city.

6 Rewrite each sentence using the words in **bold**. Do not change the meaning.

a) Unfortunately, David hasn't got a lot of friends.   **many**

.... *Unfortunately, David hasn't got many friends.* ....

b) I'm short of tea.   **haven't**

....

c) There isn't a lot of sugar left.   **much**

....

d) Can you tell me about hotels in the centre?   **information**

....

e) Gerry owns this furniture.   **Gerry's**

....

f) We have run out of milk.   **any**

....

7 Correct each sentence or question.

a) The police here <u>is</u> very helpful.   .... *are* ....

b) Can you give me an advice?   ....

c) The news this evening were interesting. ....

d) The city centre was full of peoples.   ....

e) Thank you for the informations.   ....

f) I haven't got time enough.   ....

Think about grammar! Are the sentences true or false?

a) Countable nouns have no plural.

b) *Any* is used only in questions.

c) *Too much* is the opposite of *not enough*.

Advice, agreeing/ disagreeing, apologizing

Explanations

A function is language we use for a purpose. What we say depends on the:

- place: private or public?
- person: same age? friend? stranger?, etc.
- topic: everyday (borrowing a pen) or more important (borrowing money)?

Asking for advice

What do you think I should do?
What would you do?

Giving advice

I think you should (go to the doctor's).
If I were you, I'd (go to the doctor's).
Why don't you (go to the doctor's)?

What about (going to the doctor's)?
How about (going to the doctor's)?

Agreeing and disagreeing

Agreeing

I agree.
That's right.
I like this film. So do I.
I don't like this film. Neither do I.

Disagreeing

I don't agree. I don't think so.

Apologizing

I'm sorry. Sorry, it was my fault. I'm very sorry.

Replying to apologies

Never mind. That's all right. Don't worry.

- We say *Excuse me* when we want to pass someone who is in the way. The usual reply is *Sorry*.
- We say *Excuse me* at the beginning of questions to strangers.

Practice

1   **Complete the speech bubbles (1–6) with the sentences (a–f).**

1    2    3

4    5    6

a) Never mind.   d) Sorry, I've broken this cup.

b) How about trying a larger size?   e) If I were you, I'd go to the dentist's.

c) So do I.   f) What do you think I should do?

2   **Write one word in each space.**

a) I've lost your football. ....*Sorry*...... .

b) How about .... to the cinema?

c) 'This film is good, isn't it?' 'No, I don't think ....'

d) Sorry about the mess. It's my ....

e) If I .... you, I'd stay at home today.

f) 'I really love this place.' 'So .... I.'

g) .... me, I can't get in.

h) What's your advice? What do you think I .... do?

3   **Choose the best reply (1–6) for each sentence (a–f).**

a) What's your advice?   1 Neither do I.

b) I really enjoy going to the beach.   2 So do I.

c) Who broke the window?   3 Don't worry.

d) If I were you, I'd use a dictionary.   4 I think you should talk to your teacher about it.

e) I don't like doing homework!   5 I did. Sorry!

f) Sorry, I've lost your book.   6 Good idea!

Descriptions, directions, excuses, greetings

Explanations

Asking for a description and replying	*What's George like?*	*He's very friendly.*
	What's Cairo like?	*It's a big city.*
	What does Tina look like?	*She's tall and she's got long hair.*

Asking for directions	*Where's (the bus station)?*	(informal)
	Excuse me, do you know the way to (the bus station)?	↓
	Excuse me, could you tell me the way (to the bus station)?	(formal)

Giving directions

Go down this street and turn left/right.
It's at the end of this street.
It's on the left/on the right.
It's opposite/next to (the supermarket).

Making excuses

I'm sorry I'm late.
I'm sorry I'm late, but (I missed the bus).

Saying goodbye

Bye!
Bye for now!
See you tomorrow.

Greeting and replying to greetings

Greeting	Reply	
How do you do?	*How do you do?*	(formal)
Hello, how are you?	*Fine, thanks. And you?*	(informal)

Asking and replying about health

Question	Reply
How are you?	*I'm all right, thanks.*
	Not so good.
How do you feel?	*I feel fine/great/awful,* etc.

Practice

1 **Rewrite each sentence beginning as shown. Do not change the meaning.**

a) Can you describe Jack?
   What ..... *does Jack look* ..... like?

b) I apologize for being late.
   I'm .... late.

c) Where's the Apollo cinema?
   Do you .... to the Apollo cinema?

d) How are you today? Are you still ill?
   How do .... today? Are you still ill?

e) Do you know the way to the city centre, please?
   Could .... to the city centre, please?

f) What's your opinion of Paris?
   What .... like?

2 **Write one word in each space.**

a) ..... *Go* ..... down this street and turn right.

b) How .... you do?

c) Do you know the .... to the centre?

d) Bye! I'll .... you tomorrow.

e) I'm .... I'm late.

f) What is David .... ?

g) 'Hello, ... are you?' 'Fine, thanks.'

h) Could you .... me the way to Green Street?

i) How .... you feel today?

j) It's next .... the bank.

3 **Choose the most suitable reply (1–8) for the questions (a–h).**

a) What does Sam look like?   1 It's opposite the hospital.
b) How do you do?   2 Fine, thanks. How are you?
c) Where's the bus station?   3 He laughs a lot!
d) How do you feel?   4 Sorry, I don't.
e) Bye for now!   5 He's tall and thin.
f) How are you?   6 Not so good.
g) Do you know the way to Paris?   7 I'll see you tomorrow.
h) What's Jim like?   8 How do you do?

Asking for information, invitations, offers, permission

Explanations

Asking for permission

Do you know the time?   (informal)

Excuse me, could you tell me the time?   (formal)

What does this mean, please?

How do you say (.......) in English?

Inviting and replying to invitations

Inviting

Do you want to (go to the cinema)?   (informal)

Do you feel like (going to the cinema)?   (informal)

Would you like to (go to the cinema)?   (formal)

Replying

accepting   *Thanks, I'd love to (go).*

refusing   *I'm sorry but (I'm going to a party).*

              I'm afraid I can't.

Making an offer

Can I help (you)?

Shall I help (you)?

Offering something

Do you want (some tea)?   (informal)

Would you like (some tea)?   (formal)

Asking for, giving and refusing permission

Asking	Giving	Refusing	
Can I (leave early)?	*Yes, you can.*	*No, you can't.*	
Is it alright if I (leave early)?	*Sure. That's OK.*	*Sorry, no.*	(informal)
May I (leave early)?	*Yes, you may.*	*No, you may not.*	(formal)
Do you mind if I (open the window)?	*That's fine.* *Go ahead.* *All right.* *No problem.*	*Sorry, but (I'm cold).*	

Practice

1 **Choose the best reply (1–6) for the questions (a–f).**

a) What does this mean? ......*3*......

b) Would you like to play tennis tomorrow? ....

c) Shall I help you with those books? ....

d) Would you like some ice-cream? ....

e) Do you mind if I sit here? ....

f) Could you pass me the salt, please? ....

1 That's very kind of you. Thanks very much.

2 Thanks, but I'd rather have a drink.

3 Why don't you use the dictionary?

4 Sure, here you are.

5 I'm sorry, but I'm afraid I'm going to the cinema.

6 That's fine, please do.

2 **Rewrite each question beginning as shown. Do not change the meaning.**

a) Let's go to the cinema.

How......*about going to the cinema?*..................................

b) Would you like a sandwich?

Do ....

c) Do you want to sit down?

Would ....

d) Can you open the window, please?

Would you **mind** ....

e) Do you want me to carry your bag?

Shall ....

f) Do you know the time?

Could ....

3 **Read the answers. Write a question for each answer.**

a) ......*Would you mind helping me?*...................................

No, of course I wouldn't mind helping you.

b) ....

Yes, I'd like to go to the disco.

c) ....

No, I'm afraid you can't leave early.

d) ....

Thank you, my books are very heavy.

e) ....

No, not the park. Let's go shopping instead.

Preferences, promises, reminding, requesting, suggesting, warning

Explanations

Preferences	*I prefer (tea) to (coffee).*
	I'd rather have (tea) than (coffee).
Promises	*I'll be home at 8.30.*
	I won't be late again!
Reminders	*Don't forget to (bring your dictionary on Wednesday).*
	Remember to (bring your dictionary on Wednesday).

Making requests

Can you (open the window), please? (informal)

Could you (open the window), please?

Would you mind (opening the window), please? (formal)

Replying to requests

Can you .../Could you ...?   *Of course. Sure.*

Would you mind ...?   (no answer; an action is enough)

Making suggestions

Shall we (go for a walk)?

Let's (go for a walk).

Why don't we (go for a walk)?

What about (going for a walk)?

How about (going for a walk)?

Warning

Be careful!

Watch out!

Look out!

Mind out!

Careful!

Practice

1 Underline the most suitable reply.

a) Do you want tea or coffee?

   1 I would have tea.   2 I'd rather have tea.

b) Could you open the door, please?

   1 Sure   2 Yes, I could open.

c) Will you be late?

   1 I'll be home at 8.00.   2 I come home at 8.00.

d) Do you have any ideas?

   1 We go to the cinema.   2 Let's go to the cinema.

e) Shall we go to the shops?

   1 Good idea.   2 Yes, we shall.

f) Would you prefer a hot dog or a hamburger?

   1 I'd prefer a hamburger.   2 I prefer a hamburger.

2 Write one word in each space.

a) What ...._about_.... going for a ride on our bikes?

b) Would you .... opening the window?

c) .... you tell me the time, please?

d) How .... having a party?

e) Look ....! You might fall!

f) .... you help me carry this, please?

g) I .... cake to biscuits.

h) .... go to the cinema tonight.

3 Choose a word or phrase from the box to complete each sentence. Use each word or phrase once only.

How about	Could you	I'll	~~Look out~~	Shall
Of course	I'd rather	Would you mind		

a) ...._Look out_............. ! There's a bus coming.

b) .... open the door for me, please?

c) .... playing tennis this afternoon?

d) Don't worry. .... be home before 10.00.

e) 'Can you help me?' '................................. .'

f) .... carrying these books?

g) .... we listen to my new CD?

h) .... have an orange than a banana.

121

Explanations

Writing

British English: *2/11/02   2(nd) November   2nd Nov   Monday 2nd November, 2002*

US: *11/2/02   November 2(nd)   Nov 2nd   Monday November 2nd 2002*

Speaking

British English: *the second of November, 1999   November the second, 1999*

US: *November second*

Years

Writing		Speaking
1999	=	*nineteen ninety-nine*
2001	=	*two thousand and one*

Days

■ Days of the week

Monday, Tuesday, Wednesday, Thursday, Friday, Saturday, Sunday

*I'll see you **on** Monday.*

■ Other times

Future: tomorrow, the day after tomorrow, next week, next Monday

Past: yesterday, the day before yesterday, last week, last Monday

Months

January, February, March, April, May, June, July, August, September, October, November, December

■ Short forms

Jan Feb Mar Apr Aug Sept Oct Nov Dec

(*May, June, July* do not have short forms)

I'll be back in March.

■ Other times

Future: *next month*

Past: *last month*

Seasons

spring, summer, autumn, winter

It's lovely here in Spring.

I'm going to Spain in the summer.

■ Other times

Future: *next summer*, etc.

Past: *last winter*, etc.

Practice

1 **Write the words as numbers.**

a) The twenty-second of October.   _22/10_

b) The first of January.   ....

c) The nineteenth of August.   ....

d) The fifth of June.   ....

e) The thirtieth of September.   ....

f) The fourteenth of May.   ....

g) The eighth of March.   ....

h) The thirteenth of November.   ....

2 **Write the dates as words.**

a) 21/6   _The twenty-first of June_ ....

b) 19/3   ....

c) 2/8   ....

d) 31/10   ....

e) 15/2   ....

f) 1/5   ....

g) 20/1   ....

h) 16/11   ....

3 **Choose the correct word or phrase for each space.**

a) Today is Monday. So Wednesday is _B_ .

   A) the day before yesterday   B) the day after tomorrow   C) yesterday

b) How do you say the year 1996? ..... .

   A) nineteen nine six   B) one thousand nine hundred and ninety-six

   C) nineteen ninety-six

c) What are you going to do ..... ?

   A) next summer   B) last summer   C) the summer

d) I'll talk to you again ..... .

   A) yesterday   B) last month   C) tomorrow

e) It's really cold here ..... .

   A) the winter   B) last winter   C) in the winter

f) I haven't seen James since ..... .

   A) last Monday   B) next Monday   C) tomorrow

Explanations

Parts of the day

in the morning   in the afternoon   in the evening
at night   at midday (noon)   at midnight

am and pm

midnight to midday = am 1.00 am   midnight = 12.00 am
midday to midnight = pm 4.45 pm   midday = 12.00 pm

24-hour clock

14.45   fourteen forty-five
18.15   eighteen fifteen

Telling the time

two o'clock

Other numbers

*1.11   eleven minutes **past** one*
*5.41   nineteen minutes **to** six*

Digital system

1.10	*one ten*		*2.15*	*two fifteen*
3.25	*three twenty-five*		*4.30*	*four thirty*
5.40	*five forty*		*6.45*	*six forty-five*

Asking the time

What's the time?   It's three o'clock.
What time is it?   It's ten to eight.

We cannot say: *They **are** six o'clock.*

Practice

1 **Write the times as numbers.**

a) Ten to nine. ....*8.50*.........

b) A quarter past eleven. ....

c) Twenty past five. ....

d) A quarter to six. ....

e) Twenty-five past eight. ....

f) Five to five. ....

g) Ten past eleven. ....

2 **Write the time. Use *past* and *to*.**

a)

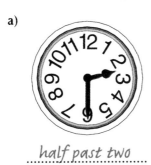

...........*half past two*...........

b)

....

c)

....

d)

....

e)

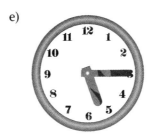

....

f)

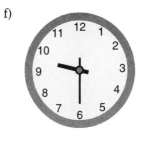

....

3 **Write one word in each space.**

a) 8.45 .....*(a)*..... *quarter* .....*to*..... nine.

b) 7.00 am Seven o'clock ....

c) 12.00 pm ....

d) 2.30 Half ....

e) 8.30 pm Half past eight ....

f) 2.56 Four .... three.

g) 12.00 am ....

1 <u>Underline</u> the correct words in each sentence.

a) 'I really love ice-cream!' '*And I too./ <u>So do I.</u>*'

b) '*What does Tony like/What's Tony like*?' 'He's very friendly.'

c) *I'm sorry I'm late/Excuse me that I'm late*.

d) It's *half past three/thirty past three*.

e) I'm sorry the window is broken. It was *my blame/my fault*.

f) If I were you, *I am going to the doctor's/I'd go to the doctor's*.

g) Today is *20 of November/20th November*.

h) '*What is Edinburgh like/How is Edinburgh*?' 'It's an interesting city.'

2 <u>Underline</u> the correct reply.

a) Is it all right if I wait here?

    1 All right.   2 <u>Sure, that's OK.</u>   3 Yes, you are.

b) Do you want to play basketball tonight?

    1 I'm afraid I'm not.   2 Sorry, I can't.   3 I wouldn't love to.

c) How do you do?

    1 I do fine.   2 Very well, thanks.   3 How do you do?

d) Shall I help you with that?

    1 Yes, you will.   2 Thanks a lot.   3 Yes, you do.

e) Do you mind if I leave my bike here?

    1 Of course.   2 Fine thanks.   3 Go ahead.

f) What's the time?

    1 Yes, it is.   2 Five o'clock.   3 Yes, the time is.

g) How do you feel?

    1 Terrible!   2 Yes, I do.   3 Yes, I feel.

3 Write one word in each space.

a) If I ..... *were* ..... you, I'd have a rest.

b) What's Helen .... ? Is she very friendly?

c) Excuse me, could you tell me the .... to the police station?

d) .... you like some orange juice? Or do you want some water?

e) I've got a good idea. .... go to the park and play football.

f) .... forget to bring your dictionary tomorrow.

g) 3.44: it's nearly a quarter .... four.

h) Would you .... opening the window?

4 Underline the correct word(s) in each sentence.

a) Do you feel like *go/going* to the theatre?

b) Don't forget *arriving/to arrive* early tomorrow.

c) I haven't seen you for ages. *How do you do/How are you*?

d) That's heavy. *Do/Shall* I help you?

e) The film *finishes/has finished* at midnight.

f) Do you mind if I *open/will open* the window?

g) I don't drink coffee. I think *I'd rather have/I like* tea, please.

h) Bye for now. I*'ll see/see* you later.

5 Rewrite each sentence using the words in **bold**. Do not change the meaning.

a) Can you close the door, please?   **would**

Would you mind closing the door, please?

b) Tell me about Paris.   **like**

....

c) May I close the door?   **mind**

....

d) Do you want to go swimming?   **feel**

....

e) Do you want some chocolate?   **like**

....

f) Let's have a party on Friday.   **don't**

....

6 Write the end of the sentence correctly.

a) Do you know <u>where is the cinema</u>?   *where the cinema is*

b) Let's meet <u>three o'clock.</u>   ....

c) What <u>is the look of your English teacher?</u>   ....

d) Why don't you <u>going to bed early?</u>   ....

e) 'I think you should buy it now.' '<u>I don't think.</u>'   ....

f) <u>Could you telling me</u> the way to the city centre?   ....

g) How about <u>you go</u> to the theatre?   ....

Think about grammar! Are the sentences true or false?

a) The British and the Americans write the date in the same way.

b) *Could* is more polite than *can*.

c) There are fifteen minutes in a quarter of an hour.

Prepositions of place and position

Explanations

in

We use *in* when things or people are contained by other things.

*There are some cups **in** that cupboard.*

Examples

*Jack lives **in** Spain. We arrived **in** Manchester. (a city)*
*Paul lives **in** Green Street.   Jim sat **in** an armchair.*
*I live **in** the country, not in the city.   Sarah is ill and is **in** hospital.*

on

We use *on* when things or people are touching other things.

*Jane put her books **on** the table.*

We use *on* when we talk about the cinema, radio, telephone and television.
    *What's **on** at the cinema?*
    *There's a good film **on** television tonight.*

Examples

    *It was crowded **on** the plane/bus/train.*
    *Our house is **on** this side of the street.*
    *There's a cinema **on** the left.*

at

We use *at* when we talk about position in general.
    *You can buy stamps **at** the post office.*
    *We arrived **at** London Airport.   Compare: We arrived **in** London.*

at the front, at the back, at the end
    *There's a school **at** the end of the street.*
    *Do you sit **at** the front of the class?*

at home, at work, at school

> *Mary is **at** school.*   (We don't know which classroom.)
> *She isn't **at** home.*
> *Mr King was **at** work yesterday.*   (We don't know where exactly.)

Examples

> *The bus stopped **at** the train station.*
> *My sister isn't **at** work. She's at the doctor's.*
> *My garden is **at** the back of the house.*
> *Wait for me **at** the crossroads.*

to

We use *to* when we talk about movement.

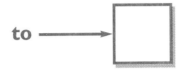

> *Last night we went **to** the cinema.*

Examples

> *I went **to** the cinema last night.*
> *Are you coming **to** the party?*
> *David brought his dog **to** school.*
> *Tina took her sister **to** the circus.*

- We do not use *to* with *home*.   *I have to go home now.*
- We do not use *to* with *here* or *there*.   *Sam is coming here tomorrow.*

into

We use *into* when we talk about moving from the outside to the inside.

> *Tom ran **into** the room and sat down.*
> *The children climbed **into** the car.*
> *I went **into** the shop.*

Practice

1 <u>Underline</u> **the correct word in each sentence.**

a) Jim and Maria have bought a house *at/<u>in</u> the country.*

b) The cupboard is *in/at* the room, on the left.

c) What have you got *in/on* your bag?

d) George walked *at/into* the room and sat down.

e) Please put your books *at/on* my desk.

f) Will you be *in/at* home this evening?

g) Clare lives *at/in* the end of the street.

h) Are you going *at/to* school tomorrow?

i) Come on! Get *on/in* your bike.

j) I saw your mum *in/on* the television.

2 **Choose** *at* **or** *to* **for each space.**

a) I'll be ....*at*........the station at 7.30.

b) Have you ever been .... Rome?

c) You can buy batteries .... the corner shop.

d) Don't forget to send a postcard .... the neighbours.

e) Do you usually walk .... school?

f) Helen flew .... New York to visit her penfriend.

g) David is studying .... university.

h) There's a phone .... the end of the corridor.

i) Tony was sent .... the head teacher's office.

j) We arrived .... our hotel just before midnight.

3 **Choose** *in* **or** *at* **for each space.**

a) Is there any milk ....*in*....... the fridge?

b) Is Sam .... the basketball team?

c) I'll wait for you .... the bus-stop.

d) I've lived .... this city for more than ten years.

e) Paolo had an operation and is still .... hospital.

f) John's house is .... the corner of the street.

g) Mary is .... work at the moment, but she'll be home soon.

h) What's on .... the cinema this week?

i) Nick lives .... Italy at the moment.

j) Lily always sits .... the back of the class.

4 **Write one word in each space.**

a) Have you heard? Pat is ......*in*...... hospital at the moment.

b) Excuse me, is George .... home?

c) Ann and Sue went to Prague .... the bus.

d) I liked the scene with the dog .... the end of the film.

e) Jean has bought a cottage .... the country.

f) Is Katerina .... school today?

g) Peter put his suitcase .... the seat next to him.

h) Nick ran .... the room and shut the door with a bang.

i) Carmen took her pet mouse .... school.

j) There are some good pictures .... this book.

5 **Choose *in* or *on* for each sentence.**

a) Kate lives ......*in*...... the house at the end of the street.

b) The library is not .... this side of the street.

c) Mark's flat is .... the fifth floor.

d) You can go up to the fifth floor .... a lift.

e) I visited Jo last week because there was a good film .... television.

f) We sat .... the living-room and watched it and ate pizza.

g) Clare put her pizza .... a small table and her dog ate it!

h) After that we put the dog .... the bedroom.

i) The boys put their toys away .... the cupboard.

j) We got .... the bus in Oxford.

6 **Choose *at, to* or – for each space.**

a) Have you ever been ......*to*...... Rome?

b) Why don't we walk .... the city centre?

c) When we arrived .... the hotel, it was late.

d) Have you been .... here before?

e) Was Helen .... school yesterday?

f) I'll meet you .... the bus station.

g) I'm going .... home now. I'll see you later.

h) Are you going .... the basketball match tomorrow?

i) My mum went .... hospital last week.

j) Mike worked .... the airport for six years.

Explanations

inside

inside is stronger than *in*.

There was nobody **inside** the burning house.

outside

outside means not *in* or not *inside*.

There was someone standing **outside** the classroom.

We can use *inside* and *outside* without an object.

Helen was standing **outside**.

Is there anyone **inside**?

in and *out* with no object

Tom is **out**.   Tom has gone **out**.   (not at home)

Jill is **in**.   (at home)

next to

We use *next to* when we talk about things or people at the side of something or someone.

Jim sits **next to** Tom.

near

near means the same as *close to*.

Ahmet's house is **near** the sports centre.

opposite

We use *opposite* when we talk about things or people that are on the other side, exactly.

> *There is a school **opposite** my house.*

> *The boy is sitting **opposite** his mother.*

out of

We use *out of* when we talk about moving from the inside to the outside.

> *Helen ran **out of** the room.*

in front of

in front of means *before* someone or something.

> *Helen sits **in front of** me.*
> *The motorbike is **in front of** the car.*

behind

behind means *after* someone or something.

> *David was **behind** me.*   *Anna sits **behind** me.*

Practice

1 <u>Underline</u> **the correct words in each sentence.**

a) Is Jack <u>in</u>/*into* at the moment?

b) There is a shop *next/opposite* our house, on the other side of the road.

c) Someone is waiting *outside/out*.

d) Kate was sitting *in front of me/outside me* on the bus.

e) Excuse me, is there a post office *near/next to* here?

f) The children ran *out of/at* the classroom.

g) David sits *next to/opposite* me, so I share his book.

h) I opened the parcel, but there was nothing *inside/in*.

i) I went to see Jane but she was *out/outside*.

j) Ther is a man *next to/behind* us. I think he is following us.

2 **Choose the correct word for each space.**

a) Look! There's someone ..*B*... the garden.

   A) on   B) in   C) inside

b) I like sitting ..... a comfortable armchair.

   A) inside   B) in   C) at

c) Take the first turning ..... the left.

   A) on   B) opposite   C) at

d) Jane isn't here at the moment. She's ..... .

   A) on   B) in   C) out

e) Is there anything good ..... television tonight?

   A) near   B) in   C) on

f) Peter likes lying ..... the floor.

   A) on   B) at   C) near

g) When you arrive ..... Paris, phone me.

   A) in   B) into   C) inside

h) Who sits next ..... Nick?

   A) –   B) at   C) to

i) What time do we go ..... home?

   A) –   B) to   C) at

j) Can you wait ....., please?

   A) out   B) out of   C) outside

3 **Tick (✔) the correct sentence.**

a) 1 Kevin is in the garden. He is out.

    2 Kevin is in the garden. He is outside. ✔

b) 1 The supermarket is next the post office.

    2 The supermarket is next to the post office.

c) 1 Is Jean in her bedroom?

    2 Is Jean inside her bedroom?

d) 1 Cristina sits near of Marcin.

    2 Cristina sits next to Marcin.

e) 1 There's nobody inside.

    2 There's nobody in.

f) 1 Roy sits opposite Lara.

    2 Roy sits opposite to Lara.

4 **Write one word in each space.**

a) When I looked in the box, there was nothing _inside_ .

b) There was a big red bus .... front of us.

c) Sorry, but Ann has gone .... Can I take a message?

d) Suddenly George ran .... of the room.

e) We can't play .... because it's raining heavily.

f) The woman .... me was pushing my back.

g) Who sits .... to Paul?

h) Excuse me, is there a bank .... here?

i) 'Go back ....! You should be in bed.'

j) There was a tall man sitting in .... of me and I couldn't see the film.

5 **Write a word or phrase in the space which is the opposite of the word or phrase underlined.**

a) There was an empty desk in front of Tina. _behind_

b) David is out. He's not at home. ....

c) A lot of people were waiting outside the bank. ....

d) My house is a long way from the railway station. ....

e) I live on the same side of the road as the supermarket. ....

f) Is Harry in? A policeman wants to talk to him. ....

g) Who sits behind you in the English class? ....

h) Suddenly Misha walked into the room. ....

Explanations

Indefinite and definite

*There was **a book** on the desk.*
We do not have any information about this book.   (indefinite)

*Where's **the book** with the answers?*
We know something about this book.   (definite)

Indefinite article: *a/an*

- with general descriptions
  *A **footballer** is a person who plays football.*
  *An **apple** is a type of fruit.*

- with a person's job
  *Mary is **a doctor**.   I'm **an engineer**.*

- with a person's character or status
  *Helen is **a genius**!   Paul is **a star**!*

Definite article: *the*

We use *the*:

- with unique objects and known references
  *The **moon** circles around the earth.*   (There is only one moon.)
  *The **Tower of London** is very old.*   (There is only one.)
  *I'm going to **the shop**.*   (We know which shop we are talking about.)

- with nationalities and other groups of people
  *The **Spanish** love dancing.*
  *The **Beatles** were a famous pop group.*

- with adjectives to describe groups of people
  *Jane has a job helping **the poor**.*
  *The **rich** usually live in big houses.*
  *The **old** need our help.*

- with collective nouns
  *Call **the police**!*
  *The **government** is very unpopular.*

- with geographical features
Rivers	**the** Loire, **the** Rhine
Oceans	**the** Atlantic, **the** Pacific
Seas	**the** Mediterranean, **the** Red Sea
Deserts	**the** Sahara, **the** Gobi

- with musical instruments
  *Do you play **the violin**?*
  *Can you play **the piano**?*

Practice

1 Choose *a, an* or *the* for each space.

a) What's ......*the*...... matter? Are you all right?

b) Kate has bought .... new car.

c) Some people think that .... moon is made of cheese!

d) I'm collecting money for .... poor.

e) Brian hasn't found .... job yet.

f) Can you play .... guitar?

g) Helen is .... idiot!

h) Don't forget to turn off .... television.

2 Complete each sentence with *a/an* and *the*.

a) There's ......*a*...... knife in ......*the*...... second drawer.

b) I'm going to .... baker's to buy .... loaf.

c) .... Rolling Stones are .... very old rock group.

d) There's .... cat in .... garden!

e) David is .... doctor at .... local hospital.

f) We missed .... beginning of .... lovely film.

g) Mary plays .... violin in .... quartet.

h) It's .... long time before .... train arrives.

3 Rewrite each sentence using the words in **bold**. Do not change the meaning.

a) Jane teaches English. **teacher**
   Jane is an English teacher.

b) There aren't any buses after this one. **last**

c) Have you seen today's paper? **the**

d) English people like tea. **the**

e) Telescopes help you to see things that are far away. **a**

f) Ann is a team-member. **of**

g) The road finishes here. **end of**

h) Tim studies at university. **student**

137

Explanations

■ We do not always use *a/an* or *the* in front of nouns. We call this 'zero article'.

General statements	*Cars are not allowed to park here.* *Teachers work very hard.*
Uncountables	*Sugar is bad for you.*
Abstract ideas	*Love makes the world go round.* *War is a terrible thing.*

Note that abstract words can be used in a definite way.
> ***The war** ended two years later.*

Food and drink	*I usually drink milk.* *I love eating chocolate.*
Languages	*Do you speak Turkish?* *I'm learning Spanish.*
Materials	*This coat is made of plastic and leather.* *I'm going to put some wood on the fire.*
Buildings	*Sue is in prison.* (She committed a crime.) *Richard is in hospital.* (He's ill.)

Also: *bed, class, school, college, university*

When we talk about the building only, we use an article.
> *Paul works **at the prison**.*   (He's not a prisoner.)

Note that we also think of work as a place.
> *Sam is at work.*

We also use the zero article with:

Countries, states and cities	*Paolo comes from Italy.* *My favourite European city is Tarragona.*

Countries which are plural or a group use the definite article *the*.
> *the* Netherlands   *the* United States

Streets	*I bought these trousers from a shop in Green Street.* *Which street do you live in?*

Geographical features	We use the zero article with regions, lakes, mountains and islands. *We visited Lake Como. It's in Northern Italy.* *Diana climbed Mont Blanc in record time.*

Transport	We use the zero article with *by* for general forms of transport. *We went there by train.* *I love travelling by boat.*

But: *on* foot
> *It was quicker to go **on** foot.*

Practice

1 <u>Underline</u> the correct word or – in each sentence.

a) Tom has got <u>*a*</u>/– new leather coat.

b) Do you like *an*/– orange juice?

c) Kate teaches at *a*/– school in Leeds.

d) Have you ever been to *the*/– Italy?

e) *The*/– Chinese have a very difficult language.

f) I'm tired. It's time to go to *the*/– bed.

g) Could you pass *the*/– sugar, please?

h) We went to Scotland by *a*/– car.

2 Choose *a, an, the* or – for each space.

a) Where's ......*the*...... milk? I thought you bought some.

b) .... students must not leave their bags here.

c) Paul went to .... prison for stealing two cars.

d) Is this chair made of .... wood?

e) It's much quicker on .... foot.

f) A large crowd welcomed .... President of the USA.

g) .... smoking is not allowed in the dining-room.

h) Do you want .... sugar in your tea?

3 Rewrite each sentence using the words in **bold**. Do not change the meaning.

a) Sue isn't up yet.   **bed**

...*Sue is still in bed.*...

b) We walked to the city centre.   **foot**

....

c) David wears plastic glasses.   **made of**

....

d) George came here on the bus.   **by**

....

e) Naomi is a French speaker.   **speaks**

....

f) Martin is a prisoner.   **prison**

....

g) I'm not a tea drinker.   **drink**

....

h) Carlos is Spanish.   **Spain**

....

Explanations

Subject pronouns

I	*he*	*we*
you	*she*	*they*
	it	

These come before the main verb:
> *I think it's awful.*
> *Do you like this film?*

Object pronouns

me	*him*	*us*
you	*her*	*them*
	it	

These come after the main verb:
> *I sent them a letter.*
> *Ellen told us the answer.*

Possessive pronouns

mine	*his*	*ours*
yours	*hers*	*theirs*
	its	

> *Is this pen yours or mine?*

■ No apostrophe before *s* with possessive pronouns.

this* and *that

singular	*this*	*that*
plural	*these*	*those*

We use *this* and *these* when we talk about things which are here. We use *that* and *those* when we talk about things which are there.
> *What's this?*   (The thing in my hands.)
> *I'd those, please.*   (The things in your hands.)

With nouns

> ***These** shoes are nice.*   *Is that blue car **yours**?*

one*/*ones

> *I like that **one**.*
> *I don't like the blue **ones**.*
> *'Did you buy a loaf?' 'I bought a small **one**.'*
> *That was a nice biscuit. Can I have another **one**?*

Practice

1 <u>Underline</u> the correct word in each sentence.

a) Tony gave *we/<u>us</u>* a lift.

b) Tina and Mike say that we can borrow *theirs/they*.

c) Could you pass me *that/those* paper?

d) Is it your turn, or is it *my/mine*?

e) Do *this/these* trees belong to you?

f) Paula wants you to help *she/her*.

g) Excuse me, but this is *my/mine* seat.

h) Shall we phone *them/they* now?

2 Choose *this, that, these, those, one* or *ones* for each space.

a) I've just found .....*this*..... watch. Is it yours?

b) There are a lot of bags here. Which .... is yours?

c) Do you like .... houses at the end of the street?

d) Anna, ... is my friend Sam. Have you met before?

e) Have one of .... chocolates. They're my favourite!

f) 'What's .... ?' 'What?' 'The animal over there.'

g) I like the black trousers, but I don't like the green ....

h) Did you enjoy that ice-cream? Would you like another .... ?

3 Rewrite each sentence beginning as shown. Do not change the meaning.

a) Is this your bike?

Is this bike ....*yours*.... ?

b) That house belongs to me.

That house is ....

c) Paul likes Jane. They're friends.

Paul and Jane are friends. He likes ....

d) I want to know the time.

Can you tell .... the time, please.

e) We own this car.

This car is ....

f) I invited John to my house for a talk.

I wanted to talk to John so I invited .... to my house.

g) Jane has arrived. Those are her suitcases.

Jane has arrived. Those suitcases are ....

h) Sam stayed in London because he liked the clubs there.

Sam stayed in London because he liked .... clubs.

Explanations

someone/somebody	For an unknown person **Someone/Somebody** *is knocking at the door.*
something	For an unknown thing **Something** *is wrong!*
anyone/anybody	For questions and negatives *Is* **anyone/anybody** *going to help me?* *There isn't* **anyone/anybody** *here.*
anything	For questions and negatives *Is there* **anything** *in the box?*
no one/nobody	A negative meaning. We do not use *not*. *I'm sure that* **no one/nobody** *saw me.*
none	None means 'not one'. We do not use *not*. *Can I have a biscuit? There are* **none** *left.* *Can I have some milk? There is* **none** *left.*
none of	We usually use a singular verb. **None of** *the children was tired.*
nothing	A negative meaning. We do not use *not*. *I pressed the button, but* **nothing** *happened.*
everyone, everybody	All the people. We use a singular verb. **Everyone** *knows the answer.*
everything	All the things. We use a singular verb. **Everything** *is beautiful.*

Practice

1 Complete each sentence with a pronoun beginning *some-, any-, no-* or *every-*.

a) Can I ask you ....*something*.... ?

b) .... has gone wrong today! It's been terrible!

c) .... has taken my bike, and I'm going to find out who!

d) There is .... nicer than a warm bath.

e) Does .... here have a pen I could borrow?

f) I feel so unhappy! .... loves me!

g) .... somewhere, wants a phone call from you!

h) .... I have is yours!

2 Change the <u>underlined</u> words to one word.

a) <u>Not one</u> of the people in the room welcomed Peter. ....*None*....

b) <u>All the people</u> in the room clapped loudly. ....

c) <u>Not one of the people</u> I asked knew the way. ....

d) Does <u>one of the people</u> here know the time? ....

e) <u>Not one person</u> laughed at the head teacher's joke. ....

f) There isn't <u>one single thing</u> to eat. ....

g) <u>All the things</u> Roger planned went badly wrong. ....

h) There's <u>a person</u> at the door. ....

3 Rewrite each sentence using the words in **bold**. Do not change the meaning.

a) There isn't anyone at home. **no one**
   There is no one at home.
   ....

b) We all know that. **everyone**
   ....

c) There is nothing to do. **anything**
   ....

d) The box was empty. **nothing**
   ....

e) There aren't any left. **none**
   ....

f) I met a person who knows you. **somebody**
   ....

g) I didn't eat anything. **nothing**
   ....

h) Do you know any people in this town? **anybody**
   ....

1 **Choose the most suitable word for each space.**

a) Tom wasn't *C* work today. Is he ill?

   A) to   B) in   C) at

b) There was a queue in the street ..... the cinema.

   A) to   B) into   C) outside

c) Are you going ..... school tomorrow?

   A) at   B) to   C) in

d) Mario took his pet snake ..... his English class.

   A) to   B) at   C) in

e) A new music shop has opened ..... the town centre.

   A) to   B) in   C) into

f) There's a good film ..... the Arts Cinema this week.

   A) at   B) in   C) to

2 <u>Underline</u> **the correct word in each sentence.**

a) Have you got <u>*a*</u>/*one* bike?

b) Cindy is *a/an* young American.

c) Sorry I'm late. I missed *a/the* bus.

d) Excuse me, is there *a/the* cinema near here?

e) Ann's house is at *a/the* end of the street.

f) Once upon *a/the* time, there were three bears.

g) Can you tell me *a/the* time please?

h) I'm sorry, but I could only buy *a/one* ticket for the match.

3 **Complete the sentences. Choose *a, an*, the or – .**

a) Kate is ....*a*........ genius and always knows all ....*the*........ answers.

b) .... Nile is one of .... longest rivers in .... world.

c) All we are saying is give .... peace a chance.

d) Most of .... people in .... world enjoy .... music.

e) Paul lives in .... old house on .... small island.

f) We learned .... Spanish by listening to .... radio.

g) .... young usually enjoy .... sport.

4 **Rewrite the sentences using the words in bold. Do not change the meaning.**

a) There is nothing in the cupboard.   **isn't**
There isn't anything in the cupboard.

b) All the people enjoyed the party.   **everyone**

....

c) Everyone was at home.   **out**

....

d) There is a person in the garden.   **someone**

....

e) I promise to say nothing.   **won't**

....

f) There was no one on the bus.   **wasn't**

....

5 **Write one word in each space.**

a) The dog has lost ......*its*...... collar.

b) Has anyone seen .... wallet? I think I've lost it.

c) My pencil broke so I borrowed .... from a friend.

d) Jo and Steve have got two children. .... names are Ian and Megan.

e) This book is .... It's got my name on it.

f) We live in this house. It's ....

g) This bike is mine and .... one is Jim's.

h) Anna says that this bag is ...., not Maria's.

6 **Correct each sentence or question.**

a) The love makes world go round!   *Love makes the world go round!*

b) Help! Call police!   ....

c) Kate enjoyed her holiday at Turkey. ....

d) Have you met mine brother?   ....

e) No one of the questions was easy.   ....

f) Those bags are there's.   ....

g) It's quicker to go to the station by foot. ....

h) Everything I wrote were wrong.   ....

Think about grammar! Are the sentences true or false?

a) Nouns don't always have an article.

b) *Mine* can only be used at the end of a sentence.

c) *Near* is the same as *at*.

Reported speech
Past perfect

Explanations

What is reported speech?

'I'm leaving at six,' she said.
This is direct speech, or the words that we hear.

She said that **she was leaving** at six.
She said she **was leaving** at six.
This is indirect or reported speech. Someone tells us what she said.

Tense changes

- Present simple to past simple

*'Tim **wants** some coffee.'*	*He said (that) Tim **wanted** some coffee.*
*'Tim **is** late.'*	*He said (that) Tim **was** late.*

- Present continuous to past continuous

*'**I'm washing** my hair.'*	*She said (that) she **was washing** her hair.*

- Present perfect to past perfect

*'Helen **has lost** her wallet.'*	*He said (that) Helen **had lost** her wallet.*

- *will* to *would*

*'**I'll** be late.'*	*She said (that) she **would** be late.*

- Past simple to past perfect

*'Kate **took** my keys.'*	*He said (that) Kate **had taken** his keys.*

Past perfect

Forming the past perfect: | *had* + past participle |

I had started	*he had started*	*we had started*
I'd started	*he'd started*	*we'd started*
you had started	*she had started*	*they had started*
you'd started	*she'd started*	*they'd started*
	it had started	
	it'd started	

- Words which describe time and place change in reported speech.

Practice

1 **Change each sentence to direct speech.**

a) She said that she was leaving at six.   *'I'm leaving at six,'* she said.

b) He said Peter often went fishing.   .... he said.

c) She said she would be back later.   .... she said.

d) I said that I had just seen Mark.   .... I said.

e) Alan said that they had left at 6.00.   .... Alan said.

f) Helen said that she was working.   .... Helen said.

g) I said that we were late.   .... I said.

h) He said he would phone back.   .... he said.

i) David said that he felt all right.   .... David said.

j) She said she loved ice-cream.   .... she said.

2 **Change each sentence to reported speech.**

a) 'I'm leaving,' she said.

She said ......*(that) she was leaving.*...

b) 'I saw the film on Monday,' Tom said.

Tom said ....

c) 'I've missed the bus,' Maria said.

Maria said ....

d) 'We live in Marsden Street,' they said.

They said ....

e) 'I'll phone at 6.00,' Anna said.

Anna said ....

f) 'I'm having a good time,' said Carol.

Carol said ....

g) 'We're arriving at 9.00,' they said.

They said ....

h) 'I forgot to do my work,' said Al.

Al said ....

i) 'I'm wrong,' he said.

He said ....

j) 'I've hurt my arm,' said Harry.

Harry said ....

Explanations

Present simple passive

is started	*are started*	*(regular)*
is eaten	*are eaten*	*(irregular)*

will passive

will be started	*(regular)*
will be eaten	*(irregular)*

Present perfect passive

had been started	*have been started*	*(regular)*
has been eaten	*have been eaten*	*(irregular)*

Past simple passive

was started	*were started*	*(regular)*
was eaten	*were eaten*	*(irregular)*

Examples

Present simple
Active   *Archaeologists often discover ancient coins.*
Passive   *Ancient coins **are** often **discovered** by archaeologists.*

will
Active   *They will finish the new road next year.*
Passive   *The new road **will be finished** next year.*

Present perfect
Active   *Your cat has eaten my pet mouse!*
Passive   *My pet mouse **has been eaten** by your cat!*

Past simple
Active   *The whole class wrote the play.*
Passive   *The play **was written** by the whole class.*

Uses

When we make an active sentence passive, the object becomes the subject. We do this when we want to put information at the beginning of the sentence because it is more important.

>   *A lot of money is spent in London by tourists*
A lot of money is important.

>   *Tourists spend a lot of money in London.*
Tourists is important.

■ We use the passive more in writing and in formal speech.

Practice

1 <u>Underline</u> the correct words in each sentence.

a) Last year more than a million cars <u>*were stolen*</u>/*are stolen*.

b) Helen *has decided/has been decided* to visit China.

c) America *visited/was visited* by the Vikings.

d) The police *have not found/have not been found* the missing dog.

e) More interesting facts *are discovered/are discovering* every year.

f) The basketball team *is chosen/chooses* by the captain.

g) The next meeting *will hold/will be held* on 14 December.

2 Complete each sentence in the passive.

a) The police arrested fifteen people.

Fifteen people ....*were arrested*............ by the police.

b) They have found little Jimmy safe and well.

Little Jimmy .... safe and well.

c) We plant hundreds of trees every year.

Hundreds of trees .... every year.

d) We will sell most tickets on the day of the match.

Most tickets .... on the day of the match.

e) They took the injured people to hospital.

The injured people .... to hospital.

f) They have discovered a new planet.

A new planet ....

3 Rewrite each sentence in the passive, beginning as shown. Do not change the meaning.

a) They built the bridge in 1996.

............*The bridge was built in 1996.*...

b) A dog has eaten my sandwich!

....

c) They'll deliver the letter tomorrow.

....

d) They have cancelled our train.

....

e) One of the students broke a window in the classroom.

....

f) People eat millions of bars of chocolate every day!

....

Explanations

With the agent *by*

This tells us who does the action.

*Peter was kidnapped **by aliens** from another galaxy.*

In this sentence; who did it = aliens.

With the agent *with*

This tells us what was used to do the action.

*The door was opened **with a special key**.*

In this sentence; what was used = a special key.

■ An agent is not always necessary.

Not known, Not important, Obvious, Impersonal

The window was broken last night.
We do not know who did it.

The castle was built in the 18th century.
We are interested in the date, but not in the architect.

The money was stolen.
We know that robbers, thieves, etc. steal things.

*The money was stolen **by robbers wearing masks**.*
We are interested in who did the stealing.

The match has been cancelled.
The person or people who decided to cancel the match are not named.

Careful!

born is always passive
*Jim **was born** in Australia.*

■ What is passive in your language but not in English?

Practice

1 Rewrite each sentence using *with* or *by*. Do not change the meaning.

a) A friend gave Tina a lift to school.

Tina *was given a lift to school by a friend.*

b) Tom Smooth will play the part of Hamlet.

The part of Hamlet ....

c) They used a screwdriver to open the window.

The window ....

d) A lot of farmers in Greece grow olives.

Olives ....

e) A ball broke the classroom window.

The classroom window ....

f) A Japanese millionaire bought the painting.

The painting ....

g) Howard Carter discovered the tomb of Tutankhamun in 1922.

The tomb ....

h) Millions of people enjoy Susan's books.

Susan's books ....

i) Heavy traffic causes a lot of pollution.

A lot of pollution ....

2 Change each sentence to the passive. Do not use the words underlined.

a) Workers build thousands of new houses every year.

Thousands of new homes are built every year.

b) The two teams will play the match on Sunday.

....

c) Nowadays people cut down many trees for no reason.

....

d) The police asked Jim to go to the police station.

....

e) Someone has stolen my bike.

....

f) People delivered our new washing-machine yesterday.

....

g) Three masked men kidnapped the bank manager.

....

h) Everyone has decided to have another meeting on Wednesday.

....

Imperatives

Explanations

Situations

We use imperatives to give orders, instructions and directions. They are also used to give advice and make requests in informal English.

Orders

We give an order when we tell someone to do something.

> ***Stand up! Stop talking!***

Instructions

Instructions tell us how to do something.

> ***Press escape*** *to cancel.*
> ***Choose*** *the most suitable word for each space.*

Directions

Directions are instructions for finding places.

> ***Turn right*** *at the bank.*
> ***Go straight on***.

Informal Advice/Requests

In informal situations it isn't necessary to be polite.

> ***Pass*** *the salt.*
> ***Don't buy*** *that one.*

Examples

Stop!	*Don't stop!*
Listen!	*Don't listen!*
Go away!	*Come back!*
Sit down!	*Stand up!*
Come here!	*Go over there!*

Practice

1 Write an instruction for each situation. Use a verb from the box.

| close | come | stop | open | site | lend | take | ~~turn off~~ |

a) A young child is reading in bed late at night. His mother says to him:
   Turn off the light!

b) A man's dog is running away. The man shouts at the dog:
   ....

c) It is the first class of the day and the students have their books on their tables.
   The teacher says:
   ....

d) The front door of the house is open. The father says to his son:
   ....

e) Lots of students are standing up in a class. The teacher says:
   ....

f) You need to borrow a pen. You say to your friend:
   ....

g) You are talking to your friend in class. The teacher says:
   ....

h) Your friend asks where the disco is. You know it's in the next street on the left.
   You say:
   ....

2 Write the opposite.

a) Stand up!   ....*Sit down!*................
b) Go away!   ....
c) Turn on the light!   ....
d) Start work!   ....
e) Open the window!   ....
f) Go to sleep!   ....
g) Pull the door!   ....
h) Get off the bus!   ....

Gerunds

Explanations

Gerund

The gerund is the noun form of the verb, ending in *-ing*. We can use it as a subject or an object.

Subject

> ***Jogging*** *is good fun!*   ***Cycling*** *is good exercise.*

Object

> *Do you like **jogging**?*   *Are you interested in **cycling**?*

Verb	Gerund	Verb	Gerund
read	*reading*	*eat*	*eating*
run	*running*	*swim*	*swimming*
cycle	*cycling*	*write*	*writing*
play	*playing*	*pray*	*praying*
cry	*crying*	*fly*	*flying*

Examples

> ***Cycling*** *is not allowed on the pavement.*
> ***Speaking*** *is forbidden during the examination.*
> *Do you like **camping**?*
> *I love **studying**!*
> *I can't stand **getting up** early.*
> ***Cycling*** *is excellent exercise.*

Practice

1 **Complete each sentence with a gerund (-ing). Use the verb in brackets.**

a) Kate is good at (run) .... *running* ....

b) (take) .... a long walk is relaxing.

c) What do you think of (collect) .... stamps?

d) (eat) .... too much isn't healthy.

e) All my friends like (play) .... basketball.

f) (shout) .... at people is rude!

g) Is Harry interested in (sail) .... ?

h) (cross) .... the road here is dangerous.

i) Do you feel like (go) .... to the cinema?

j) (jog) .... is good for you.

k) Mary can't stand (drive) .... in cities.

l) (play) .... in the street is dangerous.

2 **Change each sentence so that it starts with a gerund (-ing).**

a) It's tiring to study late at night.
.... *Studying late at night is tiring.* ....

b) It's hard to get up early.
....

c) It takes time to learn a language.
....

d) You are forbidden to park here.
....

e) It's interesting to visit other countries.
....

f) You are not allowed to talk.
....

g) It's not necessary to book a table.
....

h) It's wrong to copy other people!
....

i) It's relaxing to listen to music.
....

j) You are not allowed to smoke.
....

Contractions

Explanations

Contractions

When we speak we often shorten words like *am, are, have, has* in verb forms (auxiliary or 'helping' verbs). When we write these short forms (contractions) we put an apostrophe (') to show that letters are missing.

be

I am	you are	he is	she is	it is	we are	they are
I'm	you're	he's	she's	it's	we're	they're

Examples

I'm leaving tomorrow.
Jack's going home in a moment.

have

I have	you have	he has	she has	we have	they have
I've	you've	he's	she's	we've	they've

Examples

I've eaten your sandwiches.
Anna's left her books at school.

■ *he's* and *she's* = *he has, she has* or *he is, she is*.

With the modal *have to* we do not make contractions.
   I have to leave. (no contraction possible)

can and *could*

cannot	could not
can't	couldn't

do

do not	does not
don't	doesn't

will

will not	shall not
won't	shan't

would

I would	you would	he would	etc.	would
I'd	you'd	he'd	etc.	wouldn't

I'd, etc. can also be a contraction for *I had* in the past perfect simple.

Practice

1 **Write the full form of the words.**

a) <u>It's</u> very cold today. .... *It is* ....

b) <u>I'll</u> be back tomorrow. ....

c) <u>What's</u> the time? ....

d) <u>Don't</u> worry. It <u>won't</u> rain. ....

e) I <u>can't</u> see the blackboard. ....

f) My bike! <u>It's</u> been stolen. ....

g) If I were you, <u>I'd</u> leave. ....

h) <u>Jane's</u> got two sisters. ....

2 **Write each sentence with contractions.**

a) I will not be home early. *I won't be home early.*

b) Who is coming to your party? ....

c) We are interested in football. ....

d) I would not do that if I were you. ....

e) Paula could not lift the chair. ....

f) They have sent me a letter. ....

g) Helen has got a dog. ....

h) It is very cold today. ....

3 **Complete the sentences. Add the apostrophes if necessary.**

a) Its time for the news. *It's time for the news.*

b) Ive decided to buy some boots. ....

c) Whose books are these? Are they yours? ....

d) Sues borrowed my paints. ....

e) This new boats ours. Its got sails and oars. ....

f) I think the dogs hurt one of its legs. ....

g) These are my photos. Id like to see yours. ....

h) My names Toby. Whats yours? ....

4 **Write each sentence with contractions.**

a) If you asked me, I would not tell you. *If you asked me, I wouldn't tell you.*

b) I do not know where he has gone. ....

c) You have not done it yet. ....

d) I will see you when you are back. ....

e) Jane has not finished her homework. ....

f) We were not ready so we could not begin. ....

g) If you are nervous, do not worry. ....

1 **Change each sentence to reported speech.**

a) 'I'll be late,' said Jim.

Jim said ....*that he would be late.*..

b) 'Kate knows the answer,' said Bill.

Bill said ....

c) 'Mary is leaving at 8.00,' said Alan.

Alan said ....

d) 'I can't find the keys,' said Dave.

Dave said ....

e) 'The bus is going to be late!' said Mark.

Mark said ....

f) 'I've lost my books,' said Mr Green.

Mr Green said ....

g) 'I'm ready!' said Tina.

Tina said ....

2 <u>Underline</u> **the correct words in each sentence.**

a) The window *has been broken/was been broken*.

b) The match *will played/will be played* on Monday, not Sunday.

c) Tom's new book *is published/publishes* by Smith and Co.

d) The book *was filmed/was film* in 1997.

e) Some fingerprints *were find/were found* on the gun.

f) The new swimming pool *will been opened/will be opened* tomorrow.

g) TV programmes *are often changed/are often change* at the last minute.

h) An ancient tomb *has been discovered/is been discovered*.

3 <u>Underline</u> **the unnecessary words in each sentence. Not all sentences contain unnecessary words.**

a) The car was stolen <u>by someone</u>.

b) This photo was taken by a famous photographer.

c) The book was written by a writer in the 18th century.

d) My cheese was eaten by mice.

e) Three men have been arrested by the police.

f) My suitcase has been opened by someone.

g) The bikes are produced by workers in our Nottingham factory.

h) Millions of newspapers are read by people every day.

4 Rewrite each sentence beginning as shown. Do not change the meaning.

a) We waste a lot of water.

A lot of ..... *water is wasted.* ....

b) They have introduced a new law.

A new law ....

c) They will open the new sports centre next week.

The ....

d) A falling tree injured three people.

Three people ....

e) Someone has stolen my wallet!

My wallet ....

f) Someone will meet you at the airport.

You ....

g) A French person teaches my sister.

My sister ....

5 Write one word in each space.

a) Please come into the room and .... *sit* .... down.

b) .... books in a foreign language is a good way to learn.

c) Stop bothering me and .... away!

d) .... me your pen! I've broken mine.

e) .... is not allowed in the examination room.

f) .... letters takes a long time, so I usually phone people.

g) .... up early in the morning can be difficult!

h) .... park outside this building. It is forbidden.

6 Write the contractions in full.

a) They're building a new cinema.   .... *They are* ....

b) We've forgotten our books.   ....

c) It's a nice day today.   ....

d) I won't be late.   ....

e) It's started to rain.   ....

f) I'd like some tea, please.   ....

g) Jim doesn't live here.   ....

h) Mary's broken her arm.   ....

Think about grammar! Are the sentences true or false?

a) Passive sentences are used when the object is not important.

b) Contractions are not used in formal writing.

c) The gerund is for continuous activities.

Explanations

Possession means having or owning things.

Possessive adjectives						
my	*your*	*his*	*her*	*its*	*our*	*their*

*This is **my** bike.   Those are **our** books.*

Possessive pronouns						
mine	*yours*	*his*	*hers*	*its*	*ours*	*theirs*

*This bike is **mine**.   Those books are **ours**.*

We cannot say:
   This is mine bike. ✗
   This bike is the mine. ✗

whose?

> **Whose** bike is this?   *It's **mine**.*
> **Whose** books are these?   *They're **ours**.*
>
> **Whose** is this bike?
> **Whose** are these books?

- *Who's* (who is) does not have the same meaning as *whose* (of who), but it has the same pronunciation.

have got

> *Jane **has got** a sports car.*
> ***Have** you **got** a computer?*

The meaning of *have got* (or *have*) depends on the context.
   ***Have** you **got** a minute?*   (I want to talk to you.)
   ***Have** you **got** a pen?*   (I want to borrow it.)

- US and some GB speakers prefer *have*.
   *Jane **has** a sports car.*
   *Do you **have** a computer?*

→ SEE ALSO

Grammar 61: Pronouns 1

Practice

1 <u>Underline</u> the correct word in each sentence.

a) Are these books <u>*yours*</u>/*your*?

b) Is this *her/hers* house?

c) This car is *my/mine*.

d) This isn't *us/our* suitcase.

e) *Their/Theirs* bags are missing.

f) Is that *your/yours* pullover?

g) This is *my/mine* brother.

h) That bike is *her/hers*.

i) *Whose/Who's* bag is this?

j) I love *it's/its* colour!

2 Rewrite each sentence using the words in **bold**. Do not change the meaning.

a) Do they own that big house?   **theirs**
   Is that big house theirs?
   ....

b) Who owns this bike?   **whose**
   ....

c) These are my books.   **mine**
   ....

d) Does she own that boat?   **hers**
   ....

e) Do you own a computer?   **got**
   ....

f) Is that your dog?   **yours**
   ....

g) We own these houses.   **ours**
   ....

h) This is her seat.   **hers**
   ....

i) This is their classroom.   **theirs**
   ....

j) Who does this CD belong to?   **whose**
   ....

Possession 2: apostrophe, *of*

Explanations

Possessive apostrophe

We use an apostrophe when we talk about things belonging to people.
Singular ('s)

> This is **Jane's** house.   That's **my friend's** bike.

Plurals (s')

> These are the **boys'** desks.

Two words with apostrophes together.

> Is that **Ann's aunt's** car? = Is this the car that belongs to the aunt of Ann?

Belonging to two people.

> This is **Carol and Tony's** house.

Names ending in *s*.

> *St James' Park*   or   *St James's Park*

- No apostrophe in front of the *s* of plural words.
- No apostrophe in possessive pronouns: *yours, hers, its, ours, theirs.*

of

We can use *of* when we talk about things belonging to things.

> **The roof of the house** was damaged.

of is not always necessary

> I saw this dress in the **shop window**.

of is often used for formal names

> The University **of** Westminster

own and *belong*

> **I own** this bike.   Do you own this bike?
> This bike **belongs** to me.   Does this bike belong to you?

Careful!

Many people make mistakes with the apostrophe – including English speakers!

Practice

1 **Add apostrophes to these sentences if necessary.**

a) Is that book yours or Sams? *Is that book yours or Sam's?*

b) Davids sisters cats name is Syrup. ....

c) Have you met Pats brothers? ....

d) Are those shoes hers? ....

e) These are the girls fathers. ....

f) Those are the teachers cars. ....

g) These sandwiches are ours, not yours. ....

h) My books are in my friends bag. ....

i) Whose gloves are these? ....

j) That is Jacks fathers bike. ....

2 **Write compound words.**

a) the window of the shop   *the shop window*

b) the leg of the table   ....

c) the door of the car   ....

d) the playground of the school   ....

e) the wheel of the bicycle   ....

f) the handle of the door   ....

3 **Rewrite each sentence beginning as shown. Do not change the meaning.**

a) This desk belongs to Jim.
This *is Jim's desk* .

b) That belongs to her.
That's ....

c) Does this belong to you or him?
Is this .... ?

d) Who does this ruler belong to?
Whose .... ?

e) Do the empty seats belong to them?
Are the .... ?

f) We own this house.
This .... us.

g) Joe and Ella own this caravan.
This is ....

h) Does that bag belong to Sarah's teacher?
Is that .... bag?

Adjectives, nationalities

Explanations

Adjectives

Adjectives tell you more about the size, shape, colour, etc. of nouns.
We put them before nouns. They do not have plural *s* or other changes.

> It was a **lovely** day.   These are **tasty** apples.
> He is **tall**.   She is **tall**.   They are **tall**.

When we use an adjective with a noun, the adjective must come before the noun.

> Look at my **new coat**!   What a **lovely hat**!   You **lucky thing**!
> an **old man**   a **young woman**

■ The article belongs to the noun, not the adjective. So, it is not possible to say:
what a lovely, you lucky, an old, a young

What's it like?

We use this question when we ask someone to give an opinion about, or describe, something or someone. We use the adjective in the answer.

> What's your teacher like?   She's **fantastic**!
> What's Joe's house like?   It's **enormous**!

Classes and nationalities

Adjectives can become nouns if we add *the.*

■ Groups of people

> *the young   the old   the rich   the poor*

■ Some nationalities

the French	*the Chinese*
the Japanese	*the Portuguese*
the Swiss	*the British*
the English	*the Dutch*
the Irish	*the Spanish*
the Welsh	*the Danish*

■ Some nationalities use noun plurals.

> *the Italians   the Turks   the Greeks   the Germans   the Americans*

Verbs of sensation

Adjectives with verbs of sensation: feel, look, taste, smell, sound.

> This **tastes** good.   I **feel** ill.
> The washing-machine **sounds** terrible.
> This cheese **smells** bad.
> It **looks** great.
> It **feels** very soft.

too and enough

> We can't swim. The water is **too cold**.
> We can't swim. The water is **not cold enough**.

Practice

1 **Write questions with *What ... like?***

a) ...... *What's your teacher like?* ......

My teacher? She's a very nice person.

b) ....

The end of the film? Wait and see!

c) ....

My parents? When you meet them, you can decide!

d) ....

The weather in my country? It rains a lot.

e) ....

My next door neighbours? They make a lot of noise!

f) ....

Helen's new boyfriend? I haven't met him yet.

g) ....

The city centre? There are some shops and a cinema.

h) ....

The desks in my classroom? Old and uncomfortable!

2 **Write one word in each space.**

a) Mm, this tastes ..... *good* ..... How did you cook it?

b) The .... come from Switzerland.

c) The .... sometimes feel ill and lonely.

d) You look .... Do you feel all right?

e) The .... come from Japan.

f) The .... usually live in enormous houses.

g) The .... come from China.

h) Your bike sounds .... Is there something wrong with it?

3 **Complete each sentence with *too* or *enough*.**

a) I can't work today. It's ..... *too* ..... hot!

b) I'd like to buy those shoes, but they are .... expensive.

c) We need another ladder. This one isn't long ....

d) I can't do this exercise because it's .... difficult.

e) Nobody bought my bike because it was .... old.

f) We had to change rooms because our room wasn't big ....

g) John didn't win the race because his car wasn't fast ....

h) Don't play near the railway line. It's .... dangerous.

Order of adjectives
Problem adjectives

Explanations

More than one adjectives

Two adjectives
Jim has become happy and rich.

Three adjectives
Jim has become happy, rich and famous.

Order of adjectives

There are four main groups of adjectives, numbered here 1 to 4.

Position: 1 One or more of these types of adjective:
1a Opinion: *beautiful*
1b Size: *large*
1c Age: *old*
1d Shape: *round*
1e Temperature: *cold*

Position: 2 Colours: *green, blue*, etc.

Position: 3 Material (what it is made of): *wooden, plastic*, etc.

Position: 4 Purpose (what it is for): *a **running** shoe*

Position: 5 Noun

Examples

1c   3   4   5
an old, leather, football boot   (notice the use of commas)

1c   2   3   4   5
some new, orange, lycra, cycling shorts

1a   2   3   5
a beautiful, green, silk shirt

- A word, usually a noun (e.g. *football*), can be used as an adjective.
football boot   tennis racket

Problems with adjectives

Similar forms ending in -*ed* and -*ing*.
I am tired. (I feel tired.)
My work is tiring. (It makes me tired.)

bored	*interested*	*excited*	*worried*	*fascinated*
boring	*interesting*	*exciting*	*worrying*	*fascinating*

Practice

1 **Write the words in the correct order.**

a) shirt cotton a new lovely   *a lovely new cotton shirt*

b) large wooden old a house   ....

c) apples large two green beautiful   ....

d) film an new interesting science-fiction   ....

e) green vase old a beautiful   ....

f) short a coat red plastic   ....

g) carpet a old beautiful blue   ....

h) puppy little a sweet black   ....

2 **Write compound words.**

a) a boot for playing football   *a football boot*

b) a shoe for running in   ....

c) a road in the country   ....

d) a stadium for athletics   ....

e) a costume for swimming   ....

f) a village on a mountain   ....

g) a student at university   ....

h) a bus for the school   ....

3 **Complete each sentence with a word ending in -ed or -ing.**

a) I think this film is b. *oring* .

b) I don't find politics i................... .

c) Walking makes me t................... .

d) This book is really e................... .

e) Kate is doing her exams and is w................... .

f) Are you i................. in basketball?

g) Dick always feels b................. at the beach.

h) Jane finds computers very c................. .

4 **Underline the correct word in each sentence.**

a) I couldn't concentrate at school today because I was very *tired*/*tiring*.

b) Sarah was *shocked*/*shocking* by her friend's news.

c) There's an *amazed*/*amazing* robot display at the Science Museum.

d) We were very *disappointed*/*disappointing* with our poor exam results.

e) I don't understand this film. It's very *confused*/*confusing*.

f) It's been a long, *tired*/*tiring* day and now I want to go home and relax.

g) Joe's parents were really *worried*/*worrying* when he ran away from home.

h) My brother told a very *amused*/*amusing* joke at dinner last night.

167

Making comparisons 1: comparative adjectives

Explanations

Comparatives compare two things. We use *than* with comparatives.

> Lisa is **older than** Clara.
> Paula is a **faster swimmer than** Jane.

We use *(just) as ... as* when the things compared are equal.
> Harry is **(just) as good as** Jack.
> Harry is **(just) as good a player as** Jack.

We use *not as ... as* when we compare things negatively.
> Cathy is **not as good as** Mary.
> Cathy is **not as good a player as** Mary.

We use *more than* and *less than* for longer adjectives.
> This game is **more interesting than** the last one.
> I think this game is **less interesting than** that one.

Comparative adjectives

One syllable words add *-er* to the adjective.
> *long* ⟶ *longer*

One syllable words ending with one consonant, double the final consonant.
> *big* ⟶ *bigger*

Words ending in consonant +*y* change *y* to *i*.
> *dry* ⟶ *drier*

Two or more syllables use *more*.
> *modern* ⟶ ***more** modern*
> *interesting* ⟶ ***more** interesting*

Exceptions

Some adjectives with two syllables can be formed in either way.
> *healthy* ⟶ *healthier* OR *more healthy*

Others include: *quiet, tired* and words ending *-ow, -y, -le* and *-er*.

Irregular adjectives

> *good* ⟶ *better*
> *bad* ⟶ *worse*
> *little* ⟶ *less*

old for family members

> *old* ⟶ *elder*
> *This is my elder sister.*

Practice

1 Write a sentence for each picture. Use the comparative form of the adjective in brackets.

a) (tall) *The girl is taller than the boy.*

b) (young) ....
....

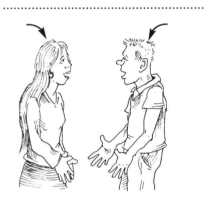

c) (expensive) ....
....

d) (short) ....
....

e) (small) ....
....

f) (big) ....
....

2 **Write the comparative form of each adjective.**

a) big   .... *bigger* ....

b) happy   ....

c) beautiful   ....

d) angry   ....

e) bad   ....

f) important   ....

g) dry   ....

h) good   ....

i) hot   ....

j) expensive   ....

3 **Write one word in each space.**

a) This book is better ..... *than* ..... the other one.

b) Jim is not .... tall as his sister.

c) I don't like running. It's .... interesting than swimming.

d) This film is funnier .... the last one we saw.

e) Do this exercise first. It's .... important.

f) These boots are cheaper .... the other ones.

g) Don't worry! It's not .... bad as you think!

h) This road is longer .... I thought.

4 **Rewrite each sentence using a comparative form of the adjective in brackets. Do not change the meaning**

a) Tim is older than Sarah. (young)

Sarah is ..... *younger than Tim.* ....

b) Our house is larger than yours. (small)

Your house is ....

c) Bill is not as tall as David. (short)

Bill is ....

d) Jack's marks are worse than mine. (good)

My marks ....

e) This book is the same price as that one. (expensive)

That book is ....

f) Your bike is slower than mine. (fast)

My bike ....

5 Read the information about France and Spain. Complete the sentences about the countries, using the words in brackets

France

Size	550,000 sq km
Population	56 million
Summer temperature	32° C
Winter temperature	20° C
Rainfall	350mm

Spain

Size	500,000 sq km
Population	40 million
Summer temperature	35° C
Winter temperature	18° C
Rainfall	300mm

a) France ... *is bigger than* .... Spain. (big)

b) Spain .... France. (small)

c) Spain's population .... France's population. (large)

d) France's population .... not .... Spain's population. (small)

e) Spain .... France, in summer. (hot)

f) France .... not .... Spain, in winter. (cold)

g) Spain .... not .... France. (rainy)

h) France .... Spain. (rainy)

Making comparisons 2: superlative adjectives

Explanations

Meaning of comparatives and superlatives

Comparatives compare two things.
> *She is a faster runner **than John**.*

Superlatives compare one thing in a group with all the other things in that group.
> *She is the fastest runner in **the world**.*

Superlative adjectives

Add *-est* to the adjective and put *the* before the noun.
> *This is **the longest river** in our country.*
> *I am **the greatest**!*

long	⟶	longest
big	⟶	biggest
dry	⟶	driest

Adjectives with two or more syllables use *most*.

modern	⟶	most modern
interesting	⟶	most interesting

Exceptions

Adjectives ending in consonant +*y*.

happy	⟶	happiest

Some adjectives with two syllables can be formed in either way.

common	⟶	commonest or most common

Others include: *quiet, tired* and words ending *-ow, -y, -le* and *-er*.

Irregular superlatives

good	⟶	best
bad	⟶	worst
little	⟶	least
old	⟶	eldest (for family members)

Practice

1 **Write the superlative form of each adjective.**

a) long ....*the longest*..........

b) fit ....

c) funny ....

d) terrible ....

e) good ....

f) wide ....

g) nasty ....

h) strange ....

2 <u>Underline</u> **the correct word in each sentence.**

a) This is the *better/<u>best</u>* restaurant in the town.

b) This castle is one of the *older/oldest* in Europe.

c) Your hotel is *more/most* comfortable than ours.

d) This is the *worse/worst* holiday I have ever had!

e) Bill is the *richer/richest* person in the world.

f) George is *happier/happiest* than he was.

g) This film is *more/most* interesting than the last one.

3 **Look at the picture and write sentences using the superlative form of the words in brackets.**

a) Dave (tall) ....*Dave is the tallest.*.........

b) Tom (short) ....

c) Jim (old) ....

d) Tom (young) ....

e) Tom (heavy) ....

f) Jim (light) ....

Consolidation 11

1 **Write one word in each space.**

a) Excuse me, does this umbrella ....*belong*.... to you?

b) Kate is .... tallest in the class.

c) Sorry, but your work isn't good ....

d) Jane is older .... Peter.

e) Kate hasn't .... any money for the bus.

f) My bike isn't .... fast as yours.

g) .... bike is this? Is it Helen's?

h) Both stories are good, but I think this one is .... than the other.

2 **Rewrite each sentence twice using the words in brackets. Do not change the meaning.**

a) This pen belongs to me.
   ....*This is my pen.*.. (my)
   ....*This pen is mine.*.. (mine)

b) Those bags belong to the students.
   .... (their)
   .... (theirs)

c) Tom owns that house.
   .... (Tom's)
   .... (Tom)

d) That's Paul and Julie's baby.
   .... (their)
   .... (theirs)

e) Who owns this farm?
   .... (belong)
   .... (whose)

f) Does that bike belong to you?
   .... (your)
   .... (yours)

g) Oscar and Cathy own that boat.
   .... (Oscar and Cathy's)
   .... (their)

3 **Choose the most suitable word or phrase for each space.**

a) We stayed in a ..*B*.. house.

   A) country beautiful old   B) beautiful old country   C) old beautiful country

b) 'Did you like the film?' 'No, I thought it was ..... .'

   A) boring   B) bores   C) bored

c) Is your friend Tom ..... ?

   A) England   B) an English   C) English

d) Ann bought a ..... skirt.

   A) lovely blue   B) blue lovely   C) blue and lovely

e) Brian and Julia are a ..... .

   A) young couple married   B) young married couple

   C) married young couple

f) This is ..... school in the country.

   A) a best   B) the best   C) best

4 **Rewrite each sentence using the words in bold. Do not change the meaning.**

a) My tea isn't hot enough.   **cold**

   ....*My tea is too cold.*...

b) That film was great!   **what**

   ....

c) You are too young to see this film.   **old**

   ....

d) Describe your brother.   **like**

   ....

e) This piece of string is too short.   **long**

   ....

f) I don't find sport interesting.   **interested**

   ....

Think about grammar! Are the sentences true or false?

a) Adjectives come after the noun they describe.

b) Superlatives are stronger than comparatives.

c) Possessive plural nouns do not need an apostrophe.

Adverbs: formation and position, irregular adverbs

Explanations

Types of adverbs

Adverbs generally give us more information about an action and tell us how it was done.

> *Jim wrote the letter **quickly**.*

Forming adverbs

Add *-ly* to an adjective. Adjectives ending in *-y* change it to *-ily*. Adjectives ending in *-ic* add *-ally*.

beautiful	⟶	*beautifully*
happy	⟶	*happily*
terrific	⟶	*terrifically*

Position of adverbs

Adverbs usually come after the subject or after the object.

> *Jim **quickly** wrote the letter.* (Jim is the subject.)
> *Jim wrote the letter **quickly**.* (The letter is the object.)

- We cannot say: *Jim wrote quickly the letter.* ✗

When the verb does not have an object, the adverb goes after the verb.

> *Tom runs quickly.*

- We cannot say: *Tom quickly runs.* ✗

Phrases describing place or manner

> *Jim ran <u>up the stairs</u>.*

The adverb goes before the verb, or after the phrase.

> *Jim **quickly** ran up the stairs.*
> *Jim ran up the stairs **quickly**.*

Irregular adverbs

adjective	*good*	*fast*	*hard*
adverb	*well*	*fast*	*hard*

→ **SEE ALSO**

Grammar 2: Frequency adverbs
Grammar 20: Time expressions

Practice

1 **Write the adverb form of each adjective.**

a) quick   *quickly*   f) special   ....

b) fast   ....   g) good   ....

c) wonderful   ....   h) slow   ....

d) happy   ....   i) beautiful   ....

e) bad   ....   j) sad   ....

2 **Complete each sentence with an adverb from the box.**

beautifully	completely	~~freshly~~	frequently	greatly
sincerely	specially	well		

a) All the food in our restaurant is ....*freshly*........ prepared.

b) I am .... grateful for your help.

c) The head teacher was .... loved by the whole school.

d) Lidia passed the test because she was .... prepared.

e) This is a .... made piece of jewellery.

f) We made this cake .... for you.

g) The game is not .... finished yet.

h) Buckingham Palace is one of London's .... visited sights.

3 **Change each sentence. Use the underlined word to make an adverb.**

a) Jim is a <u>good</u> worker.
    Jim works well. ....

b) Ann is a <u>wonderful</u> dancer.
    ....

c) Carol is an <u>accurate</u> writer.
    ....

d) Tina is a <u>bad</u> singer.
    ....

e) Sam is a <u>secret</u> smoker.
    ....

f) Ruth is a <u>fast</u> runner.
    ....

g) Pablo is a <u>careful</u> driver.
    ....

h) Liz is a <u>quick</u> reader.
    ....

Explanations

it, its and *it's*

Subject or object pronoun
> *It stops here.*   *Do you like it?*

Possessive form of *it*
> Look at **its** beautiful eyes!

Contracted form of *it is* or *it has*
> **It's** on the shelf.   **It's** got six legs.
> **It is** on the shelf.   **It has** got six legs.

there, their and
they're

Pronoun for something that exists
> **There** is a strange dog in the garden.

Possessive form of *they*
> Tim and Ann have brought **their** car.

Contracted form of *they are*
> 'Where are my gloves?'   'They're on the seat.'

there is/are

Saying that something exists
> **There's** a spider in the bath. **There are** lots of trees in your street.

it is/they are

Something already mentioned:
> **There's** a spider in the bath. **It's** not very big.
> **There are** lots of trees in your street. **They're** beautiful!

Expressions with *it*

> **It's** raining.   **It's** snowing.
> **It's** cold/hot/sunny.   **It's** a lovely day.
> **It's** half past two.   **It's** late.
> **It's** lovely to be here.   **It's** a pity about the weather.
> **It's** a good idea to arrive early. **It** doesn't matter.

Other tenses are also possible.
> **It was** three o'clock.   **It didn't** matter.

Expressions with
there

> **There's** a phone in the office.   **There's** a bus-stop near here.

Practice

1 <u>Underline</u> the correct word in each sentence.

a) Is *there/their/they're* any milk left?

b) Oh no! *It's/Its* snowing again.

c) Tim and Jean have lost *there/their/they're* tickets.

d) We're nearly at the cinema. *It's/Its* not far.

e) *There/Their/They're* are lots of people here today.

f) This isn't your bag. I think *it's/its* Tom's.

g) Most of my friends say *there/their/they're* happy.

h) The dog hurt *it's/its* leg so we took it to the vet.

i) When *there/their/they're* letter arrives, can you tell me what they say?

j) I'm sorry, *it's/its* too late to go out now.

2 Complete each sentence with *it, its, it's, there, their* or *they're*.

a) The others are outside. ...*They're*... waiting for us.

b) The school has invited all .... old pupils to a party.

c) What an awful day! .... raining again!

d) .... doesn't matter about money. You can pay me back later.

e) .... is no way I can get to school before 8.30.

f) Some people lose .... keys very easily!

g) .... a lovely day today.

h) I like your new shoes. .... very fashionable!

i) Kate stopped and listened. .... was something wrong!

j) .... a pity about John's accident.

3 Write one word in each space.

a) ...*It*... wasn't a good idea to ring the doorbell.

b) Are .... any good restaurants in this town?

c) Is .... any cheese in that sandwich?

d) Has anyone forgotten .... homework?

e) .... was a pity that we missed the beginning of the film.

f) Is .... a cinema near here, please?

g) Is that an Indian elephant? .... has got very small ears.

h) The dog has left .... bone in my bed again!

i) Is .... any chance of meeting David tonight?

j) .... was snowing when we arrived.

Problem verbs

Explanations

have

We can use *have* as an auxiliary or 'helping' verb and as a main verb.

auxiliary   *I **have** eaten a pizza.*
main   *Carlos **has** a new bike.*

Auxiliary

Present

Statements	Negative	Questions
*I/you/we/they **have***	*I **have not/haven't***	***Have** I?*
*he/she/it **has***	*he **has not/hasn't***	***Has** he?*

Past

***had** (all persons)*	*I **had not/hadn't***	***Had** I?*

Main verb

Same as the auxiliary but with some differences.
Present negatives and questions

*I don't **have***   *Do I **have**?*
*he/she/it doesn't **have***   *Does he **have**?*

**Past negatives
and questions**

*I didn't **have***   *Did I **have**?*

Examples

auxiliary   ***Has** Jim written his letters?*
main verb   *Do you **have** a sister?*

have got

The past form of *have got* is *had*.
*Ann **has got** a new car.*
***Has** Ann **got** a new car?*   *Ann **hasn't got** a new car.*

Past forms do not use *got*.
*Ann **had** a car when she was a student.*
***Did** Ann **have** a car?*   *Ann **didn't have** a car.*

■ US prefer *have*, to *have got*.
   British English: *I've got a dog and two cats.*
                       Have you got any pets?   *I haven't got any pets.*
   US English: *I have got a dog and two cats.*
                       Do you have any pets?   *I don't have any pets.*

get

Get has a number of different meanings in everyday use.

*Can you **get** me some milk at the shops?*	(buy)
*I **got** a letter this morning.*	(receive)
*Are you **getting** tired?*	(become)
*How much do you **get**?*	(earn)
*When did you **get** here?*	(arrive)
*I'll just go and **get** my coat.*	(collect)
*How far have you **got**?*	(reach)

■ We do not usually use *get* in writing or formal speech.

Practice

1 **Change the statements into questions or negatives.**

a) Jane has got a new car. (question)

......*Has Jane got a new car?*...

b) I've got a stamp. (negative)

....

c) Jim had a cold last week. (question)

....

d) We've got a problem. (question)

....

e) You have a test today. (negative)

....

f) Paul has a sister. (question)

....

2 **Change each sentence or question into the past tense.**

a) I've got a cat.

......*I had a cat.*...

b) Have you got a bike?

....

c) Jim hasn't got any time.

....

d) David's got an exam.

....

e) We haven't got a house.

....

f) Has Tina got a cold?

....

3 **Replace the underlined words with a verb from the box.**

arrive in	become	buy	collect	~~earn~~	receive

a) How much do you get ....*earn*.... in your new job?

b) Did you get .... any letters this morning?

c) Could you get .... me some stamps when you go shopping?

d) Put your coat on. You don't want to get .... cold.

e) I have to get .... my trousers from the cleaner's today.

f) What time do we get to .... London?

Problem verbs
Phrasal verbs

Explanations

make and do

We *do* an action.
We *make* something that was not there before.

do *your work/homework*	***make*** *a cake*
do *the cooking/ironing, etc.*	***make*** *a mistake*
do *your hair/teeth, etc.*	***make*** *a noise*
do *nothing*	***make*** *a cup of tea/coffee*
do *exercises*	***make*** *an offer*

Expressions

*What **do** you **do**?*	(What's your job?)
*How **do** you **do**?*	(a greeting: the reply is *How do you do?*)

go/come + -ing

*to **go**/**come** shopping*	*to **go**/**come** sailing*
*to **go**/**come** skating*	*to **go**/**come** fishing*
*to **go**/**come** skiing*	*to **go**/**come** swimming*

Phrasal verbs

Examples with two words:

get up (in the morning)	=	leave your bed
look up (a word in the dictionary)	=	try to find
fill in (a form)	=	write the details on
go on (doing something)	=	continue
come across (something)	=	find

Examples with three words:

get on (well) *with* (someone)	=	have good relations with
look forward to (something)	=	think you will enjoy
run out of (something)	=	have no more of

■ Always check in a dictionary when you come across a new example.

Practice

1 Complete each sentence with a suitable form of *make* or *do*.

a) Wait a minute. I'm ..... *doing* ..... my hair at the moment.

b) Please don't .... so much noise!

c) My father .... most of the cooking in our house.

d) Oh dear, I think I've .... a mistake.

e) Are you going to .... Michael a birthday cake?

f) They .... Harry an offer which he couldn't refuse.

g) Don't forget to .... your homework before you go out.

h) When you have .... this exercise, try the next one.

2 Complete each sentence with a suitable form of *go* or *come*. More than one answer may be possible.

a) Pat and Sam ..... *went* ..... shopping in New York last month.

b) Do you want to .... swimming with us tomorrow?

c) My brother .... to my house yesterday.

d) Kate usually .... skiing in Switzerland.

e) I used to .... swimming a lot, but I stopped.

f) Mary loves .... shopping with her sister.

g) I .... skating last year for the first time.

h) Do you feel like .... fishing tomorrow?

3 Match each sentence (1–8) with a sentence (a–h) which means the same.

a) I tried to find the word in a dictionary.   ..... 6 .....

b) I have good relations with my neighbours.   ....

c) I wrote down all my personal details on the form. ....

d) The teacher asked me to stop talking, but I didn't. ....

e) I think I'm going to enjoy my holiday.   ....

f) I haven't got any more food.   ....

g) I spent my childhood near London.   ....

h) I've stopped eating sweets.   ....

1 I filled it in.

2 I get on well with them.

3 I've given them up.

4 I'm looking forward to it.

5 I've run out.

6 I looked it up.

7 I went on talking.

8 I grew up there.

82 | Verbs with prepositions, gerund or infinitive

Explanations

Verbs followed by prepositions

about

dream	I **dreamt about** Switzerland last night.
know	Do you **know** a lot **about** physics?
talk	What are you **talking about**?

at

look	**Look at** these lovely flowers.

for

apologize	I **apologize for** being late.
pay	Tim **paid for** my ticket.
wait	I'll **wait for** you outside.

in

believe	Do you **believe in** ghosts?

to

belong	Does this **belong to** you?
explain	Could you **explain** something **to** me please?
lend	Kate **lent** her pen **to** me.
listen	You're not **listening to** me!
talk	Jill was **talking to** her sister.

Verbs followed by -ing

Examples: *dislike, enjoy, fancy, can't stand*

I **dislike getting up** early.

Pat **enjoys using** a computer.

Do you **fancy going** to the cinema?

I **can't stand travelling** by bus.

Verbs followed by infinitive + to

Examples: *ask, choose, help, manage, offer, refuse, want*

I **chose to walk** to the station.

Sue **asked us to wait**.

Jack **helped me (to) do** my homework.

I **managed to find** a taxi.

Helen **offered to help** me.

Joe **refused to sit** down.

Paula **wanted to go** home.

Practice

1 <u>Underline</u> **the correct words in each sentence.**

a) I hate <u>*walking*</u>/*walk* in the rain.

b) I fancy *to go/going* to the cinema tonight.

c) Don't listen to Bob. He's talking *of/about* cars again.

d) Sue offered *to/at* find me a job.

e) Kevin can't stand *to cook/cooking*.

f) Harry still believes *on/in* giants!

g) Carl doesn't want *to go/going* home yet.

h) We apologized *for/to* the girl's bad behaviour.

i) All children dislike *doing/to do* homework.

j) Please wait *to/for* me in the restaurant.

2 **Write one word in each space.**

a) I've lost my wallet, so I can't pay ......*for*...... my ticket.

b) Do you .... going to the cinema this evening?

c) What do you .... about the Eiffel Tower?

d) Alan doesn't .... to get up before midday.

e) You don't really .... in ghosts, do you?

f) I really dislike .... homework!

g) The customer didn't like the meal, and .... to pay.

h) Could you lend a pen .... Jim? He's lost his.

i) Do these books belong .... you?

j) I must apologize .... being late. I'm very sorry.

3 **Complete each sentence with a verb from the box.**

| apologize | can't stand | choose | enjoy | know |
| lend | listen | ~~manage~~ | refuse | wait |

a) Students who do not ....*manage*........ to finish now, can come back later.

b) Jan .... doing the washing-up.

c) If drivers .... to stop, the police arrest them.

d) I .... for damaging your bike.

e) Do think you could .... for me outside?

f) Did you .... to the football match on the radio?

g) I don't really .... working at weekends.

h) Ann and Pat .... a lot about wildlife.

i) Tim used to .... his calculator to his friends.

j) Some students .... to study Spanish instead of French.

4 **Rewrite each sentence beginning as shown. Do not change the meaning.**

a) Jim said that he would pay for my ticket.

Jim offered ....*to pay for my ticket*.. .

b) Tony really doesn't like playing football

Tony can't ....

c) Could you give me an explanation of this?

Could .... me?

d) 'Please wait,' the teacher asked us.

The teacher asked us ....

e) You were in my dreams last night.

I dreamt ....

f) Carol would like to go to the cinema tonight.

Carol wants ....

g) Ann wants to go to the park.

Ann fancies ....

h) Is this pencil yours?

Does .... ?

i) Clare finished the race in three minutes!

Clare managed ....

j) The waiter offered me some cakes. I took the chocolate one.

I chose ....

5 **Correct each sentence or question.**

a) Do you fancy <u>to go</u> swimming tomorrow?

  Do you fancy going swimming tomorrow ?

b) Can you lend to me your phone, please?

  .... ?

c) We managed sailing home despite the bad weather.

  ....

d) She apologized stealing the money.

  ....

e) Tim paid at the meal.

  ....

f) I want for visiting the museum this afternoon.

  ....

g) They don't know very much in British history.

  ....

h) Sue doesn't enjoy to watch television.

  ....

6 **Choose the most suitable word for each space.**

I want to tell you the story of a dream I had last night. I dreamt (1) *A* Australia. I was staying in Sydney with my uncle and aunt and we were going to drive across Australia by car. This was really strange because I can't stand (2) ..... by car, I prefer trains. Anyway I refused (3) ..... get in the car and my uncle got very cross with me. He said he wanted (4) ..... to Perth and it would be an adventure for us all. I tried to explain (5) ..... him that I was always very sick in a car, but he wasn't listening (6) ..... me. My aunt said I would enjoy (7) ..... across the desert, seeing all the animals and birds. I thought that maybe she was right so I apologized (8) ..... being rude and we all got in the car to drive across Australia.

When I woke up the next morning, my mum was talking (9) ..... her sister in Australia. My uncle and aunt were really planning to drive across the desert. It was so strange – do you believe (10) ..... dreams?

1)	**A** about	**B** at		**C** for
2)	**A** travel	**B** travels		**C** travelling
3)	**A** to	**B** with		**C** in
4)	**A** going	**B** to go		**C** go
5)	**A** for	**B** about		**C** to
6)	**A** with	**B** to		**C** too
7)	**A** driving	**B** drive		**C** drives
8)	**A** at	**B** about		**C** for
9)	**A** to	**B** in		**C** at
10)	**A** with	**B** in		**C** about

Be with adjectives and prepositions

Explanations

be + adjective
followed by a
preposition

about

	excited	We were all **excited about** the match.
	right	You were **right about** it.
	sorry	I'm **sorry about** that.

at

	bad	Sorry, I'm **bad at** adding up!
	good	Bill is really **good at** cooking.

for

	famous	Our country is **famous for** its mountains.
	late	Sam was **late for** school yesterday.
	ready	Are you **ready for** your lunch?

from

	different	This house is **different from** ours.

in

	interested	Are you **interested in** computers?

of

	afraid	Michael is **afraid of** spiders.
	frightened	Lisa is **frightened of** the dark.
	full	My sleeping bag is **full of** ants!
	tired	I'm **tired of** the same old things!

on

	keen	I'm not very **keen on** fried food.

to

	married	Ellen is **married to** Jack.

with

	angry/annoyed	I'm really **angry/annoyed with** you.
	bored	We're **bored with** this film.
	pleased	Kate's teacher is **pleased with** her.

Careful!

Many adjectives have different meanings with different prepositions. Always
check in a dictionary.

Practice

1 Underline the correct word.

a) Brazil is famous *for/in* its beautiful beaches.

b) I'm not very good *for/at* maths.

c) Your computer is different *from/with* mine.

d) Kate is afraid *of/for* mice.

e) My teacher was very pleased *with/to* me.

f) Helen was very excited *for/about* her prize.

g) Peter isn't very keen *on/for* playing golf.

h) My town is famous *for/with* its soap factory.

i) Why are you so angry *for/with* me?

j) Is your brother interested *in/to* football?

2 Write one word in each space.

a) Are you ....*ready*.... for bed yet? It's very late.

b) Stop shouting! Why are you .... with me?

c) Joe's school bag is .... of dirty pieces of paper!

d) I'm .... of doing the same old things every day!

e) Diana is .... at physics and always gets top marks.

f) Paula has decided to get married .... the boy next door.

g) You were .... about my wallet. It was on my desk, as you said.

h) Lots of people I know are .... of the dark.

i) I'm not very .... on Chinese food.

j) Clive is really .... with his new bike. He says it's great.

3 Rewrite each sentence using the words in **bold**. Do not change the meaning.

a) George arrived at school late.   **for**
   ....*George was late for school.*....

b) I find staying at home boring.   **with**
   ....

c) Ann and Chris are married.   **to**
   ....

d) I apologize for my behaviour.   **about**
   ....

e) Joaquim is a very good cyclist.   **at**
   ....

f) Do you find history interesting?   **in**
   ....

Consolidation 12

1 **Choose the most suitable word or phrase for each space.**

a) I like your new bike. ..*B*.. really fast!

    A) Its   B) It's   C) It

b) Oh no! ..... a huge traffic jam!

    A) There's   B) Its   C) It has

c) ..... seems to be something wrong with my camera.

    A) It   B) There   C) It's

d) Hurry up! ..... half past seven already.

    A) There's   B) Its   C) It's

e) Tina's house is very large. ..... got six bedrooms.

    A) It is   B) There is   C) It has

f) ..... no doubt about it. Helen is the winner!

    A) There's   B) It's   C) It

g) Someone has left ..... watch in the classroom.

    A) there   B) their   C) they're

h) You can phone from here. ..... a phone in the corridor.

    A) It has   B) There's   C) It's

2 **Complete each sentence with an adverb from the box.**

badly	carelessly	hard	loudly	politely	quickly	secretly	~~well~~

a) I slept ....*well*.... , thank you.

b) Deborah studied .... for her exams.

c) Paul did his homework ....

d) Mary took the money ....

e) Harry drove .... to the hospital.

f) David always behaves ....

g) Ann shouted ....

h) Sarah speaks French ....

3   **Write one word in each space.**

a) The police told Jim to stop, but he ....*refused*.... to obey them.

b) Nobody .... to Tim when he starts talking.

c) I don't .... in magic and ghosts and things like that.

d) Jane is very .... with her new car. She likes it a lot.

e) Luckily, when it started raining we .... a place to wait.

f) Susan is really .... at making clothes.

g) Are you .... in history or archaeology?

4   **Rewrite each sentence using the words in bold. Do not change the meaning.**

a) Birds frighten Ann.   **of**
    ....*Ann is frightened of birds.*............................

b) Tina arrived at school late yesterday.   **for**
    ....

c) I'm sorry I missed you.   **apologize**
    ....

d) Harry finds his lessons boring.   **is**
    ....

e) I don't like getting up early.   **stand**
    ....

f) There are lots of people in the cinema.   **full**
    ....

g) Ricardo is a very bad footballer.   **at**
    ....

5   **Write one word in each space.**

a) Paula .....*went*..... swimming yesterday afternoon.

b) Why don't you look .... the word in your dictionary?

c) I really hate .... up early.

d) I'm looking .... to going on holiday.

e) Are you interested .... computers?

f) I think we've .... out of milk.

g) Have I .... any mistakes?

h) Do you fancy .... to the theatre?

Think about grammar! Are the sentences true or false?

a) *Do* is used for an action, *make* is used when we create something new.

b) There is no difference in meaning between *have you got* and *do you have*.

c) Adverbs usually follow the verb.

85 Punctuation

Punctuation helps the reader understand what we write, and is an important part of writing.

Basic punctuation

Symbol	Name	Use	Example
.	full stop	at end of sentence	*This is a sentence.*
		in abbreviations	*E.U.*
,	comma	separates clauses	*If it rains, we'll get wet.*
		in lists.	*It was dark, wet and windy.*
?	question mark	end of questions	*What's your name?*
'	apostrophe	contractions	*I'm not happy.*
		possessives	*Peter's room.*
!	Exclamation mark	for emphasis – informal	*I've won!*

- Full stops are often left out in *Mr* and *Mrs*.

- *it's* and *its*
  The possessive form of *it* is *its*.
  > I like **its** colour.

  It's is the contracted form of *it is* or *it has*.
  > **It's** *a lovely day!*
  > **It's** *rained three times this week*.

- Apostrophe with *o'clock*.
  > *It's six o'clock.*
  > *It's nine o'clock.*

 SEE ALSO

Grammar 72: Possession 2: apostrophe, *of*

Practice

1   **Choose the sentence with the correct punctuation.**

a) 1 Have you seen my pen, I'm looking for it?
   2 Have you seen my pen I'm looking for it?   ✔
   3 Have you seen my pen? I'm looking for it.

b) 1 We bought some oranges some apples and, a loaf.
   2 We bought some oranges, some apples and a loaf.
   3 We bought, some oranges, some apples, and a loaf.

c) 1 What's the matter? with your bike, is it broken?
   2 What's the matter? with your bike? Is it broken?
   3 What's the matter with your bike? Is it broken?

d) 1 Two boys in football kit ran across the playground.
   2 Two boys, in football kit, ran, across the playground.
   3 Two boys in football kit ran, across the playground.

e) 1 Go down this street turn left and then cross the road.
   2 Go down this street, turn left, and then cross the road.
   3 Go down, this street, turn left, and then, cross the road.

f) 1 Look out! You'll fall off the bus if you're not careful.
   2 Look out? You'll fall off the bus if, you're not careful.
   3 Look out you'll fall off the bus, if you're not careful!

g) 1 First of all I think, this idea is wrong.
   2 First of all, I think, this idea is wrong.
   3 First of all, I think this idea is wrong.

h) 1 If I, were you, I'd go to bed earlier.
   2 If I were you, I'd go to bed earlier.
   3 If I were you I'd go, to bed earlier.

i) 1 Its got a lovely pattern, but the material is too thin.
   2 It's got a lovely pattern, but the material is too thin.
   3 Its' got a lovely pattern, but the material is too thin.

j) 1 These are Paul's magazines and Jame's books.
   2 These are Paul's magazine's and James' books.
   3 These are Paul's magazines and James' books.

2 **Add apostrophes if necessary.**

a) Its six o clock. Its time for the news.
...... *It's six o'clock. It's time for the news.* ......

b) Ive decided to buy Jims old boots.
....

c) Whose books are these? Are they yours?
....

d) Sues borrowed Carols paints.
....

e) This new boats ours. Its got sails and oars.
....

f) My sisters are going to Janes party.
....

g) I think the dogs hurt one of its legs.
....

h) Wheres Helens brothers bike?
....

3 **Correct each sentence or question. Write the punctuation where necessary.**

a) Whats the matter with Mrs Smiths dog
...... *What's the matter with Mrs Smith's dog?* ......

b) Carols got two brothers a sister and three cousins
....

c) Thats not yours Its mine
....

d) I bought some bananas two apples and some sandwiches
....

e) Dont worry The boys will borrow their friends bikes
....

f) Theres something wrong with Anns car
....

g) Have you seen the swimming pool Its fantastic
....

h) Its eight o clock Its time for the bus
....

4 **Add commas where necessary.**

a) There was a big, red bus.

b) We had meat potatoes and vegetables for lunch.

c) He was an angry old man.

d) We took a book a pen and a ruler.

e) My brother sister and mother were there.

f) We watched an old scary film.

g) The teacher shouted screamed and ran out of the class.

h) I got a new blue jumper.

5 **Rewrite this letter. Add punctuation where necessary.**

Dear Miss Green

Im writing to you to tell you that Steven isnt coming to school today because hes not feeling very well Hell be in class again on Friday morning If youd like to talk to me you can call me at home

When is the last day of term

Best wishes

John Roberts

....
....
....
....
....
....
....
....
....
....
....

Explanations

How to improve your spelling

Always use a dictionary to check the spelling of new words. Use the spelling of other words you know to help you. Make lists of the words you usually spell wrongly. When you come across words which are difficult to spell, follow these four steps. First, look at the correct spelling. Then cover it. Next write the word. Finally check your word.

Adding -ing to verbs

One syllable words which end in one vowel (*a, e, i, o, u*) and one consonant – double the last consonant.

    swim ⟶ *swimming*   *put* ⟶ *putting*

Compare these words which do not double the consonant:

    shoot ⟶ *shooting*   *lift* ⟶ *lifting*

Two syllable words which end in one vowel and one consonant – double the last consonant when the stress is on the second syllable.

    begin ⟶ *beginning*   *control* ⟶ *controlling*

Compare these words with the stress on the first syllable:

    wonder ⟶ *wondering*   *threaten* ⟶ *threatening*

Exceptions to this rule in British English are verbs ending in -l.

    travel ⟶ *travelling*   *cancel* ⟶ *cancelling*

Words which end in one vowel, one consonant and -*e* - drop the final -*e*.

    write ⟶ *writing*   *drive* ⟶ *driving*

Words ending in -*ful*

The suffix -*ful* has only one -*l*.

    beautiful   *successful*

When -*ly* is added for adverbs, the *l* is doubled.

    beautifully   *successfully*

***ie* or *ei*?**

There is a useful rule: *i* before *e* except after *c*, when the sound is /i:/.

    field niece but *receive receipt*

Commonly misspelled words 1

accommodation	*believe*
address	*biscuit*
advertisement	*careful*
almost	*chocolate*
answer	*diary*
argument	*different*
beautiful	*disappear*
beginning	*disappointed*

Practice

1 **Write new words. Use *-ing, -ful* or *-ly*.**

a) swim + *ing* ......*swimming*......   e) beauty + *ful* ....

b) write + *ing* ....   f) success + *ful* ....

c) begin + *ing* ....   g) wonder + *ful* ....

d) decide + *ing* ....   h) careful + *ly* ....

2 <u>Underline</u> the correct spelling.

a) Would you like some *choclate/chocolate*?

b) It's a really *beautiful/beatiful* day today.

c) Gerry *awnsered/answered* all the questions.

d) Could you give me your *adress/address*?

e) We're looking for *accommodation/acommodation*.

f) We missed the *begining/beginning* of the film.

g) We were *almost/allmost* late for the concert.

h) Helen was very *dissapointed/disappointed* when she failed the exam.

3 **There is one spelling error in each sentence. Correct the word.**

a) I don't beleive that aliens have ever visited our planet.   ...*believe*...

b) Mary writes in her secret dairy every night.   ....

c) Would you like a chocolate buiscit? They're very tasty.   ....

d) Put your books in the cuboard at the end of the lesson.   ....

e) Helen is still changeing her clothes.   ....

f) George and I go to diferrent schools.   ....

g) This swimming pool is deepper than the other one.   ....

h) When I cut myself, there was a lot of blud on the floor!   ....

4 <u>Underline</u> the correct spelling.

a) Suddenly the glass of water <u>*disappeared*</u>/*dissappeared*!

b) I'm sorry, but I just can't *believe/beleive* your lies.

c) Harry gets really *angry/angery* sometimes.

d) I like the television *advertisment/advertisement* for Choco-Bars.

e) Mandy and her sister belong to *diferrent/different* sports clubs.

f) An *apple/appel* a day keeps the doctor away.

g) How many people are *coming/comeing* to your party?

h) Tom's plane *arives/arrives* at 6.30.

5 **In your notebook, make a list of words you will learn to spell correctly tomorrow.**

GRAMMAR 87

Same pronunciation, different spelling

Explanations

Words with the same pronunciation

There are many words with the same pronunciation, but different spelling and different meanings. Check the meanings of these words.

brake	*break*	*hour*	*our*
know	*no*	*meat*	*meet*
past	*passed*	*piece*	*peace*
right	*write*	*see*	*sea*
some	*sum*	*son*	*sun*
steal	*steel*	*there*	*their*
whose	*who's*	*won*	*one*
week	*weak*	*wood*	*would*
wear	*where*		

q and u

The letter *q* is always followed by *u*.

question   squid   acquire

Words with a syllable which is not pronounced

Some words appear to have more syllables than they actually have when pronounced. Examples which are often spelled wrongly:

temperature	*library*	*Wednesday*
vegetable	*interesting*	*comfortable*

Nouns and verbs with c and s

Noun:	*advice*	*practice*	*licence*
Verb:	*advise*	*practise*	*license*

Commonly misspelled words 2

discuss	*fruit*
doctor	*half*
February	*hundred*
foreign	*immediately*
fortunately	*independent*
forty	*know*
friend	*laugh*

Practice

1 <u>Underline</u> the correct spelling.

a) George left at the end of <u>*February*</u>/*Febuary*.

b) Tim invited all his *freinds*/*friends* to his party.

c) Hurry up! It's half past *eight*/*eigth*.

d) There were over three *hunndred*/*hundred* people at the concert.

e) We sat around the table and *discussed*/*discused* the problem.

f) More than *harf*/*half* the students passed the exam.

g) The Little Princess used to be my *favourite*/*faverite* book.

h) Please bring me my lunch *immediatly*/*immediately*.

2 There is one spelling error in each sentence. Correct the word.

a) More than fourty people needed accommodation.   *forty*

b) Helen knows more than ten forein languages.   ....

c) We had a light lunch of friut and salad.   ....

d) Tim crashed into a tree, but fortunatly he wasn't injured.   ....

e) Can I have something to eat? I'm really hungrey.   ....

f) All Tina's friends visited her in hospittal when she was ill.   ....

g) Make a gess if you don't know the answer.   ....

h) We really enjoied ourselves at the party last night.   ....

i) If your shoes are derty, take them off at the door.   ....

j) Let me introduce you to the other members of my familly.   ....

3 <u>Underline</u> the correct word.

a) Our team has <u>*won*</u>/*one* the school swimming competition.

b) Could you go to the butcher's and buy some *meat*/*meet*?

c) Jim is Mr Brown's *son*/*sun*.

d) I'd like to play football, but I feel really *weak*/*week*.

e) Joe and Dave *were*/*where* on opposite teams in the football match.

f) Sorry, I don't *know*/*no* the answer to that question.

g) Mary saw the old man *steal*/*steel* the box of biscuits.

h) Don't forget to *right*/*write* me a letter.

i) Excuse me. *Who's*/*Whose* bags are these?

j) Melanie was happy when she *passed*/*past* her driving test.

4 In your notebook, make a list of words you will learn to spell correctly tomorrow.

British and American spelling

Explanations

There are many differences between British and American spelling.

British	American
centre	*center*
colour	*color*
defence	*defense*
dialogue	*dialog*
jewellery	*jewelry*
neighbour	*neighbor*
practise (verb)	*practice*
programme	*program*
theatre	*theater*
traveller	*traveler*
tyre	*tire*

Commonly misspelled words 3

library	*said*	*village*
minute	*science*	*Wednesday*
mountain	*should*	*where*
necessary	*success*	*which*
neighbour	*swimming*	*wonderful*
receive	*tomorrow*	*writing*
remember	*uncomfortable*	*written*
right		

Task

Make a list of your own spelling problems and successes.

Practice

1 **Underline the correct spelling.**

a) Have you been to the *library/libary*?

b) I'll see you on *Wenesday/Wednesday*.

c) Is it really *neccessary/necessary* to do this?

d) This new chair is really very *uncomfortable/uncomfortible*.

e) Helen has decided to become a *sceintist/scientist*.

f) *Witch/Which* one of you is Mrs Henley?

g) Will Jack be here *tommorrow/tomorrow*?

h) What do you think of our new *neighbours/neibours*?

2 **There is one spelling error in each sentence. Correct the word.**

a) I don't think you shoud do so much unnecessary work.   *should*

b) We discussed the possibility of going swiming tomorrow.   ....

c) There's an interesting programe on television tonight.   ....

d) I haven't writen to my aunt to thank her for her invitation.   ....

e) I became a succesful businessman after studying economics.   ....

f) Ron has to complete his writeing before Wednesday.   ....

g) Were have you been? I've been looking for you all day.   ....

h) Tony has started puting on weight, so he is going on a diet.   ....

3 **There are two spelling errors in each sentence. Correct both words.**

a) I received three leters this morning but I haven't writen any.

    ....*letters*...........   ....*written*...........

b) We're leaveing early in the morning, so set the alarme clock.

    ....

c) We're goeing on holliday to France with some old friends.

    ....

d) Did you rember to do your sience homework on Wednesday?

    ....

e) While we were chooseing our meal, the waiter brougth some water.

    ....

f) I'm writting a letter to my penfreind with all my news.

    ....

g) I had a wonderfull journy to the mountains with my friends.

    ....

h) The first astronauts succesfully landded on the moon in 1969.

    ....

Prefixes, suffixes, phrasal verbs, compound words

Explanations

Prefixes

A prefix goes at the front of a word to make a new word. It changes the meaning of the word.

interesting	***un***interesting*
like	***dis***like*

The prefixes: *dis-, un-,* and *im-* usually mean: *not*
The prefix: *re-* usually means: *again*

Suffixes

A suffix goes at the end of a word to make a new word. It changes the grammar of the word.

danger	*danger**ous***
care	*care**ful***

Phrasal verbs

Phrasal verbs can be difficult to remember. It is a good idea to keep a record of all the new phrasal verbs you see.

Examples

fill in (an application form)	*switch/turn on* (lights/computer)
get up (in the morning)	*switch/turn off* (lights/computer)
grow up	*take off* (a plane)
look after (a child)	*take part in*
look forward to (an event)	*try on* (a dress)
look something up (in a dictionary)	

Prepositions after adjectives and verbs

Keep a record of which nouns are followed by which prepositions.
Try making a list of the prepositions which are used differently in your language.

Compound words

We can make new words by joining a noun with another noun.

bath + room = bathroom
car + park = carpark

have, make, do, take, go

Examples

***have** dinner*	***make** a mistake*	***go** shopping*	***do** the shopping*	***take** a photo*
***have** a shower*	***make** a cake*	***go** swimming*	***do** the ironing*	
	***make** a noise*			
	***make** friends*			
	***make** an excuse*			

→ **SEE ALSO**

Grammar 81: Phrasal verbs
Grammar 82: Verbs with prepositions, gerund or infinitive
Grammar 83: *Be* with adjectives and prepositions

Practice

1 Write a prefix from the box in the space. You can use a prefix more than once.

| dis-   un-   im-   re- |

a) I can't answer this question. It's ....*im*..possible.

b) Kate started crying because she was so ....happy.

c) Paul never waits in queues. He is too ....patient.

d) Stealing other people's pens is ....honest!

e) A million pounds was given to the hospital by a/an ....known person.

f) When you ....write this, make it a bit shorter.

g) Mary was wearing a/an ....usual hat, shaped like a giant flower.

h) I don't think you are right. I ....agree completely.

2 Write a suffix from the box in the space. Use each suffix once only.

| -ing   -ed   -ance   -ful   -able   -ly   ~~-ous~~   -er |

a) Don't stand near the water! It's danger ..*ous*............. . You might fall in!

b) Thank you for your advice. You have been very help.................. .

c) Our new science teach.................. is very young.

d) Harry didn't think the book was very interest.................. .

e) I don't like this fish. It's not very well cook.................. .

f) I like this town. The people are very friend.................. .

g) If you have a haircut, it will change your appear.................. .

h) That was a great film! It was really enjoy.................. .

3 **Match each sentence half (a–j) with an ending (1–10).**

a) When little Johnny grows ....6..........

b) Don't forget to turn ....

c) Can I try ....

d) Mary always takes ....

e) What time do you usually get ....

f) Jim is really looking ....

g) If you don't know a word, look it ....

h) Will you look ....

i) The plane took ....

j) Could you fill ....

1 off more than two hours late.

2 after my cat while I'm away?

3 forward to his holiday in Spain.

4 up at the weekend?

5 in this application form, please?

6 up, he wants to be a pilot.

7 off the lights when you leave.

8 on these trousers please?

9 part in class activities.

10 up in a good dictionary.

4 <u>Underline</u> **the correct word in each sentence.**

a) Do you believe *for/<u>in</u>* ghosts?

b) Dave is very good *at/for* tennis.

c) What's the difference *of/between* these two words?

d) Mr Smith is very different *of/from* the rest of our teachers.

e) I'm not very keen *on/at* outdoor sports.

f) Carol spent a lot of money *on/for* a new car.

g) Peter isn't very interested *in/of* basketball.

h) Bill likes listening *to/at* music late at night.

5 **Choose a word from the box to complete each sentence.**

~~bath~~	book	home	motor	sea	suit	rain	under

a) Tim is in the .... *bath* .. room having a shower.

b) The weather is really bad, so take your umbrella and wear a ....coat.

c) Our teacher didn't give us any ....work today.

d) Peter packed his ....case and left the hotel.

e) We went on holiday to the ....side and swam every day.

f) I went to the ....shop to buy a new dictionary.

g) Jane decided to ....line important words with a red pen.

h) Kate got on her ....bike and rode quickly away.

6 **Choose the most suitable word for each space.**

a) Would you like to .A. for a walk later?

   A) go   B) have   C) make

b) Martin said he couldn't come and ..... an excuse.

   A) did   B) made   C) took

c) Sue ..... friends with the family next door.

   A) did   B) made   C) took

d) I'm going to ..... a bath now.

   A) have   B) make   C) go

e) Did you ..... shopping yesterday?

   A) do   B) go   C) make

f) Let's ..... some photos of the class.

   A) do   B) make   C) take

g) I think I've ..... a mistake.

   A) done   B) made   C) taken

h) What time are we ..... lunch?

   A) doing   B) having   C) taking

i) I always ..... the ironing on Sunday afternoon.

   A) go   B) make   C) do

j) Please don't ..... so much noise!

   A) make   B) do   C) take

k) Joe ..... several stupid mistakes in his driving test.

   A) did   B) took   C) made

Consolidation 13

1 **Choose the sentence with the correct punctuation.**

a) **A** This ones your's, but who's got their's?

    B This ones yours but whos got theirs?

    C This one's yours, but who's got theirs? ✔

b) **A** We got up late, had lunch, and watched television.

    B We got up, late had lunch, and watched television.

    C We got up late, had lunch and watched, television.

c) **A** Whats the matter with David's bike?

    B What's the matter with David's bike?

    C What's the matter, with Davids's bike?

d) **A** At the end of the film, we found the boys' coats under the seats.

    B At the end, of the film, we found the boys' coat's under the seats.

    C At the end of the film we found, the boys coats under the seats'.

e) **A** If I were you, I'd stop using yours and try hers'.

    B If I, were you, I'd stop using your's and try hers.

    C If I were you, I'd stop using yours and try hers.

f) **A** Jack's brother's name's Paul, isn't it?

    B Jack's brothers' name's Paul, isnt it?

    C Jack's brother's, names Paul, isn't it?

g) **A** If any letter's come here, I'll bring them, to Sam's house.

    B If any letters come here, I'll bring them to Sams's house.

    C If any letters come here, I'll bring them to Sam's house.

h) **A** Go down, this road, turn left, at the end, and then turn right.

    B Go down this road, turn left at the end, and then turn right.

    C Go down this road, turn left, at the end, and then turn right.

i) **A** Its nearly time for me to take the dog for its walk.

    B It's nearly time for me to take the dog for its walk.

    C It's nearly time for me to take the dog for it's walk.

j) **A** Watch out? You nearly hit that cyclist?

    B Watch out. You nearly hit that cyclist!

    C Watch out! You nearly hit that cyclist!

2 **There are two spelling errors in each sentence. Correct both words.**

a) It was a lovly afternoon, so we decided to spend the day at the beech.

...........*lovely*........... ....*beach*...........

b) The holiday was so succesful that we plan to go agian next summer.

....

c) I have seen an advertisment for some holiday accomodation in the countryside.

....

d) This answer isn't quite write. I believe it should be diferent.

....

e) Last Febuary I had a wonderful time staying in my friend's vilage.

....

f) My advise would be to discuss the problem with you're doctor.

....

3 **There are two spelling errors in each sentence. Write each sentence correctly.**

a) I was very dissapointed when I couldn't awnser the questions.

...*I was very disappointed when I couldn't answer the questions.*...

b) A climing holiday is diferent, but it's a bit dangerous.

....

c) Fortunately, all Helen's freinds remebered her birthday.

....

d) Peter trys to learn a new foriegn language every year.

....

e) Are you comeing with us to the cinema tommorow?

....

f) Do you beleive that people can travell through time?

....

g) Jim has just writen two leters to his uncle.

....

h) Oh bother! I've forgoten my keays. I'll have to go back.

....

i) Carol likes walking in the countery and seeing wild annimals.

....

j) Which is your faverite avertisement on television?

....

4 **Write one word in each space.**

a) I'd like to try ....._on_...... these shoes, please.

b) Tom grew .... in France.

c) Mary is looking .... to her party.

d) Why don't you look the word .... in the dictionary?

e) Jack is still in bed. He hasn't got .... yet.

f) What time does our plane take .... ?

g) Anna looked .... her dog for an hour, but couldn't find it.

h) I can't see. Can you turn .... the light?

5 **Complete each sentence with a word made from the word in brackets.**

a) If the word is important, (line) ..._underline_... it.

b) Thank you for inviting me. It was an (enjoy) .... evening.

c) I enjoyed this programme. It was really (interest) ....

d) Harry was (honest) .... and stole his friend's money.

e) Thank you very much. You've been very (help) ....

f) We've decided to spend two weeks at the (sea) .... this year.

g) Mary cried all night, and felt very (happy) ....

h) David couldn't wait in the queue. He was too (patient) ....

i) You can buy cheap books from that (book) ....

j) Don't touch the lion! That's (danger) ....

6 **Choose the most suitable word for each space.**

a) Would you like to .._A_. to the cinema later?

   A) go   B) have   C) stay

b) We stayed in a ..... on our holiday.

   A) beach   B) hotel   C) country

c) Jane is learning a new ..... language.

   A) foregn   B) forein   C) foreign

d) Go down the street and turn right ..... the post office.

  A) in   B) on   C) at

e) Can I have a ..... of cake, please?

  A) piece   B) peace   C) peas

f) It costs ..... Euros.

  A) fourty   B) forthy   C) forty

g) I'm going to be a doctor, when I grow ..... .

  A) in   B) up   C) to

h) My little brother believes ..... ghosts.

  A) of   B) about   C) in

7 **Choose the most suitable word for each space.**

Dear Jim

I am (1) .A.. to tell you that I won't be able to come to lunch with your family on Saturday the (2) ..... of April.

The (3) ..... is my cat is very ill and I have to take her (4) ..... the vet. I have asked my dad and he says he (5) ..... take her, but he has to go to the dentist at the same time and (6) ..... the same day. What a pain! I can't ask my mum as she is afraid (7) ..... cats and won't go near Tibbles.

I would love to come, but maybe when you have a party I will be there.

Best (8) .....

Simon

1) **A** writing	**B** writting	**C** to write
2) **A** twenteth	**B** twentyeth	**C** twentieth
3) **A** problem	**B** peroblem	**C** problim
4) **A** see	**B** to see	**C** seeing
5) **A** will	**B** wouldn't	**C** would
6) **A** on	**B** of	**C** for
7) **A** for	**B** of	**C** at
8) **A** whishes	**B** wishers	**C** wishes

Think about grammar! Are the sentences true or false?

a) You can put a question mark anywhere in a sentence.

b) A dictionary can teach you how to spell.

c) British spelling is more difficult than American spelling.

Personal details

1 <u>Underline</u> the correct word or phrase in each question.

a) <u>*What's your name*</u>/*What do you call*?

b) How *old/age* are you?

c) Where do you *stay/live*?

d) What's your *house/address*?

e) Which country do you *come/live* from?

f) What's your date of *birthday/birth*?

g) How long do you want to *stay/pass* here?

h) Have you got a *work/job*?

2 Choose the most suitable answer below for the questions from exercise 1.

1 1146, Black Lion Drive ....*d*...........

2 Three weeks ....

3 I'm nineteen. ....

4 In Los Angeles ....

5 No, I'm a student. ....

6 The United States ....

7 Ann-Marie Davis ....

8 3 November, 1980 ....

3 Complete each sentence. Use a word from the box.

| boy | children | family | foreigner | girl | friend | teenager | ~~woman~~ |

a) Our teacher is a tall ....*woman*..... called Mrs Green.

b) Is Helen your .... ?

c) Who is that .... ? Is it George?

d) Has Jean got any .... ?

e) How many people are there in your .... ?

f) Do you know that .... ? Her name's Anna.

g) Now that I'm thirteen, I'm a ....

h) I don't come from this country. I'm a ....

4 **Choose the most suitable word for each space.**

a) What's Tim like? He's ..*B*.. .

  A) high   B) tall   C) big

b) Ann ..... glasses.

  A) uses   B) carries   C) wears

c) Jane's only nine. She's ..... .

  A) young   B) modern   C) new

d) Can you ..... Peter?

  A) describe   B) look   C) appear

e) How many brothers and sisters ..... you got?

  A) do   B) have   C) are

f) Are you ..... ?

  A) study   B) a student   C) student

g) Where do you ..... from?

  A) arrive   B) do   C) come

h) What colour ..... your hair?

  A) has   B) is   C) are

i) Are you ..... or single?

  A) doubled   B) married   C) marriage

j) I ..... sixteen years old.

  A) have   B) get   C) am

k) James has ..... a beard.

  A) wears   B) got   C) carries

l) ..... your address?

  A) What   B) What's   C) Where's

m) What does Lucy look ..... ?

  A) after   B) alike   C) like

Family matters

1 **Look at the family tree. Write the answers.**

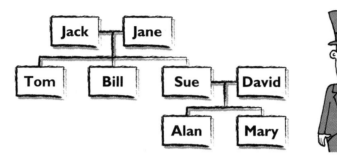

a) Who are Jack and Jane's children?   *Tom, Bill and Sue*

b) Who are Tom, Bill and Sue's parents?   ....

c) Who are Jack and Jane's sons?   ....

d) Who is Jack and Jane's daughter?   ....

e) Who is Tom's brother?   ....

f) Who is Tom and Bill's sister?   ....

g) Who is Sue's husband?   ....

h) Who is Jack's wife?   ....

i) Who is Alan and Mary's father?   ....

j) Who is Alan and Mary's grandfather?   ....

k) Who is Alan and Mary's mother?   ....

l) Who is Alan and Mary's grandmother?   ....

2 **Underline the correct word in each sentence.**

a) Christine is married *to/with* an Italian.

b) More than fifty of Rick's *parents/relatives* came to the wedding.

c) Ann is the only *people/person* I really like!

d) The *old/olds* often think about the past.

e) I've never met him before. He's a *stranger/foreigner*.

f) I *knew/met* your new English teacher yesterday.

g) Sue and her sister Mary are *twins/pairs*.

h) My brother Mark is the *eldest/elderly* child in the family.

3 Use the family tree on page 212 to answer the clues and complete the crosword.

Clues

Across

1 Jack is Jane's …
5 Tom is Jack's …
8 Sue is Mary's …
10 Jack is Alan's …

Down

2 Mary is Alan's …
3 Sue is Jack's …
4 David is Mary's …
6 Tom is Bill's …
7 Sue and David are Mary and Alan's …
9 Jane is Jack's …

4 Complete each sentence. Use a word from the box.

brother	children	~~daughter~~	husband	sister	son	twins	wife

a) Ted and Alice were happy when Emily, their _daughter_ was born.

b) Harry asked Ann to be his ...., and they got married six months later.

c) Jim and Mary's ...., David was their second child.

d) Richard and Stephen are ...., but they don't look exactly the same.

e) Mark and his .... Sue went shopping with their mother.

f) When the school bell rang, a crowd of .... ran out of the school.

g) Jane met her .... Philip at a friend's wedding.

h) Liz and her .... Mike like listening to their grandmother's stories.

Elem Lang Practice
M. Vince Macmillan

1 Choose the most suitable use (a–h) for each picture (1–8).

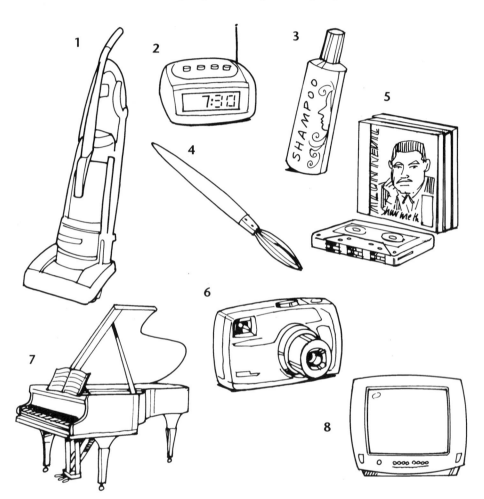

a) taking photos ....6......
b) doing the housework ....
c) listening to music ....
d) playing the piano ....
e) waking up ....
f) washing your hair ....
g) watching television ....
h) painting a picture ....

2 <u>Underline</u> the correct words in each sentence.

a) Are you interested *for/<u>in</u>* photography?

b) This is my *best/favourite* book. It's *David Copperfield*, by Dickens.

c) I've decided to *make/join* the local swimming club.

d) Kate usually *passes/spends* most of her time reading.

e) Tim has a very interesting *fun/hobby*. He builds small boats.

f) What do you like doing in your *empty/spare* time?

g) Wendy is a *member/team* of the drama club.

h) Sue likes going *to the cinema/cinema*.

3 Choose the most suitable word for each space.

What do you like doing best (1) .*C*. your spare time? My cousin Paul likes going (2) ..... in the country and (3) ..... photos. Sometimes he (4) ..... with his friends, and they (5) ..... at the park or at the beach. They always (6) ..... a good time. His brother Chris isn't (7) ..... on walking. He spends most of the (8) ..... at home.

1) **A** for	**B** when	**C** in	**D** at
2) **A** for walks	**B** walks	**C** a walk	**D** to walk
3) **A** making	**B** having	**C** taking	**D** doing
4) **A** travels	**B** gets up	**C** sees	**D** goes out
5) **A** enjoy	**B** hobby	**C** go	**D** have fun
6) **A** have	**B** make	**C** do	**D** like
7) **A** interested	**B** out	**C** decided	**D** keen
8) **A** other	**B** time	**C** people	**D** money

4 Choose the most suitable word or phrase for each space.

a) You need a pencil if you want to make a .*C*. .
   A) painting   B) planning   C) drawing

b) Kate's mother thinks that skateboarding is ..... .
   A) danger   B) dangerous   C) in danger

c) Sarah has a wonderful ..... collection.
   A) stamping   B) stamp   C) stamps

d) Does your sister play ..... ?
   A) the piano   B) pianos   C) a piano

e) Carol writes pop ..... in her spare time.
   A) songs   B) sings   C) singing

f) Harry spends a lot of time playing ..... .
   A) computer's games   B) games of computer   C) computer games

1 **Use a word from the box to complete each label (a–h).**

| ~~ceiling~~ | chair | light | door | floor | wall | window | radiator |

a) _ceiling_

b) ....

c) ....

d) ....

e) ....

f) ....

g) ....

h) ....

2 **Choose the most suitable word for each sentence.**

| kitchen | dining room | ~~bedroom~~ | living-room | bathroom | study |

a) You usually sleep in this room.   _bedroom_

b) You sit at your desk in this room.   ....

c) You sit on the sofa and watch television in this room.   ....

d) You cook meals in this room.   ....

e) You take a shower in this room.   ....

f) You eat in this room.   ....

3 <u>Underline</u> the correct word in each sentence.

a) Don't forget to <u>*turn off*</u>/*close* the light when you leave.

b) Can you *shut*/*stop* the door? It's cold in here.

c) Jim and Tina usually *have*/*get* lunch in the kitchen.

d) Our house is dirty because nobody likes *making*/*doing* housework.

e) Someone is *hitting*/*knocking* at the door.

f) Why don't you *put*/*take* a picture on this wall?

g) Can you *open*/*turn on* the light? I can't see.

h) Tom is *living*/*staying* with his sister for a few days.

4 Complete each sentence. Use a word from the box.

armchair   bathroom   ceiling   desk   floor   furniture   ~~upstairs~~   window

a) Our house has two floors, and my bedroom is ..*upstairs*.. .

b) If I stand on a chair, I can touch the ....

c) Peter does his homework at his .... in his bedroom.

d) I can't move in your room! There is too much ....

e) From my ...., I can see the park at the end of the street.

f) Kate dropped a glass on the .... and it broke.

g) Jack is in the .... He's taking a shower.

h) When I read, I like sitting in a comfortable ....

5 Choose the most suitable word for each space.

I like my house because it has lots of (1) ..*B*.. . It's a flat, and it has a hall, a
(2) ....., three bedrooms, a kitchen and a bathroom. My bedroom is small, but
I can see the park from my (3) ..... . I've got posters on the (4) ....., and a carpet on
the (5) ..... . There isn't a lot of (6) ....., just (7) ....., a bed and a (8) ..... for my
clothes. I used to (9) ..... the room with my brother, but he's a student now and
lives in a student (10) ..... .

1)	**A** place	**B** space	**C** floors	**D** area
2)	**A** living-room	**B** bedsit	**C** cottage	**D** saloon
3)	**A** door	**B** mirror	**C** curtain	**D** window
4)	**A** bed	**B** chair	**C** bookcase	**D** walls
5)	**A** wall	**B** floor	**C** window	**D** ceiling
6)	**A** furniture	**B** table	**C** armchair	**D** central heating
7)	**A** an office	**B** a library	**C** a desk	**D** a study
8)	**A** cupboard	**B** curtain	**C** carpet	**D** wardrobe
9)	**A** live	**B** part	**C** share	**D** double
10)	**A** hostel	**B** home	**C** college	**D** accommodation

217

Places

1 **Choose the correct name for each place.**

> baker's   bank   butcher's   chemist's   ~~greengrocer's~~
> newsagent's   market   post office

a) You can buy fresh fruit and vegetables here.   *greengrocer's*

b) You can put money in your account here.   ....

c) You can buy things outside in the street here.   ....

d) You can buy medicine here.   ....

e) You can buy bread and cakes here.   ....

f) You can buy meat here.   ....

g) You can buy stamps, and send letters here.   ....

h) You can buy magazines and sweets here.   ....

2 <u>Underline</u> **the correct word in each sentence.**

a) Have you been to Grimton? It's not a very nice *part/place*.

b) It's good to get away from the city and visit the *field/country*.

c) Paris is the *head/capital* of France.

d) You can get a bus from here to the city *central/centre*.

e) Would you rather live in a city, a small town or a *villa/village*?

f) When you leave the *land/country*, you have to show your passport.

g) David comes from a small *centre/town* in Wales.

h) Everest is the highest mountain in the *world/earth*.

3 **Choose the most suitable word or phrase for each space.**

a) Excuse me, how do I _B_ to the post office from here?
A) find   B) get   C) come

b) When you come to the end of the street, turn ..... .
A) to left   B) left   C) the left

c) Could you tell me the ..... to the bus station, please?
A) road   B) direction   C) way

d) I don't know where we are. I'm completely ..... .
A) lost   B) missed   C) absent

e) ..... the next turning on the right.
A) Make   B) Go   C) Take

f) How ..... is it from here to the museum?
A) far   B) distance   C) journey

g) Go ..... at the traffic lights.
A) over   B) straight on   C) through

h) The cinema is ..... the left.
A) on   B) at   C) by

Elementary Language Practice
Vince Macmillan

4 **Choose the correct name for each place.**

block of flats	station	cinema	hotel	library
~~police station~~	restaurant	theatre		

a) You can ask for help here.   _police station_
b) You can stay here.   ....
c) You can borrow books from here.   ....
d) You can watch a film here.   ....
e) You can catch a train here.   ....
f) You can see a play here.   ....
g) You can live here.   ....
h) You can have dinner here.   ....

6 Jobs

1 <u>Underline</u> the correct word in each sentence.

a) Mark works for an Australian *job/company*.

b) Ann got a job in an office as a *typewriter/typist*.

c) When I had toothache I went to the *doctor's/dentist's*.

d) Bob trained as an *electrician/electric*.

e) My mother used to work as a *cook/cooker* in a school.

f) Do you like our new English *teacher/professor*?

g) The police *was/were* waiting for Jim outside the bank.

h) Helen has found a *work/job* in a bank.

2 Choose the best ending (1–8) for each sentence (a–h).

a) The mechanic   1 milked the cows.

b) The carpenter   2 sent the thief to prison.

c) The vet   3 gave Lisa some medicine for her sick cat.

d) The judge   4 brought Ann a drink on a tray.

e) The plumber   5 repaired the table and chairs.

f) The farmer   6 made Paul's new suit.

g) The tailor   7 repaired my car.

h) The steward   8 fixed the broken pipe in the bathroom.

3 Complete each sentence. Use a word from the box.

actor	~~architect~~	electrician	gardener	lawyer	musician
nurse	sailor	scientist	soldier		

a) Sam's new house was designed by a well-known ....*architect*.... .

b) After he was arrested, Paul was allowed to phone his ....

c) Being a/an .... is enjoyable, until there is a war.

d) A/an .... looked after Bob when he was in hospital.

e) When all the lights went out, the manager called a/an ....

f) Once a week, a/an .... comes and cuts the grass.

g) Helen trained as a/an .... and now plays in an orchestra.

h) Ann is a famous .... and works at a university.

i) The best .... in the play played the part of the King.

j) David didn't enjoy being a/an .... because he got seasick.

4 **Read these descriptions of jobs and complete the words.**

a) My dad helps children learn things. t _ea_ _cher_

b) This person helps people who are ill. d _ _ _ _ _

c) He/She performs in the theatre, on TV or in films. a _ _ _ _

d) This person sells things in shops. s _ _ _ a _ _ _ _ _ _ _

e) I study in a university. s _ _ _ _ _ _

f) This person writes books and plays. w _ _ _ _ _

g) My cousin looks after people's teeth. d _ _ _ _ _ _

h) He makes houses and other offices. b _ _ _ _ _ _

5 **Choose the most suitable word for each space.**

My sister has got a new (1) .A. in a hospital. She's not a nurse or a doctor. She
(2) ..... in the kitchen, she's a (3) ..... . She prepares special food for the patients in
the hospital.

She saw an (4) ..... in the paper, and wrote a letter telling them about her work
cooking for people in a vegetarian restaurant. She has lots of (5) ..... working in a
kitchen. The hospital (6) ..... asked her to come for an (7) ..... . They liked her very
much, but before they (8) ..... her the job, they checked her (9) ..... .

She loves her new job and says that cooking for patients in a hospital is much
better than working in a small (10) ....

1) **A** job	**B** work	**C** employment
2) **A** is	**B** work	**C** works
3) **A** cooker	**B** cook	**C** cooks
4) **A** sign	**B** notice	**C** advertisement
5) **A** experience	**B** past	**C** previous
6) **A** doctor	**B** manager	**C** dentist
7) **A** interview	**B** review	**C** references
8) **A** give	**B** offered	**C** told
9) **A** referee	**B** references	**C** review
10) **A** company	**B** job	**C** cooker

Inside the house

1 **Use a word from the box to complete each label (a–h).**

| poster | carpet | ~~curtains~~ | lamp | shelf | table | bed | wardrobe |

a) _curtains_   e) ....

b) ....   f) ....

c) ....   g) ....

d) ....   h) ....

2   **Choose the things you usually find in each room.**

a) kitchen

    ① cooker   2 sofa   3 bath   ④ fridge

b) bedroom

    1 blanket   2 dustbin   3 wardrobe   4 pillow

c) living-room

    1 bed   2 armchair   3 carpet   4 table

d) bathroom

    1 mirror   2 television   3 bookshelf   4 shower

e) study

    1 bed   2 desk   3 bookshelf   4 cooker

f) dining room

    1 table   2 bath   3 chair   4 wardrobe

3   **Choose the most suitable word for each space.**

a) To stop the light coming in the window we need some .A. .

    A) curtains   B) radiators   C) shelves

b) It's very cold. Why don't you turn on the ..... ?

    A) central heating   B) cooker   C) stove

c) In the evening I like to relax in ..... .

    A) a chair   B) a seat   C) an armchair

d) Laura sat at her ..... and turned on her computer.

    A) study   B) desk   C) office

e) My school books are in the ..... in the living-room.

    A) library   B) bookcase   C) bookshelf

f) There was a lovely fire burning in the ..... .

    A) chimney   B) central heating   C) fireplace

g) You can wash your hands in the ..... in the bathroom.

    A) basin   B) shower   C) tap

h) The biscuits are in the ..... in the kitchen.

    A) table   B) shelf   C) cupboard

1 Use a word from the box to complete each label (a–h).

| some biscuits | some bread | a chicken | some chips | some fruit |
| a salad | a sausage | ~~some spaghetti~~ | | |

a) *some spaghetti*

b) ....

c) ....

d) ....

e) ....

f) ....

g) ....

h) ....

2 **Complete each sentence. Use a word from the box.**

breakfast	take-away	dinner	food	lunch	meal
menu	picnic	~~snack~~	course		

a) When I get hungry and feel like a .....*snack*...., I eat an apple.

b) The waiter gave us the .... and we chose our meals.

c) A good .... is the best way of starting the day.

d) Peter has to take medicine an hour before every ....

e) I'm meeting Carol for .... at 1.30, so I'll be back late this afternoon.

f) .... is served every evening in the hotel dining-room.

g) Michael really loves Greek ....

h) We took some fruit and sandwiches and had a .... on the beach.

i) Helen didn't have time to cook so she phoned for a ....

j) After the starter we ordered our main ....

3 <u>Underline</u> **the correct word in each sentence.**

a) *Boil*/*Cook* some water, and pour it into the cup.

b) We usually *bake*/*fry* the fish in oil.

c) At the end of the meal we paid the *menu*/*bill*.

d) I always buy fresh food because I don't like *iced*/*frozen* food.

e) Lisa doesn't eat meat. She's a *vegetable*/*vegetarian*.

f) Don't forget to put *the meal*/*the food* in the fridge.

g) When the food is *made*/*done*, take it out of the oven.

h) Could we have some more *bread*/*loaf* please?

i) The *cook*/*cooker* put the meat in the oven.

j) Jack bought a fresh *chicken*/*kitchen* from the supermarket.

4 **Choose the most suitable word for each description.**

cup	jug	fork	knife	plate	~~spoon~~	straw	tray

a) You can eat soup with this.   .....*spoon*.....

b) You can suck drinks through this.   ....

c) You put food on this and eat from it.   ....

d) You can carry things on this.   ....

e) You can cut meat with this.   ....

f) You drink tea or coffee from this.   ....

g) You can carry food to your mouth with this.   ....

h) You can pour water from this.   ....

Animals

1 **Use a word from the box to complete each label (a–h).**

| bird | cat | chicken | dog | fish | ~~horse~~ | lizard | monkey |

a) *horse*   e) ....

b) ....   f) ....

c) ....   g) ....

d) ....   h) ....

2 Underline the correct word in each sentence.

a) Can you *take*/*run* the dog for a walk, please?

b) This is my *pet*/*toy* lizard, Larry.

c) When someone knocks at the door, the dog *shouts*/*barks*.

d) Some birds can *run*/*fly* for thousands of kilometres.

e) Lions and tigers are *wild*/*country* animals.

f) Do you know how to *ride*/*drive* a horse?

g) Monkeys are good at *climbing*/*living* trees.

h) Helen has two birds, and *feeds*/*eats* them every day.

i) There are many fish living *deep*/*low* in the sea.

j) My cat has a really long *leg*/*tail*.

3 Complete each sentence. Use a word from the box.

~~bite~~ catch ride hunt jump like live feed make sing

a) Don't worry! The dog won't ..... *bite* ..... you.

b) Monkeys can .... from one tree to another.

c) Fish can't .... out of water.

d) Parrots .... a lot of noise.

e) Not many people .... snakes.

f) Most birds .... in the morning.

g) Cats usually .... at night and sleep during the day.

h) You can use a net or a hook to .... a fish.

i) Can you .... a horse?

j) Let's got to the park and .... the ducks.

4 Choose the best ending (1–10) for each sentence (a–j).

a) A small blue fish

b) The fat white cat

c) The friendly horse

d) Mickey Mouse

e) Suddenly a small bird

f) Mary's pet chicken

g) A large black dog

h) The snake

i) The monkey

j) The small green lizard

1 laid an egg in the kitchen.

2 barked when I knocked at the door.

3 was green and two metres long.

4 took the nuts and ran away.

5 flew across the garden.

6 went to sleep on the armchair.

7 ate some grass from Tim's hand.

8 lay asleep on the rock in the sun.

9 was swimming in the glass bowl.

10 was the star of many cartoons.

1   **Look at the picture and read the descriptions. Write the names.**

Paula   Rick   Mr Davis   Mrs Green

a) She's middle-aged and she's wearing a skirt.   *Mrs Green*

b) He's got a beard.   ....

c) She's got long hair and glasses.   ....

d) He's wearing jeans and a pullover.   ....

e) She's wearing a tracksuit.   ....

f) He's wearing a suit.   ....

g) She's wearing ear-rings.   ....

h) He's old and he's tall, and he's wearing a hat.   ....

2   **Choose the most suitable word from the box for each description.**

belt   costume   earring   glove   hat   overcoat   ~~sock~~   underwear

a) You put one of these on each foot.   *sock*

b) You wear this over your clothes in cold weather.   ....

c) You wear this on your head.   ....

d) This stops your trousers falling down.   ....

e) You wear this in your ear.   ....

f) You wear one of these on each hand in cold weather.   ....

g) You wear this when you go swimming.   ....

h) You wear this under your clothes.   ....

3 **Choose the most suitable word or phrase for each space.**

a) Maria usually ..A.. sports clothes.

   A) wears   B) carries   C) dresses

b) I don't like these shoes. They hurt my ..... .

   A) hands   B) arms   C) feet

c) Peter always wears a tie and a white ..... .

   A) shirt   B) blouse   C) skirt

d) Helen went to the shops and bought ..... .

   A) a trouser   B) a pair of trousers   C) two trousers

e) David has decided to buy ..... .

   A) a new cloth   B) a new dress   C) new clothes

f) This coat is the wrong ..... . It's too big.

   A) size   B) large   C) number

g) Your clothes are wet! I think you should ..... them off.

   A) dress   B) take   C) wear

h) When it's hot, I usually wear ..... and a t-shirt.

   A) shorts   B) a short   C) short ones

i) I want to buy a new pair of ..... .

   A) ear-ring   B) ring   C) earrings

j) It's very cold outside. You must ..... on your coat.

   A) take   B) put   C) wear

4 **Complete each sentence. Use a word from the box.**

assistant	bargain	counter	customer	label	~~sale~~	size	shoplifter

a) Peter bought his jacket cheap in a ..... *sale* ..... .

b) These shoes are .... 44. Are they big enough for you?

c) Kevin left his wallet on the .... when he paid for his trousers.

d) The .... says this dress is size 10, but I think it's smaller.

e) Jane forgot to pay for the shirt, and she was arrested for being a ....

f) I only paid £5 for these shoes! They were a ....

g) Emma had to wait while the assistant served another ....

h) Helen asked the .... to help her choose a skirt.

1 **Choose the most suitable description (a–f) for each situation (1–6).**

a) It's hot. ....4..........

b) It's snowing. ....

c) It's windy. ....

d) It's raining. ....

e) It's cold. ....

f) It's cloudy ....

1

2

3

4

5

6

2 **<u>Underline</u> the correct word in each sentence.**

a) The sky was full of dark *<u>clouds</u>/rain*.

b) Before the storm started, we heard *booming/thunder*.

c) It was very cold and the river was *frozen/iced*.

d) It won't rain for a long time. It's only a *shower/bath*.

e) When the wind *whistlers/blows*, all the trees move.

f) We sat on the beach and enjoyed the *sunshine/sunburn*.

g) It started raining, and everyone got *watery/wet*.

h) During the storm the sky lit up with *rain/lightning*.

3 **Complete each sentence. Use a word from the box.**

| freezing | lightning | rain | ~~raining~~ | snowing | sunny | windy |

a) As it's ..*raining*.., take your umbrella.

b) If it's .... tomorrow, we'll go to the beach.

c) Suddenly there was a flash of .... and then loud thunder.

d) I'm ....! Can I borrow a thick pullover?

e) It was very .... yesterday, so Jim flew his kite.

f) We had very heavy .... yesterday and I got very wet.

g) Look, it's ....! All the cars are white!

4 **Choose the most suitable word for each space.**

Dear Graham

We have just come back from our summer holiday in France. During the first week the (1) ..*B*.. was terrible. Everyone said that summer in the south of France would be (2) ..... and sunny, but it wasn't. Every day was (3) ..... and one day we had a thunderstorm. It was very exciting, but the dog didn't like the (4) ..... or the thunder. It was very loud!

In the second week the weather got better. It stopped (5) ..... all the time and the sun came out. It was still quite (6) ..... on the beach, but that was OK because sometimes it got too hot. My brother got (7) ..... on his back because he fell asleep – it wasn't too bad though. One day we flew our kites from the top of a hill. That was great fun, but the (8) ..... blew and broke mum's kite. She was very cross.

We came home yesterday on the boat. It was very (9) ..... and not very nice at all. My dad said that next year we could go to Iceland for our holiday – I don't think I want to because I'm sure it would be (10) ..... and I prefer sunny holidays!

Love

Jane

1)	**A** day	**B** weather	**C** weeks
2)	**A** hot	**B** rainy	**C** cold
3)	**A** watery	**B** cloudy	**C** weathery
4)	**A** booming	**B** raining	**C** lightning
5)	**A** raining	**B** snow	**C** cloudy
6)	**A** wet	**B** windy	**C** wind
7)	**A** sunshine	**B** sunburn	**C** sunny
8)	**A** cloud	**B** rain	**C** wind
9)	**A** wet	**B** snow	**C** sun
10)	**A** iced	**B** freezing	**C** snow

1 **Use a word from the box to complete each label (a–j).**

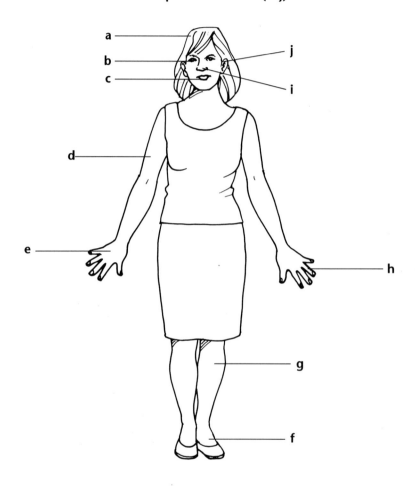

| arm | ear | eye | finger | foot | ~~hair~~ | hand | leg | mouth | nose |

a) *hair*

b) ....

c) ....

d) ....

e) ....

f) ....

g) ....

h) ....

i) ....

j) ....

2 <u>Underline</u> the correct word in each sentence.

a) Horses have got four _legs/arms_.

b) The little girl was holding her mother's _foot/hand_.

c) Tony always lies on his _back/head_ when he sleeps.

d) Gina has beautiful long _ears/hair_.

e) Jack has got a cold and his _knee/nose_ is red.

f) Anna can't write because she has broken two _fingers/toes_.

g) I've got five _fingers/toes_ on each foot.

h) A giraffe has got a very long _mouth/neck_.

3 Complete each sentence. Use a word from the box.

arm	ear	eye	foot	hand	head	~~leg~~	waist

a) Peter broke his ....._leg_...... and couldn't walk for a month.

b) When David met Mrs Greenwood, he shook her ....

c) I tried on the shoe but my .... got stuck!

d) I can't see! I've got something in my ....

e) The teacher was carrying a lot of books under his ....

f) I need new trousers, because my .... is getting bigger!

g) My .... feels cold in winter, so I wear a hat.

h) Our teacher's words go in one .... and out the other!

4 Choose the most suitable word for each space.

a) You ....._C_......... with your foot.

   A) laugh   B) click   C) kick

b) You .... with your teeth.

   A) stamp   B) bite   C) smell

c) You .... with your finger.

   A) point   B) smell   C) wink

d) You .... with your nose.

   A) blink   B) kick   C) smell

e) You .... with one eye.

   A) point   B) wink   C) bite

f) You .... with both eyes.

   A) blink   B) kiss   C) shout

13 | Staying healthy

Elementary
Language Practice
M Vince, Macmilla

1 **Underline** the correct word in each sentence.

a) I can't see! There is something wrong with my left *ear/eye*.

b) I couldn't wash because there wasn't any *soap/soup*.

c) The doctor told me that I have to *have/do* an operation.

d) These shoes are too small for me. I've got wide *feet/legs*.

e) I didn't go to school because I had *cold/a cold*.

f) Mary decided to *do/have* a hot bath.

g) Peter is *ill/bad* and has gone to the doctor's.

h) Don't forget to *wash/clean* your hands!

2 **Choose the most suitable word or phrase for each space.**

a) I've got a ..*B*.. in my leg.

 A) hurt   B) pain   C) damage

b) Tom was very ill, and had to go to ..... .

 A) hospital   B) medicine   C) doctor

c) George broke his leg in a/an ..... .

 A) chance   B) problem   C) accident

d) Kate had a ..... of 41°C.

 A) temperature   B) heat   C) thermometer

e) Ellen stayed at home because she didn't feel very ..... .

 A) ill   B) well   C) better

f) Little Jimmy was crying because he had a/an ..... .

 A) ill ear   B) earache   C) ear pain

g) The doctor didn't expect his poor ..... to pay a lot.

 A) patients   B) customers   C) users

h) When Michael ....., everyone said, 'Bless you!'

 A) hurt   B) fell   C) sneezed

i) You should put a ..... on that cut.

 A) bleeding   B) wound   C) plaster

j) Peter has decided to give up ..... .

 A) smoke   B) smoking   C) smoker

3 Complete each sentence. Use a word from the box.

| bleeding | broken | dangerous | fit | ~~healthy~~ | injured | sore | well |

a) A ....*healthy*.... diet includes lots of fruit and vegetables.

b) John is very ill and won't come to school until he is ....

c) Helen's leg was .... so the doctor put it in plaster for a month.

d) It is .... to take more than four of these tablets in 24 hours.

e) George has cut his hand and it's ....

f) David keeps .... by doing exercises in the gym twice a week.

g) Edward walked all day in his new boots, and now his feet are ....

h) The bus crashed into a tree, but luckily nobody was ....

4 Use a word from the box to complete each label (a–h).

| headache | sore throat | ~~back ache~~ | broken arm |
| stomach ache | cold | fever | dizzy |

a) ....*back ache*....

b) ....

c) ....

d) ....

e) ....

f) ....

g) ....

h) ....

235

1 Use a word from the box to complete each label (a–h).

| bush | fence | field | flower | lake | ~~hill~~ | stream | tree |

a) ....*hill*........   e) ....

b) ....   f) ....

c) ....   g) ....

d) ....   h) ....

2 <u>Underline</u> the correct word in each sentence.

a) Go along this road and up the <u>*hill*</u>/*mountain* at the end.

b) We travelled down the *river*/*stream* by boat to the sea.

c) Beside the road there were *fields*/*gardens* full of animals and plants.

d) Helen spent her holiday on a small Greek *island*/*land*.

e) The boys camped next to a small *lake*/*ocean* in Scotland.

f) The children enjoyed playing on the *beach*/*seaside*.

g) Kate stayed in a small village in the *country*/*outside*.

h) From the ship, Mark could see the distant *coast*/*side* of France.

3 <u>Underline</u> the correct word in each sentence.

a) Sarah spent the summer *at/<u>on</u>/to* an island.

b) There is a castle *at/in/above* the top of the hill.

c) It was cold so I didn't put my feet *on/in/to* the water.

d) At midday, we sat *at/below/under* a tree and had a picnic.

e) Caroline spent a lovely day *at/on/in* the seaside.

f) Would you like to have lunch *in/on/next* to the garden?

g) George and his friends camped *in/on/under* the beach.

h) We decided to have a weekend *at/in/with* the country.

4 Complete each sentence. Use a word from the box.

beach	field	forest	hill	island	mountain	~~river~~	sea

a) We couldn't cross the ...... *river* ...... because there wasn't a bridge.

b) At the back of the farm was a large .... with five horses.

c) Most fish live in the ....

d) Maria climbed the .... and looked down from the top.

e) The hill was covered with a thick .... of tall trees.

f) Tina lived on a small .... in the middle of the Aegean Sea.

g) Our school is on the top of a small ....

h) After his swim, Jim rested on the ....

1 <u>Underline</u> the correct word in each sentence.

a) The bus to the shops leaves from the *station/<u>stop</u>* outside our house.

b) Sue got *into/onto* her car and drove away.

c) Enjoy your *travel/trip*! I'll see you next week!

d) It's much quicker to go *by/on* foot.

e) I'd like a *back/return* ticket to London, please.

f) Jane arrives *home/at* home at 4.00.

g) What time does the train *leave/part*?

h) If you don't hurry, we'll *lose/miss* the bus.

2 Choose the most suitable word or phrase for each space.

a) There was a notice at the airport which said, ' ...C... to Greece.'

   A) Well come   B) Well came   C) Welcome

b) We missed the train so we decided to ..... a bus.

   A) go   B) get   C) have

c) Jim's ..... to Argentina left at 6.00.

   A) fly   B) flight   C) flying

d) As the bus left, Helen's friends said, 'Have a good ..... .'

   A) journey   B) travel   C) voyage

e) Carol ..... to Birmingham on the motorway.

   A) ran   B) drove   C) led

f) Excuse me. What time does this train ..... London?

   A) arrive   B) reach   C) come

g) Could you tell me the ..... to the bus-station?

   A) street   B) path   C) way

h) I got on the bus and bought my ..... .

   A) ticket   B) paper   C) cheque

i) If you don't have a ticket, you might be ..... .

   A) penaltied   B) fined   C) refused

j) Sarah never travels by plane because she is scared of ..... .

   A) flying   B) flights   C) flight

3 **Use the words from the box to complete each label (a–h)**

| bike | boat | ~~bus~~ | car | plane | ship | taxi | train |

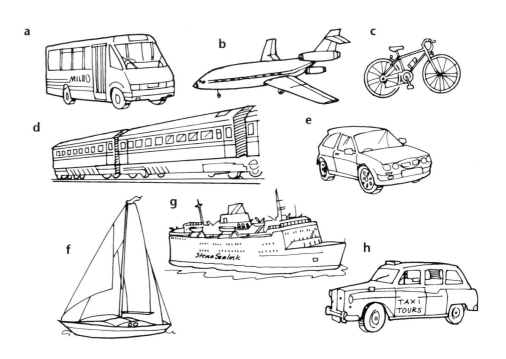

a) ...*bus*...   e) ....

b) ....   f) ....

c) ....   g) ....

d) ....   h) ....

4 **Complete each sentence. Use the words from exercise 3.**

a) When the ...*plane*... took off, Tom felt nervous.

b) Ann's .... broke down while she was driving on the motorway.

c) Peter enjoyed his voyage across the Atlantic in an old sailing ....

d) Tina got off her .... and pushed it up the hill.

e) Carlos saw the sights of London from the top of a double-decker ....

f) Helen and Sue hired a .... and rowed across the lake.

g) When the .... came into the station, Kate was waiting.

h) Joe saw a .... coming down the street. He shouted, and it stopped.

1 Use a word from the box to complete each label (a–h).

> tin opener   ~~calculator~~   dishwasher   camera   mobile phone
> video recorder   personal stereo   kettle

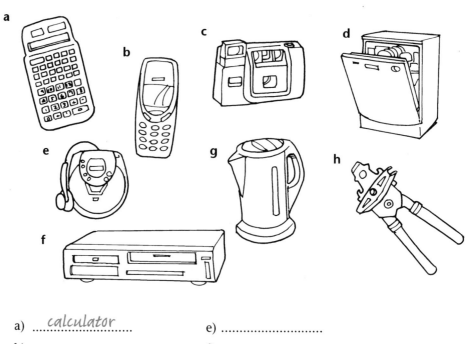

a) ...calculator...   e) ....

b) ....   f) ....

c) ....   g) ....

d) ....   h) ....

2 Choose the most suitable word from the box in Exercise 1.

a) You can use this to make copies of television programmes. *video recorder*

b) You can use this to open cans. ....

c) You can take interesting photos with this. ....

d) You can make calls from this, wherever you are. ....

e) You can do the washing-up with this. ....

f) This helps you if you have problems with maths. ....

g) You can take music with you everywhere with this. ....

h) This boils water for you. ....

3 <u>Underline</u> the correct word in each sentence.

a) My *pen/<u>pencil</u>* is broken. Have you got a sharpener?

b) Ann couldn't cut Mary's hair because she didn't have any *knife/scissors*.

c) We can't get in. The door is *locked/closed*, and I haven't got a key.

d) When the lights *went out/closed*, Jan couldn't see a thing.

e) Put the dirty clothes in the *washing/wash* machine.

f) Dave has got a bad cold and needs some *tissues/papers*.

g) If you want to draw a straight line, use a *file/ruler*.

h) There's a *clock/watch* on the wall over there.

4 **Choose the most suitable word or phrase for each space.**

a) Terry put a large ..*C*.. full of apples on the table.

    A) envelope   B) saucer   C) bowl

b) Jim put some oil into the ..... and cooked the eggs in it.

    A) frying pan   B) cooker   C) bowl

c) Can you turn on the ..... ? I can't see very well.

    A) candle   B) lamp   C) bulb

d) Kate filled the ..... with water, and boiled some potatoes.

    A) oven   B) kettle   C) saucepan

e) Do you want your coffee in a cup or a ..... ?

    A) mug   B) plastic   C) jar

f) Paul had a cup of coffee in one hand and a ..... of cakes in the other.

    A) pan   B) saucer   C) plate

1 <u>Underline</u> the correct word in each sentence.

a) You usually need a *passport*/*permission* to go from one country to another.

b) Have you ever been to a *stranger*/*foreign* country?

c) Europe and Asia are both *countries*/*continents*.

d) Have you got a *map*/*plan* of Germany?

e) We all enjoy *singing*/*eating* our National Anthem.

f) Most people would like to travel *outside*/*abroad*.

g) What is your national *meal*/*dish*? Ours is spaghetti!

h) I've always wanted to take a *trip*/*travel* to South America.

i) The plane *takes off*/*takes on* at midday.

j) The Alps and the Himalayas are both mountain *areas*/*ranges*.

2 Complete each sentence with *in*, *to* or *at*.

a) Have you ever been ......*to*...... Turkey?

b) What time does our plane arrive .... Paris?

c) I met an old friend .... Frankfurt Airport.

d) Is Milan .... the south of Italy?

e) It's very cold .... Poland at the moment.

f) Cathy has decided to go .... Spain for a holiday.

g) Anna lives .... Slovenia.

h) Tim is studying .... London University.

3 Complete the list.

a) I'm *Italian* .   I come from Italy.

b) I'm ....   I come from Spain.

c) I'm ....   I come from Germany.

d) I'm ....   I come from France.

e) I'm ....   I come from Greece.

f) I'm ....   I come from Brazil.

g) I'm ....   I come from Switzerland.

h) I'm ....   I come from Turkey.

i) I'm ....   I come from Poland.

j) I'm ....   I come from Argentina.

4 **Match the countries (1–8) with the people (a–h).**

1 Norway   a) The Dutch   4
2 Hungary   b) The Norwegians   .....
3 Mexico   c) The Swedes   .....
4 Holland   d) The Scots   .....
5 Ireland   e) The Mexicans   .....
6 Sweden   f) The Hungarians   .....
7 Egypt   g) The Irish   .....
8 Scotland   h) The Egyptians   .....

5 **Test yourself! Choose the most suitable word for each space.**

a) A is in Spain.
   A) Madrid   B) Manchester   C) Montreal

b) ..... is in Egypt.
   A) Caracas   B) Cairo   C) Cardiff

c) ..... is the Polish capital.
   A) Washington   B) Wellington   C) Warsaw

d) ..... is an Argentinian city.
   A) Berlin   B) Budapest   C) Buenos Aires

e) ..... is in Portugal.
   A) Liverpool   B) Los Angeles   C) Lisbon

f) ..... is the Greek capital.
   A) Atlanta   B) Athens   C) Alice Springs

g) ..... is in Switzerland.
   A) Berne   B) Brazilia   C) Beijing

h) ..... is in the United States of America.
   A) Santiago   B) Stockholm   C) San Francisco

6 **Put these countries into the correct column according to their stress pattern.**

Brazil	Malaysia	Holland	Japan	Singapore	Austria
Iraq	New Zealand	Bangladesh	England	Pakistan	
Poland	Germany	Mexico	Morocco		

☐☐   ☐☐   ☐☐☐   ☐☐☐   ☐☐☐

Holland
....

243

1 <u>Underline</u> **the correct word in each sentence.**

a) I have to *read/study* hard because I have a test tomorrow.

b) If you don't understand a word, *look it out/look it up* in a dictionary.

c) Please do the rest of this exercise for *homework/housework*.

d) Mrs Jackson *learns/teaches* us geography.

e) At the end of the lesson, put the books back on the *bookshelf/library*.

f) Paul tried *hard/hardly* this year, and made progress.

g) Why were you *absent/off* yesterday, Angela?

h) Jim *lost/failed* the maths test.

2 **Choose the most suitable word or phrase for each space.**

a) Could you tell me what .....*C*.. .

   A) does this word mean   B) means this word   C) this word means

b) What's the difference ..... 'say' and 'tell'?

   A) between   B) of   C) from

c) If you don't know the answer, ... a guess.

   A) do   B) make   C) say

d) Please pay ..... to what I am saying.

   A) meaning   B) knowledge   C) attention

e) If you're not sure, ... a question.

   A) make   B) ask   C) do

f) I don't understand. Can you give me a/an ..... ?

   A) example   B) sample   C) model

g) Please ..... yourself, John.

   A) behaving   B) behaviour   C) behave

h) I'm sorry, but I don't ..... the question.

   A) know   B) understand   C) realise

i) Please stop talking and ..... to your teacher.

   A) hear   B) attend   C) listen

j) Could you ..... that, please?

   A) resay   B) repeat   C) retell

3 Complete each sentence. Use a word from the box.

copy	explain	fail	have	make	mean
practise	~~share~~	take	underline		

a) We have to ....*share*.... books because there aren't enough for one each.

b) Don't worry if you .... the exam. You can take it again in December.

c) I must remember to .... this book back to the library today.

d) During the exam, Jack tried to .... Sarah's work.

e) Some teachers don't .... things very clearly.

f) What exactly does this word .... ?

g) We didn't .... a history lesson today, because our teacher was ill.

h) It's a good idea to .... important words with a pencil.

i) If you don't .... a foreign language, you soon forget it.

j) I can't .... up my mind about the answer to this question.

4 Complete each sentence. Use a word from the box.

attendance	break	class	~~lesson~~	notes	project
subject	term	timetable	uniform		

a) We had an interesting ....*lesson*.... today about Ancient Egypt.

b) At the end of the .... our teachers write reports about us.

c) Please make .... as you read chapter two.

d) This is a very small .... There are only eight students.

e) Kate's .... been good. She has only missed one lesson.

f) Our .... has changed, and now we have English on Monday at 11 o'clock.

g) The boys usually play football outside when they have a ....

h) Chris has to wear a .... at his new school.

i) Physics was Rebecca's favourite .... when she was at school.

j) I went to the library to find some information for my history ....

1 Underline the correct word in each sentence.

a) Why don't we *write/record* our song on tape?

b) Do you want to come *for swimming/swimming* tomorrow?

c) All the girls in the group are very good *singers/songs*.

d) Would you *like/want* to play basketball?

e) George and I are to going *to the cinema/the cinema* this afternoon.

f) Ann loves listening to *classical/classic* music.

g) The children saw a Mickey Mouse *cartoon/comic* at the cinema.

h) In the World Cup, Italy *beat/won* Germany 2–0.

i) Do you want to go *a walk/for a walk* this evening?

j) Jack *excused/made an excuse*, and said he couldn't come to the party.

2 Choose the most suitable word or phrase for each space.

Last week I phoned one of my friends. 'Why don't you (1) .B.. to my house?'

he said. 'We can play some computer games, if you (2) ..... .' 'I don't feel (3) .....

doing that,' I said. 'How about (4) ..... fishing?' He wasn't very (5) ..... on the idea,

so we decided to (6) ..... to the cinema, although we didn't know what was (7) ..... .

When we (8) ..... there, it was a science fiction film, and so we (9) ..... our minds.

We can't (10) ..... that kind of film.

1)	A turn up	B come round	C cross over	D go past
2)	A know	B can	C do	D like
3)	A for	B I'm	C like	D well
4)	A the	B going	C a	D it
5)	A interested	B much	C keen	D liking
6)	A go	B pass	C see	D try
7)	A on	B it	C there	D playing
8)	A reached	B were	C saw	D got
9)	A discussed	B changed	C made	D found
10)	A like	B hate	C stand	D admire

3 **Make compound words by joining a word from the box to a word (a–f). More than one answer may be possible.**

| ~~club~~ | court | field | pool | stadium | track |

a) health   *club*

b) football   ....

c) tennis   ....

d) running   ....

e) swimming ....

f) playing   ....

4 **Choose the best place from Exercise 3 for each activity.**

a) an exercise programme   *health club*

b) diving competition   ....

c) a marathon   ....

d) school sports   ....

e) a cup final   ....

f) a doubles match   ....

1 <u>Underline</u> **the correct word in each sentence.**

a) I think these trousers are the wrong *size*/*number* for me.

b) Helen wants to *buy*/*take* some new shoes.

c) Thank you very much. This is your *recipe*/*receipt*.

d) I'd like to buy this coat, but it costs a lot of *money*/*cash*.

e) I saw some red shoes in the window. Can I *try*/*have* them on?

f) I'm sorry, but the shop *closes*/*ends* in five minutes.

g) Could I have a small white *bread*/*loaf*, please?

h) Please *name*/*sign* on this line.

i) Could you put these things in a *bag*/*sack*, please?

j) Excuse me, could you tell me how much this *costs*/*prices*?

2 **Choose the best reply (1–10) for each sentence (a–j).**

a) Can I help you?

b) Have you got size 7?

c) How much is this?

d) Can I try this on?

e) Do you take credit cards?

f) This one doesn't fit.

g) Have you got any money?

h) Do you like this red one?

i) Can I return this?

j) What time do you close?

1 Yes, the changing room is over there.

2 At 5.30 today.

3 Try this larger one.

4 It doesn't go with your coat.

5 I'm afraid we don't have any left.

6 No, I've spent every penny I had!

7 Did you buy it here?

8 No thanks, I'm just looking.

9 Sorry, only cash or cheques.

10 It's £8.95.

3 **Answer the questions with a suitable word or phrase from the box.**

At the baker's	At the grocer's	At the travel agent's	At the newsagent's
At the café	At the post office	At the chemist's	At the butcher's

a) Where do you buy a newspaper? *At the newsagent's*

b) Where do you post a parcel? ....

c) Where do you buy medicine? ....

d) Where do you buy meat? ....

e) Where do you buy bananas? ....

f) Where do you book a holiday? ....

g) Where do you buy a cake? ....

h) Where do you have a coffee? ....

Elem. Lang Practice
M. Vince Macmillan

4 **Choose the most suitable word or phrase for each space.**

a) Why don't we get a ..A.. of mineral water?

   A) bottle   B) jar   C) bag

b) Why don't we buy Julia a ..... of flowers?

   A) bunch   B) pile   C) crowd

c) I need a ..... of toothpaste.

   A) box   B) packet   C) tube

d) Don't forget to buy Wendy a ..... of chocolate.

   A) lump   B) bar   C) cube

e) I'd like ..... cheese, please.

   A) a kilo of   B) half kilo   C) half kilo of

f) Could you buy me two ..... of biscuits?

   A) packets   B) parcels   C) containers

g) I've decided to buy a new ..... of shoes.

   A) couple   B) pair   C) double

h) We need a ..... of matches.

   A) bag   B) box   C) bunch

5 **Choose the most suitable word for each space.**

Nowadays lots of people drive to large supermarkets to (1) ..D.. their shopping.
These supermarkets have (2) ..... , so you can buy several (3) ..... of shopping. You
can fill your (4) ..... , and then push it to your car. Some people prefer to use
(5) ..... shops. These small shops are usually more (6) ..... than supermarkets.
Some towns have an open air (7) ..... in the centre, where you can buy (8) ..... fruit
and (9) ..... , but you have to (10) ..... your shopping home.

1)	A make	B take	C have	D do
2)	A cars	B car-parks	C places	D roads
3)	A bags	B shops	C customers	D bargains
4)	A pocket	B bag	C trolley	D wallet
5)	A sale	B local	C centre	D various
6)	A cheaper	B often	C parking	D expensive
7)	A place	B sale	C square	D market
8)	A cheap	B the	C there	D a
9)	A fishes	B meats	C vegetables	D green
10)	A walk	B carry	C manage	D with

Formation rules

1 Tenses

Present simple

positive:	I/you/we/they like	he/she/it likes
negative:	you don't like	he doesn't like
question:	Do you like...?	Does he like...?

Present continuous

positive:	I am going. He/she/it is going.	You/we/they are going.
negative:	I am not going. She isn't going.	You aren't going.
question:	Am I going? Is she going?	Are you going?

Present perfect

positive:	I/you/we/they have left.	He/she/it has left.
negative:	They haven't left.	He hasn't left.
question:	Have they left?	Has he left?

Past simple

1 Regular	positive:	I/you/he/she/it/we/they started.
	negative:	You didn't start.
	question:	Did you start?
2 Irregular	positive:	I/you/he/she/it/we/they went.
	negative:	You didn't go.
	question:	Did you go?

Past continuous

positive:	I/he/she/it was going.	You/we/they were going.
negative:	You weren't going.	She wasn't going.
question:	Were you going?	Was she going?

2 Reported Speech

Direct	Reported
'I always drink milk.'	He said (that) he always drank milk.
'I'm leaving.'	She said (that) she was leaving.
'I'll be back soon.'	He said (that) he would be back soon.
'I've forgotten it.'	She said (that) she had forgotten it.
'I took it.'	He said (that) he had taken it.
'I was reading.'	She said (that) she had been reading.

3 Passive Tenses

Active	Passive
He helps.	He is helped.
He has helped.	He has been helped.
He helped.	He was helped.
He will help.	He will be helped.

251

Irregular verbs

Infinitive	Past simple	Past participle
be	was/were	been
beat	beat	beaten
become	became	become
begin	began	begun
bite	bit	bitten
blow	blew	blown
break	broke	broken
bring	brought	brought
build	built	built
burn	burnt/burned	burnt/burned
buy	bought	bought
catch	caught	caught
choose	chose	chosen
come	came	come
cost	cost	cost
cut	cut	cut
dig	dug	dug
do	did	done
draw	drew	drawn
dream	dreamt/dreamed	dreamt/dreamed
drink	drank	drunk
drive	drove	driven
eat	ate	eaten
fall	fell	fallen
feel	felt	felt
fight	fought	fought
find	found	found
fly	flew	flown
forgive	forgave	forgiven
get	got	got
give	gave	given
go	went	gone
grow	grew	grown
have	had	had
hear	heard	heard
hide	hid	hidden
hit	hit	hit
hold	held	held
hurt	hurt	hurt
keep	kept	kept
know	knew	known

Infinitive	Past simple	Past participle
lay	laid	laid
lead	led	led
learn	learnt/learned	learnt/learned
leave	left	left
lend	lent	lent
let	let	let
lie	lay	lain
light	lit	lit
lose	lost	lost
make	made	made
mean	meant	meant
meet	met	met
pay	paid	paid
put	put	put
read	read	read
ride	rode	ridden
ring	rang	rung
rise	rose	risen
run	ran	run
say	said	said
see	saw	seen
sell	sold	sold
send	sent	sent
shoot	shot	shot
shut	shut	shut
sing	sang	sung
sit	sat	sat
sleep	slept	slept
speak	spoke	spoken
spell	spelled/spelt	spelled/spelt
spend	spent	spent
stand	stood	stood
steal	stole	stolen
swim	swam	swum
take	took	taken
teach	taught	taught
tell	told	told
think	thought	thought
throw	threw	thrown
understand	understood	understood
wake	woke	woken
wear	wore	worn
win	won	won
write	wrote	written

Grammar index

A/an/any 44, 45
Ability 36, 39
Able to 36
Adjectives 73, 74, 75, 76, 83
Adverbs 8, 78
Advice 30, 50, 67
Advising 30, 50, 67
After 27
Ago 20
Agreeing/disagreeing 50
Already 20
Anyone, anybody, anything 62
Apologizing 50
Apostrophes 72, 85
Articles
    a/an, the 59
    zero 60
Asking for information 52

Be
    am, is, are 1
    was, were 12
    with adjectives and prepositions 83
Be able to 36
Been and *gone* 20

Can 36, 53
Can't, cannot 36, 40
Certainty 40
Come [*swimming*, etc.] 81
Comparative adjectives 75
Compound words 89
Conditional 1 sentences 29, 31
Conditional 2 sentences 30, 31
Contractions, *it's, they're, I'm, I've, he's,*
    etc. 69
Could 39, 40, 53
Countable and uncountable nouns 44,
    45, 46, 47

Dates 54
Days, months, seasons 54
Decisions 24
Descriptions 51
Direct speech 64
Directions 51
Disagreeing/agreeing 50
Do and *make* 81

Enough
    not + adjective + *enough* 73
    [*not*] *enough* + noun 47
Ever 20
Everyone, everybody, everything 62
Excuses 51
Expect 23

For 20, 82, 83
Frequency adverbs 2
Functions 50, 51, 52, 53
Future
    going to 22, 25
    plans/intentions 22, 25
    predictions 22, 23
    present continuous 26
    will 23, 25

Gerund [*-ing*] 5, 6, 26, 68, 86
Get 80
Go [*swimming*, etc.] *81*
Going to 22, 25, 26, 27
Greetings 51

Habits 2, 16
Had to 39
Have got 71, 80
Have to 37, 38, 41
How much/many 46

If I were you 30, 50
If sentences 29, 30, 31
Imperatives 29, 67
Impossibility 40
Inviting 52
Irregular verbs 10, 11, 17, 18
It and *there* 79
Its and *It's* 85

Just 20, 75

Later 27

Make and *do* 81
Making arrangements 24, 26
Making comparisons 75, 76
Making offers 52
May 40, 52
Might 40
Modals
    ability/possibility 36, 39, 40
    obligation 37, 38, 39
    past 39
    possibility/certainty 36, 40
    problems and contrasts 41
Much and *many* 46, 47
Must 37, 38, 40, 41

Nationality words 59, 73
Never 20
No one, nobody, nothing, none 62
Numbers 48

Object
    gerund as object 68
    pronouns 61
    questions 33
Obligation 37, 38, 39
Offering 52
One, ones 61

Passive voice 65, 66
Past continuous 13
    and past simple 15

Past perfect 64
Past simple 8, 9, 10, 11
    and past continuous 15
    was, were 12
Perhaps 23
Permission 52
Personal pronouns [*I, me*, etc.] 61
Phrasal verbs 81, 89
Place and position 57, 58
Plurals 43, 44, 45
Possessive
    adjectives [*my*, etc.] 71
    apostrophe 72
    of 72
    pronouns [*mine*, etc.] 71
Possibility 36, 40
Predictions 22, 23, 25, 27
Preferences 53
Prefixes 89
Prepositions/adverbials
    after adjectives 89
    after verbs 89
    of place and position
    in, on, at, to, into 57
    in front of 58
    next to, near 58
    opposite, behind 58
    out, out of 58
    outside, inside 58
    of time
    in, on 54, 55
    at 27, 55
Present continuous 4, 5
    and present simple 6
    future use 26, 27
Present perfect simple 17, 18
    and past simple 19
    and time expressions 20
Present simple 2, 3
    and present continuous 6
Probably 23

Promising 24, 25, 53

Pronouns
  object pronouns 61
  possessive pronouns 71
  someone/body/thing, etc. 62
  subject pronouns 61
Punctuation 85

Questions
  subject and object 33
  tags 34
  wh- questions 33

Refusing 24, 25, 52
Reminders 53
Reported speech 64
Requesting 53, 67

Short answers 32, 33
Should 37, 38
Since 20
Some 44, 45
Someone, somebody, something 62
Soon 27
Spelling 86, 87, 88
  and pronunciation 87
  British/American 88
  gerunds 4
Subject
  gerund as subject 68
  it and *there* 79
  pronouns 61
  questions 33
Suffixes 89
Suggesting 53
Superlative adjectives 59, 76

Tag questions 34
Telling the time 55
There and *it* 79

This, that 61
Time expressions
  ago 20
  for 20
  since 20
  with past simple and present
  perfect simple 20
  with future 27
Too + adjective 73
Too much, too many 47

Uncertainty 36, 40
Used to 16

Verbs
  followed by gerund [*-ing*] 82
  followed by infinitive 82
  followed by prepositions 82

Warning 29, 53
Was, were 12
Whose 71
Will
  and *going to* 25
  contrasts 27
  in functional language 24
  predictions 23
Word formation 89
Would
  in conditionals 31, 36
  in functional language 52, 53

Yet 20

Grammar answers

Grammar 1

1
a) *is*
b) are
c) is
d) are
e) is
f) are
g) is
h) am

2
a) *It isn't hot today.*
b) I'm not at home.
c) My friends aren't here.
d) You aren't a teacher.
e) We aren't at the cinema.
f) This isn't difficult.
g) Katy isn't happy.

3
a) *Am I late?*
b) Are you ill?
c) Are we right?
d) Is he fifteen?
e) Is it cold?
f) Is the school in this street?
g) Are my books in your bag ?

4
a) *3*
b) 1
c) 5
d) 2
e) 4

Grammar 2

1
a) *likes*
b) rains
c) lives
d) arrives
e) starts
f) teach

2
a) *live*
b) watches
c) go
d) snows
e) lives
f) clean
g) gets
h) leave

3
a) *sometimes misses*
b) never get up
c) usually have
d) often go
e) often sing
f) sometimes plays
g) never finish
h) always wears

Grammar 3

1
a) *teachers do not smoke*
b) does Helen live
c) We do not go
d) Does David ride
e) Do you play
f) does not like
g) usually have lunch

2
a) *does not like*
b) Does Peter wash
c) Do you watch
d) do not/don't often eat
e) Have we got
f) do not/don't live

3
a) *Does Jack get up at 7.00?*
b) Do Alice and Mike walk to work?
c) Does Jack leave home at 8.00?
d) Do Alice and Mike relax in the evening?
e) *Alice and Mike don't like tennis.*
f) Jack doesn't wear school uniform.
g) Alice and Mike don't use computers.
h) Jack doesn't do his homework.

Grammar 4

1
a) *I'm eating.*
b) They're listening.
c) She's coming.
d) You're moving.
e) It's raining.
f) We're singing

2
1) *are having/'re having*
2) is raining/'s raining
3) am sitting/'m sitting
4) am watching/'m watching
5) are playing/'re playing
6) is reading/'s reading
7) is making/'s making
8) is crying/'s crying

Grammar 5

1
a) *Am I making a lot of noise?*
b) Is Clare reading?
c) Are you watching the news?
d) Is it snowing?
e) Are we waiting in the right place?
f) Are you sitting here?
g) Is David enjoying the film?
h) Is the bus stopping?

2
a) *You aren't listening to me.*
b) Tim isn't studying.
c) We aren't talking.
d) You aren't writing.
e) Katherine isn't lying.
f) They aren't waiting for us.
g) Anna isn't having a good time.
h) I'm not reading at the moment.

3
a) *I'm playing tennis with my best friend.*
b) Are you coming to the cinema tonight?
c) John and Mandy aren't going to the beach.
d) Are Emma and Katy flying to America?
e) My sister is walking on the beach now.
f) We're not studying French at school this year.
g) What's that noise? Is the dog outside?
h) I'm not watching the TV. Turn it off.
i) Fred is eating a sandwich for his lunch.
j) Are they waiting for a bus?

Grammar 6

1
a) *2*
b) 1
c) 2
d) 1
e) 1
f) 2

2
a) *always gets up*
b) is waiting
c) are we going
d) don't believe
e) am/'m reading
f) Does Susan like

3
a) *B*
b) A
c) C
d) B
e) C
f) C

Grammar 7

1
a) *don't like*
b) want
c) sometimes walks
d) does the lesson begin
e) get
f) doesn't like
g) watches

2
a) *do*
b) don't/can't
c) are
d) doesn't
e) do
f) does

3
a) *C*
b) A
c) B
d) B
e) C
f) C
g) B

4
a) *Jo usually goes to school by bus.*
b) I'm not working hard.
c) Sara does not/doesn't like sport.
d) I always get up at 6.30.
e) We do not/don't or cannot/can't speak German.
f) Pierre often goes to the beach.
g) George never drinks beer.
h) We aren't/'re not having a good time.

5
a) *Do you have a motorbike?*
b) Correct
c) I'd like to buy this coat. How much does it cost?
d) What are you doing?
e) I usually get up at 6.00.
f) This book is difficult. I don't understand it.
g) Correct
h) Excuse me. Do you know the way to the museum?

Think about grammar!
a) True. This is the most common use of the present simple.
b) False. It is for actions which are not finished at the time of speaking.
c) True. Also with names, as well as pronouns.

Grammar 8

1
a) *called*
b) washed, dressed
c) walked
d) watched
e) played
f) finished
g) telephoned

2
1) *arrived*
2) started
3) worked
4) talked
5) played
6) continued
7) listened
8) finished

3
  a)   *Tom looked out of the window.*
  b)   We arrived at 6.30.
  c)   Laura watched television all afternoon.
  d)   The bus stopped at the end of the street.
  e)   I visited an old castle this week.
  f)   Sue waited for her friends for more than an hour.
  g)   They decided to come to my party.

Grammar 9

1
  a)   *Our bus didn't arrive on time.*
  b)   Sue didn't phone last night.
  c)   Maria didn't finish work early yesterday.
  d)   The train didn't stop at Harry's station.
  e)   I didn't want to go to bed early.
  f)   Carlos didn't answer my letter.
  g)   John didn't invite lots of people to his party.
  h)   The shops didn't open on Sunday.
  i)   Peter didn't like his new shoes.

2
  a)   *Did Tim arrive at 2.00?*
  b)   Did Sam phone home?
  c)   Did Helen want to make a phone call?
  d)   Did Paul visit the doctor?
  e)   Did Bill miss the bus?
  f)   Did George walk to school?
  g)   Did Jim open the window?
  h)   Did Emma help the teacher?
  i)   Did Alice wash her hair?

Grammar 10

1
  a)   *began*
  b)   felt
  c)   flew
  d)   did
  e)   got
  f)   knew
  g)   stood
  h)   wore
  i)   ate
  j)   told

2
  1)   C
  2)   A
  3)   A
  4)   C
  5)   A
  6)   A
  7)   A
  8)   B
  9)   B
  10)   C
  11)   B
  12)   C
  13)   C
  14)   C
  15)   B

Grammar 11

1
  a)   *Did Nick fly to the USA?*
  b)   Did Ana go to Italy?
  c)   Did Jack find the money?
  d)   Did Helen know the answer?
  e)   Did Alex give Sue a present?
  f)   Did Pat buy the flowers?
  g)   Did Kate send Mike a letter?
  h)   Did Alan make the cake?
  i)   Did Tina wear a hat?
  j)   Did Rick feel ill?

2
  a)   *Tom and Anna didn't have breakfast.*
  b)   Mike didn't take the bus.
  c)   Maria and Carlos didn't do the homework.
  d)   Catherine didn't get a prize.
  e)   Peter didn't know the teacher.
  f)   Sam didn't go to university.
  g)   Paula didn't eat a sandwich.
  h)   Murad and Soraya didn't run fast.
  i)   Joe didn't make mistakes.
  j)   Carla didn't come early.

3
  a)   *did you come*
  b)   didn't wear
  c)   left
  d)   did you write
  e)   did the teacher say
  f)   You didn't tell
  g)   Did you go
  h)   didn't know
  i)   did you take
  j)   Jane didn't get

Grammar 12

1
  a)   *Was Helen, wasn't at home, was at the cinema*
  b)   Were Yannis and Emma, weren't at school, were at home
  c)   Was Nick, wasn't at home, was at work
  d)   Were Liz and Jane, weren't at the cinema, were at school

2
a) *Was Jim at home last night?*
b) Were you at school on Monday?
c) Was the cinema open on Sunday?
d) Were all your friends at your party?
e) *Kevin and Mel weren't at my party.*
f) Nick wasn't in class yesterday.
g) It wasn't warm yesterday.
h) We weren't at the match yesterday.

Grammar 13

1
a) *was reading a book.*
b) were playing football.
c) was writing on the board.
d) were listening to music.
e) was looking out of the window.
f) were drawing pictures.

2
a) *Anna wasn't drawing pictures.*
b) Paula and Jim weren't looking out of the window.
c) Tim wasn't reading a book.
d) Kate and Bill weren't writing on the board.
e) Sam wasn't playing football.
f) Ed and Lisa weren't listening to music.

3
a) *Was Tim drawing pictures?*
b) Were Kate and Bill looking out of the window?
c) Were Ed and Lisa reading a book?
d) Were Paula and Jim writing on the board?
e) Was Anna playing football?
f) Was Sam listening to music?

Grammar 14

1
a) *looked*
b) took
c) read
d) closed
e) came
f) saw

2
a) *4*
b) 3
c) 6
d) 2
e) 7
f) 1
g) 5

3
a) *David didn't miss the train.*
b) Cristina didn't forget her book.
c) They didn't go out.
d) John didn't close the door.
e) Terry didn't get up.
f) Karen didn't like Chinese food.
g) Chris's team didn't win the match.
h) I didn't sit down on the bus all the way home.

4
a) *Where did you go last night?*
b) I didn't know the answer.
c) Harry made a lot of noise.
d) I didn't like my new teacher.
e) Did you take your medicine?
f) Helen came home late last night.
g) I didn't get up early this morning.
h) What did you see at the cinema?

5
a) *you working last night?*
b) Tim waiting at the bus-stop?
c) Mary talking?
d) Kate wearing jeans?
e) Ali and Mehmet playing football?
f) it raining?

6
a) *Were you playing*
b) Mary was having
c) We were watching
d) were you dancing
e) Some of the boys were looking
f) I was walking

Think about grammar!
a) True.
b) False. When actions continue for some time, use the past continuous.
c) False. *Did* is also used in questions and as a main verb.

Grammar 15

1
a) *was doing*
b) broke
c) went
d) found
e) saw
f) was having

2
a) *ate*
b) came, were playing
c) turned on, happened
d) were running, fell over
e) was listening, heard
f) broke, was doing

3
1) *A*
2) A
3) C
4) C
5) C
6) B
7) C
8) B
9) B
10) A

Grammar 16

1 a) *David used to like ice-cream, but now he hates it.*
   b) Anna used to live in the country, but now she lives in the city.
   c) Nick used to walk to school, but now he rides a bike.
   d) Kate used to get up late, but now she gets up early.
   e) Carol used to have short hair, but now she has (got) long hair.
   f) Jack used to be short, but now he is tall.

2 a) *used to ride*
   b) didn't use to drive
   c) used to go to
   d) didn't use to go to
   e) used to wash
   f) didn't use to watch
   g) used to look after
   h) didn't use to use

3 a) *Did Susan use to have a dog?*
   b) People didn't use to have mobile phones.
   c) He used to go swimming.
   d) Did they use to like jazz music?
   e) Ewa's family used to live in Moscow.
   f) We didn't use to drink coffee.
   g) My sister didn't use to watch television.
   h) Did Tony use to work in a bank?

4 (Suggested answers)
   a) *I used to be in the school tennis team.*
   b) Sophie used to have long hair (when she was at school).
   c) Mary didn't use to listen when her teachers were speaking.
   d) Ricardo used to get up at 6.00 (when he was training for the Olympics).
   e) What did you use to do on Saturday evenings?
   f) Becky used to be afraid of dogs (when she was a girl).
   g) We used to give our teachers presents at the end of term.
   h) Did you use to live next door to Mrs Harrison?
   i) My brother used to wear glasses (when he was small).
   j) Did Marcin use to learn German at school?

5 Students' own answers.

6 Students' own answers.

Grammar 17

1 (Suggested answers)
   a) *has eaten*
   b) has lost
   c) have broken
   d) has taken
   e) has finished
   f) has left
   g) has happened
   h) have found
   i) has written
   j) have bought

2 a) *has done*
   b) have found
   c) has sent
   d) have tried
   e) have eaten
   f) has bought
   g) have started
   h) has broken
   i) have lost
   j) has taken

3 a) *have missed*
   b) Have you read
   c) have spent
   d) have had
   e) have copied
   f) Have you washed
   g) has arrived
   h) haven't phoned
   i) Have you seen
   j) have made

Grammar 18

1 a) *Has he booked the hotel?*
   b) Has he invited Tim?
   c) Has he looked at the map?
   d) Has he packed his suitcase?
   e) Has he checked the timetable?
   f) Has he borrowed a guide book?
   g) Has he bought a ticket?
   h) Has he chosen his clothes?

2 a) *He's booked the hotel.*
   b) He hasn't invited Tim.
   c) He has looked at the map.
   d) He hasn't packed his suitcase.
   e) He has checked the timetable.
   f) He has borrowed a guide book.
   g) He hasn't bought a ticket.
   h) He hasn't chosen his clothes.

3 1) *have enjoyed*
   2) haven't done
   3) have spent
   4) hasn't rained
   5) has learnt
   6) haven't tried
   7) Have you received

Grammar 19

1 a) *3*
   b) 5
   c) 4
   d) 1
   e) 2
   f) 6

2 a) *'ve read*
   b) haven't finished
   c) 've lost
   d) Did you eat
   e) left
   f) haven't started
   g) Did you see

3 a) *did you go*
   b) have just hurt
   c) has written
   d) haven't finished
   e) did you invite
   f) did you meet
   g) hasn't played

Grammar 20

1 a) *4*
   b) 7
   c) 1
   d) 3
   e) 6
   f) 2
   g) 5

2 a) *ever*
   b) just
   c) already
   d) for
   e) ten years ago
   f) yet
   g) since

3 (Suggested answers)
   a) *for*
   b) already
   c) ever
   d) yet
   e) just
   f) never
   g) since

Grammar 21

1 a) was arriving   *arrived*
   b) was coming   came
   c) swam   were
                     swimming
   d) were going   went
   e) watched   was watching
   f) was losing   lost
   g) was seeing   saw
   h) was hearing   heard

2 (Suggested answers)
   a) *taken*
   b) read
   c) been
   d) eaten
   e) caught
   f) left
   g) bought
   h) broken

3 a) *has just gone*
   b) did you get up
   c) had
   d) have lived
   e) did you do
   f) hasn't finished
   g) arrived
   h) Have you seen

4 (Suggested answers)
   a) *for*
   b) yet
   c) never
   d) for
   e) just
   f) since
   g) ever

5 a) *haven't been to the cinema*
   b) used to ride her bike
   c) has gone
   d) used to play in the garden
       every day.
   e) How long did you stay
   f) has been living here for
   g) Have you visited Scotland

6 (Suggested answers)
   a) have you arrived
       did you arrive
   b) you were doing
       were you doing
   c) didn't do   haven't done
   d) was wearing   wore/used to
                      wear
   e) was missing   missed
   f) Did you meet Have you met
   g) use to   used to

Think about grammar!
a) True
b) False. Some end with *-en*, other
    don't – they are irregular!
c) False. It is for past habits.

Grammar 22

1 a) *are going to fall*
   b) is going to rain
   c) are going to hit
   d) is going to crash
   e) are going to miss

2 a) *Are you going to buy*
   b) isn't going to be
   c) am going to buy
   d) Is Helen going to catch
   e) is going to carry
   f) aren't going to get
   g) is going to take
   h) are you going to phone
   i) are we going to eat
   j) am not going to give

3 a) *Joe is going to buy a new computer next year.*
 b) We aren't going to play tennis this weekend.
 c) Is Nick going to join the sports club?
 d) What are you going to do next summer?
 e) Look! That tree is going to fall over!
 f) Are you going to work hard this year?
 g) I'm not going to get a new car.
 h) It is going to rain tomorrow.
 i) Are Mike and Pat going to make sandwiches for the party?
 j) It's going to snow.

4 a) *he's going to arrive at 4.00pm.*
 b) He's going to walk around the village
 c) he's going to visit the castle.
 d) He's going to sit on the beach
 e) he's going to see the museum.
 f) He's going to climb the mountain
 g) he's going to buy presents at the market.

5 Students' own answers.

Grammar 23

1 a) *will choose*
 b) won't have
 c) will be
 d) won't know
 e) will like
 f) Will you give
 g) won't be
 h) Will we see
 i) will read
 j) will win

2 a) *I'm sure it will be cold tomorrow.*
 b) I expect we'll win.
 c) I think I'll leave now.
 d) I'm sure Jim won't be late.
 e) I expect it won't take long./I don't expect it will take long.
 f) I'm sure you won't have any problems.
 g) I think you'll enjoy the party.
 h) I don't imagine they'll decide anything yet./I imagine they won't decide anything yet.
 i) I don't expect the train will be late.
 j) I imagine Jane will have cooked dinner.

Grammar 24

1 a) 5
 b) 3
 c) 2
 d) 4
 e) 6
 f) 1

2 (Suggested answers)
 a) *I'll have the giant pizza.*
 b) I'll be home before midnight./I won't be home after midnight.
 c) I'll meet you tomorrow at 6.30.
 d) I'll take the red pair.
 e) No, I won't (give you my book)!
 f) I'll pay you back at the end of the week.

Grammar 25

1 a) *1*
 b) 1
 c) 1
 d) 2
 e) 1
 f) 1

2 a) *is going to have*
 b) I'll see
 c) I'm going to
 d) are you going to do?
 e) is going to go to bed
 f) is going to move

Grammar 26

1 (Suggested answers)
 a) *I'm seeing the dentist at 4.30 on Saturday.*
 b) I'm staying at home on Sunday.
 c) I'm playing basketball at 3.00 on Monday.
 d) I'm doing some shopping on Tuesday afternoon.
 e) I'm going to London on Wednesday.
 f) I'm having a party on Thursday.
 g) Jim and Carol are coming to lunch on Friday.

2 a) *are you doing*
 b) am not coming
 c) is going
 d) Are you having
 e) are not going
 f) Is Mrs Simpson teaching
 g) are not arriving
 h) Is Joaquim going
 i) is not working
 j) Are you leaving

Grammar 27

1 a) *1*
   b) 3
   c) 1
   d) 1
   e) 3
   f) 2

2 a) *tomorrow*
   b) next year
   c) in
   d) later
   e) at
   f) a minute
   g) after

Grammar 28

1 a) *B*
   b) A
   c) B
   d) A
   e) A
   f) A
   g) B
   h) B

2 a) *is spending*
   b) is waiting
   c) Are you doing
   d) is reading
   e) are going
   f) am having
   g) are you doing
   h) is leaving

3 a) *We're going to the cinema this evening. Do you want to come?*
   b) Look out! That car is going to crash!
   c) Bye for now! I'll see you tomorrow.
   d) Sorry I can't meet you. I'm going to the doctor's.
   e) Have you heard the weather forecast? It's going to rain tomorrow.
   f) I've bought my ticket. I'm leaving tomorrow.

4 a) *tonight*
   b) in
   c) at
   d) this
   e) tomorrow
   f) later
   g) on

5 a) *at*
   b) next year
   c) soon
   d) after
   e) tonight
   f) in
   g) in

Think about grammar!
a) False. There are at least three tenses – *will, going to* and present continuous.
b) True.
c) True.

Grammar 29

1 a) *doesn't leave, will miss*
   b) works, will pass
   c) rains, will go
   d) doesn't practise, won't improve
   e) rains, won't go
   f) comes, will be
   g) see, will tell

2 a) *press*
   b) won't be
   c) feel
   d) come
   e) rains
   f) 'll work

3 (Suggested answers)
   a) *play basketball in the classroom, we'll break the window.*
   b) don't leave the party now, we'll miss the last bus/leave the party now, we won't miss the last bus.
   c) touch my dog, it'll bite you.
   d) stand under a tree, we won't get wet/don't stand under a tree, we'll get wet.
   e) walk, we'll get tired.
   f) hurry, we'll be late.

Grammar 30

1 a) *had, would go*
   b) found, would take
   c) had, would take
   d) met, would try
   e) spoke, would learn
   f) saw, would run

2 a) *met, would ask*
   b) had, would fly
   c) robbed, would catch
   d) won, would buy
   e) slept, would be
   f) were, would visit

3 (Suggested answers)
   a) *I were you, I would go to the*
   b) I were you, I would go to the
   c) I were you, I would ask
   d) I were you, I would talk to your
   e) I were you, I would go to
   f) I were you, I would join

Grammar 31

1
a) *1*
b) 2
c) 2
d) 1
e) 1
f) 2

2 (Suggested answers)
a) *had a bike, she would ride it to school.*
b) works hard, he'll pass his exams.
c) ate a lot, he would be fat.
d) had a car, she wouldn't walk to work.
e) practises, his English will improve.
f) hurries, she won't be late.
g) liked swimming, she would go to the beach.
h) takes his medicine, he will get better.
i) didn't live near the school, he would get up early.
j) leaves now, she will catch the bus.

3
a) *B*
b) A
c) B
d) A
e) A
f) C
g) C
h) A
i) B
j) C

4
a) *want, will ask*
b) won, would get
c) were/was, would be
d) place, appears
e) don't come, will not see
f) starts, will finish

Grammar 32

1
a) *5*
b) 7
c) 1
d) 3
e) 8
f) 4
g) 2
h) 6

2
a) *Were they working hard?*
b) Has Jim eaten yet?
c) Do you read a lot?
d) Is Tom writing a letter?
e) Did Tina leave yesterday?
f) Have we met before?
g) Was Sam watching TV?

3
a) *I haven't.*
b) he is.
c) it didn't.
d) I do.
e) I have.
f) I'm not.
g) she doesn't.
h) he wasn't.

Grammar 33

1
a) *Why are you crying?*
b) How did you get here?
c) What does Jack usually do on Saturdays?
d) How long have you lived here?
e) Where was David going?
f) Who are you talking to?
g) What were you doing?

2
a) *makes you tired*
b) did you talk to
c) did you read
d) brought the ice-cream
e) did Joe decide
f) answers most of the questions
g) house is yours
h) looks after the children

3
a) *A sandwich*
b) My teacher
c) Cartoons
d) My pen-friend
e) You
f) Somebody

Grammar 34

1
a) *didn't he*
b) do you
c) weren't they
d) does he
e) did he
f) hasn't it
g) are you
h) won't you
i) doesn't he
j) aren't you

2
a) *4*
b) 10
c) 5
d) 8
e) 3
f) 9
g) 2
h) 6
i) 1
j) 7

3
a) *hasn't he*
b) do you
c) wasn't he
d) didn't I
e) isn't she
f) aren't we
g) has he
h) were you
i) are they
j) did she

Grammar 35

1 a) *get, will catch*
   b) were, would tell
   c) lived, would spend
   d) see, will tell
   e) don't hurry, won't get OR hurry, will get
   f) had, would lend
   g) don't get, won't be
   h) landed, would soon decide

2 a) *I were you, I would go to the doctor's.*
   b) name isn't Jim, is
   c) have forgotten your homework, haven't
   d) we hurry, we won't be late.
   e) isn't going to lose, is
   f) I were you, I would go to bed early
   g) weren't at school yesterday, were
   h) If you ate breakfast, you wouldn't feel hungry.

3 a) *do, sit next to*
   b) Have you ever been
   c) are you going to do tomorrow
   d) makes you happy
   e) are you looking at me
   f) Do you like
   g) lives

4 a) *don't you*
   b) isn't it
   c) are we
   d) aren't you
   e) has he
   f) won't they
   g) were you

5 (Suggested answers)
   a) you are   *are you*
   b) does live   lives
   c) am, am   were, would
   d) got you?   have you?
   e) means this? does this mean?
   f) isn't it?   aren't you?

Think about grammar!
a) False. They are about imaginary situations.
b) True. Unless *do* is the main verb.
c) False. Some are real and some are checking.

Grammar 36

1 a) *She can walk.*
   b) She can't run.
   c) She can dance.
   d) She can smile.
   e) She can't speak English.
   f) She can't ride a bicycle.

2 a) *I can't come to your party.*
   b) Can you play basketball tonight?
   c) Can you use a computer?
   d) You can't borrow my bike.
   e) We can't answer this question.
   f) I can't help you.
   g) I can't play this game.
   h) Can you help me?

Grammar 37

1 a) *You must do it again!*
   b) You must work faster!
   c) You must turn to page 50!
   d) You must hurry up!
   e) You must stop talking!
   f) You must listen to me!
   g) You must give me your homework!
   h) You must sit down!

2 a) *Do you have to wear a uniform?*
   b) You have to/must do homework.
   c) Do you have to sit in the same place?
   d) Does he have to arrive before 8.00?
   e) She has to/must eat lunch at school.
   f) Do you have to change classrooms?
   g) Do they have to do gym?
   h) You have to/must learn German.

3 a) *you should go to the doctor's.*
   b) should wear a warm coat.
   c) should leave early.
   d) should take more exercise.
   e) you should read a lot.
   f) should do that.
   g) you should ride a bike.
   h) you should buy a dog.

Grammar 38

1 a) *You mustn't talk.*
   b) You mustn't smoke.
   c) You mustn't open the window.
   d) You mustn't enter.
   e) You mustn't park.
   f) You mustn't take photographs.

2 a) *You shouldn't smoke.*
   b) You should keep fit.
   c) You should eat healthy food.
   d) You shouldn't drink alcohol.
   e) You should go to the gym.
   f) You shouldn't take drugs.

3 a) *doesn't have to take*
   b) doesn't have to get up
   c) don't have to make
   d) doesn't have to do
   e) don't have to sit
   f) doesn't have to do

Grammar 39

1 a) *3*
   b) 4
   c) 2
   d) 6
   e) 1
   f) 5

2 a) *I had to wash the dishes. I didn't have to wash the dishes.*
   b) I had/didn't have to cook the dinner.
   c) I had/didn't have to do my homework.
   d) I had/didn't have to go shopping.
   e) I had/didn't have to go to school.
   f) I had/didn't have to write a letter.

3 a) *couldn't get home before 7.00.*
   b) had to leave at 6.00 to catch his plane.
   c) couldn't believe our luck!
   d) didn't have to wait long for the bus.
   e) could speak five languages.
   f) couldn't find your number.

Grammar 40

1 a) *It might rain.*
   b) This must be right.
   c) I might see you tomorrow.
   d) This can't be the answer.
   e) This must be the place.
   f) I might not come to your party.
   g) You can't be serious!
   h) We must be early.

2 a) *6*
   b) 3
   c) 1
   d) 4
   e) 5
   f) 2

Grammar 41

1 a) *don't have to*
   b) have to
   c) had to
   d) shouldn't
   e) 'm not able to
   f) mustn't
   g) did you have to
   h) should
   i) can't

2 (Suggested answers)
   a) *I didn't have to go to school yesterday.*
   b) This can't be right.
   c) Tina could play the piano at an early age.
   d) I may see you tomorrow.
   e) Harry was able to repair the radio.
   f) Bill had to return his library book.
   g) Carol might phone tonight.

3 (Suggested answers)
   a) *has/had*
   b) can/could
   c) must
   d) have
   e) can/should/must
   f) has/had
   g) have
   h) has/had

Grammar 42

1 a) *had to go*
   b) could walk
   c) must be
   d) didn't have to wait
   e) could be
   f) couldn't do
   g) might go
   h) was able to catch

2 a) *must*
   b) had
   c) able
   d) have
   e) could
   f) must
   g) must
   h) had

3 (Suggested answers)
   a) *can't be*
   b) should talk to your teacher about it
   c) don't have to be here before 8.00
   d) must know
   e) had to go to the doctor's
   f) might/could/may be
   g) I should

4
a) *You must be here at 6.00.*
b) I can't see you tomorrow.
c) You have to press the button twice.
d) You shouldn't eat lots of sweets.
e) Jean is unable/isn't able to come to the party.
f) You don't have to pay now.
g) You mustn't park here.
h) You should work harder.

5
a) *must*
b) may/might
c) able
d) may/might
e) couldn't
f) have
g) can't
h) can/could
i) can't
j) had

Think about grammar!
a) False. *Mustn't* = not allowed; *don't have to* = your choice.
b) True. *Must* is a rule from someone else; *have to* is a rule from yourself.
c) True.

Grammar 43

1
a) *feet*
b) knives
c) children/babies
d) teeth
e) sheep
f) glasses

2
a) *potatoes*
b) families
c) bookshelves
d) dishes
e) boxes
f) monkeys

3
a) *leaves*
b) shelves
c) matches
d) children
e) women
f) glasses

Grammar 44

1
a) *a*
b) some
c) some
d) some
e) a
f) some

2
a) *a*
b) any
c) some
d) any
e) a
f) any
g) a

3
a) *any*
b) some
c) some
d) any
e) some
f) any
g) some

Grammar 45

1
a) –
b) –
c) a
d) –
e) –
f) an
g) –
h) a

2
a) *B*
b) C
c) C
d) A
e) B
f) A
g) B

3
a) *is*
b) is
c) are
d) is
e) are
f) is
g) are
h) is

Grammar 46

1
a) *much*
b) many
c) much
d) much
e) many
f) many
g) much
h) many

2
a) *How much*
b) How many
c) How many
d) How much
e) How many
f) How much
g) How much
h) How many

3 a) *much*
b) many
c) much
d) much
e) many
f) much
g) many
h) many

4 a) *How many brothers have you got?*
b) How much does it cost?
c) How many people are there?
d) How many bicycles do you need?
e) How much rice would you like?
f) How many children has he got?
g) How much money have you got?

Grammar 47

1 a) *5*
b) 3
c) 6
d) 1
e) 4
f) 2

2 a) *2*
b) 1
c) 2
d) 1
e) 2
f) 2
g) 1
h) 1
i) 2
j) 1

3 (Suggested answers)
a) *6*
b) 8
c) 5
d) 10
e) 4
f) 2
g) 1
h) 9
i) 3
j) 7

4 a) *A*
b) B
c) A
d) C
e) C
f) A
g) B
h) B
i) A
j) B

5 a) *There are too many people.*
b) There is too much noise.
c) I've got too many things to do.
d) There are too many cars.
e) There is too much sugar.
f) There are too many books.

Grammar 48

1 a) *109*
b) 87
c) 255
d) 332
e) 2,001
f) 2,000,000
g) 200,000
h) 51,210

2 a) *eighteen*
b) ninety
c) forty-nine
d) seventy-one
e) sixty-four
f) ninety-seven
g) twenty-three
h) fourteen

3 a) *third*
b) ninth
c) twenty-first
d) thirtieth
e) fifth
f) second
g) forty-third
h) first

4 a) *2*
b) 1
c) 2
d) 1
e) 2
f) 2
g) 1

Grammar 49

1 a) *any*
b) any
c) an
d) some
e) some
f) a
g) some

2 a) *much*
b) much
c) any
d) any/enough
e) many
f) many
g) any

3
a) *are*
b) are
c) is
d) are
e) are
f) is
g) is

4
a) *much*
b) much
c) many
d) much
e) many
f) many
g) much

5
a) *enough money*
b) is
c) is
d) much
e) haven't got
f) many

6 (Suggested answers)
a) *Unfortunately David hasn't got many friends.*
b) I haven't got much tea.
c) There isn't much sugar left.
d) Can you give me some information about hotels in the centre?
e) This is Gerry's furniture.
f) We haven't got any milk.

7 (Suggested answers)
a) is   *are*
b) an   some
c) were   was
d) peoples   people
e) informations information
f) time enough   enough time

Think about grammar!
a) False. Uncountables have no plural.
b) False. *Any* is used in questions and negatives.
c) True.

Grammar 50

1
1) *c*
2) e
3) b
4) f
5) d
6) a

2
a) *Sorry*
b) going
c) so
d) fault
e) were
f) do
g) Help
h) should

3
a) *4*
b) 2
c) 5
d) 6
e) 1
f) 3

Grammar 51

1
a) *does Jack look*
b) sorry I'm
c) know the way
d) you feel
e) you tell me the way
f) is Paris

2
a) *Go*
b) do
c) way
d) see
e) sorry
f) like
g) how
h) tell
i) do
j) to

3
a) *5*
b) 8
c) 1
d) 6
e) 7
f) 2
g) 4
h) 3

Grammar 52

1
a) *3*
b) 5
c) 1
d) 2
e) 6
f) 4

2 (Suggested answers)
a) *about going to the cinema?*
b) you want a sandwich?
c) you like to sit down?
d) opening the window, please?
e) I carry your bag for you?
f) you tell me the time?

3 (Suggested answers)
a) *Would you mind helping me?*
b) Would you like to go to the disco?
c) Can/May I leave early?
d) Do you want me to carry your books?
e) Shall we go to the park?

Grammar 53

1
a) *2*
b) 1
c) 1
d) 2
e) 1
f) 1

2 (Suggested answers)
- a) *about*
- b) mind
- c) Could/Can
- d) about
- e) out
- f) Could/Can
- g) prefer
- h) let's

3
- a) *Look out*
- b) Could you
- c) How about
- d) I'll
- e) Of course
- f) Would you mind
- g) Shall
- h) I'd rather

Grammar 54

1
- a) *22/10*
- b) 1/1
- c) 19/8
- d) 5/6
- e) 30/9
- f) 14/5
- g) 8/3
- h) 13/11

2
- a) *The twenty-first of June*
- b) The nineteenth of March
- c) The second of August
- d) The thirty-first of October
- e) The fifteenth of February
- f) The first of May
- g) The twentieth of January
- h) The sixteenth of November

3
- a) *B*
- b) C
- c) A
- d) C
- e) C
- f) A

Grammar 55

1
- a) *8.50*
- b) 11.15
- c) 5.20
- d) 5.45
- e) 8.25
- f) 4.55
- g) 11.10

2
- a) *half past two*
- b) (a) quarter to two
- c) (a) quarter past four
- d) (a) quarter to four
- e) (a) quarter past five
- f) half past nine

3
- a) *quarter to*
- b) in the morning
- c) noon/midday
- d) past two
- e) in the evening
- f) minutes to
- g) midnight

Grammar 56

1
- a) *So do I*
- b) What's Tony like
- c) I'm sorry I'm late
- d) half past three
- e) my fault
- f) I'd go to the doctor's
- g) 20th November
- h) What is Edinburgh like

2
- a) *2*
- b) 2
- c) 3
- d) 2
- e) 3
- f) 2
- g) 1

3
- a) *were*
- b) like
- c) way
- d) Would
- e) Let's
- f) Don't
- g) to
- h) mind

4
- a) *going*
- b) to arrive
- c) How are you
- d) Shall
- e) finishes
- f) open
- g) I'd rather have
- h) 'll see

5 (Suggested answers)
- a) *Would you mind closing the door, please?*
- b) What's Paris like?
- c) Do you mind if I close the door?
- d) Do you feel like going swimming?
- e) Would you like some chocolate?
- f) Why don't we have a party on Friday?

6
- a) *where the cinema is*
- b) at three o'clock
- c) does your English teacher look like
- d) go to bed early
- e) I don't think so
- f) Could you tell me
- g) going

Think about grammar!
- a) False. They write them in different ways.
- b) True.
- c) True.

Grammar 57

1 a) *in*
   b) in
   c) in
   d) into
   e) on
   f) at
   g) at
   h) to
   i) on
   j) on

2 a) *at*
   b) to
   c) at
   d) to
   e) to
   f) to
   g) at
   h) at
   i) to
   j) at

3 a) *in*
   b) in
   c) at
   d) in
   e) in
   f) at
   g) at
   h) at
   i) in
   j) at

4 a) *in*
   b) at
   c) on
   d) at
   e) in
   f) at
   g) on
   h) into
   i) to
   j) in

5 a) *in*
   b) on
   c) on
   d) in
   e) on
   f) in
   g) on
   h) in
   i) in
   j) on

6 a) *to*
   b) to
   c) at
   d) –
   e) at
   f) at
   g) –
   h) to
   i) to
   j) at

Grammar 58

1 a) *in*
   b) opposite
   c) outside
   d) in front of
   e) near
   f) out of
   g) next to
   h) inside
   i) out
   j) behind

2 a) *B*
   b) B
   c) A
   d) C
   e) C
   f) A
   g) A
   h) C
   i) A
   j) C

3 a) *2*
   b) 2
   c) 1
   d) 2
   e) 2
   f) 1

4 a) *inside*
   b) in
   c) out
   d) out
   e) outside
   f) behind
   g) next
   h) near
   i) upstairs
   j) front

5 a) *behind*
   b) in
   c) inside
   d) near
   e) opposite
   f) out
   g) in front of
   h) out of

Grammar 59

1 a) *the*
   b) a
   c) the
   d) the
   e) a
   f) the
   g) an
   h) the

2 a) *a, the*
   b) the, a
   c) The, a
   d) a, the
   e) a, the
   f) the, a
   g) the, a
   h) a, the

3 (Suggested answers)
   a) *Jane is an English teacher.*
   b) This is the last bus.
   c) Have you seen the paper today?
   d) The English like tea.
   e) A telescope helps you to see things that are far away.
   f) Ann is a member of a team.
   g) This is the end of the road.
   h) Tim is a university student.

Grammar 60

1 a) *a*
   b) –
   c) a
   d) –
   e) The
   f) –
   g) the
   h) –

2 a) *the*
   b) –
   c) –
   d) –
   e) –
   f) the
   g) –
   h) –

3 (Suggested answers)
   a) *Sue is still in bed.*
   b) We went to the city centre on foot.
   c) David wears glasses made of plastic.
   d) George came here by bus.
   e) Naomi speaks French.
   f) Martin is in prison.
   g) I don't drink tea.
   h) Carlos comes from Spain.

Grammar 61

1 a) *us*
   b) theirs
   c) that
   d) mine
   e) these
   f) her
   g) my
   h) them

2 a) *this*
   b) one
   c) those
   d) this
   e) these
   f) that
   g) ones
   h) one

3 a) *yours*
   b) mine
   c) her
   d) me
   e) ours
   f) him
   g) hers
   h) its

Grammar 62

1 a) *something*
   b) Everything
   c) Someone
   d) nothing
   e) anyone
   f) No one/Nobody
   g) Someone
   h) Everything

2 a) *None*
   b) Everyone/body
   c) No one/body
   d) anyone/body
   e) No one/body
   f) anything
   g) Everything
   h) someone/body

3 (Suggested answers)
   a) *There is no one at home.*
   b) Everyone knows that.
   c) There isn't anything to do.
   d) There was nothing in the box.
   e) There are none left.
   f) I met somebody who knows you.
   g) I ate nothing.
   h) Do you know anybody in this town?

Grammar 63

1 a) *C*
   b) C
   c) B
   d) A
   e) B
   f) A

2 a) *a*
   b) a
   c) the
   d) a
   e) the
   f) a
   g) the
   h) one

3 a) *a, the*
   b) The, the, the
   c) –
   d) the, the, –
   e) an, a
   f) –, the
   g) The, –

4 (Suggested answers)
   a) *There isn't anything in the cupboard.*
   b) Everyone enjoyed the party.
   c) No one was out.
   d) Someone is in the garden.
   e) I promise I won't say anything.
   f) There wasn't anyone on the bus.

5 a) *its*
   b) my
   c) one
   d) Their
   e) mine
   f) ours
   g) that
   h) hers

6 a) *Love makes the world go round!*
   b) Help! Call <u>the</u> police!
   c) Kate enjoyed her holiday <u>in</u> Turkey.
   d) Have you met <u>my</u> brother?
   e) <u>None</u> of the questions was easy.
   f) Those bags are <u>theirs</u>.
   g) It's quicker to go to the station <u>on</u> foot.
   h) Everything I wrote <u>was</u> wrong.

Think about grammar!
a) True.
b) True.
c) False. The meaning of the two words is similar, in some contexts, but they are not the same.

Grammar 64

1 a) *'I'm leaving at six,'*
   b) 'Peter often goes fishing,'
   c) 'I will be back later,'
   d) 'I have just seen Mark,'
   e) 'They/We left at 6.00,'
   f) 'I am working,'
   g) 'We are late,'
   h) 'I will phone back,'
   i) 'I feel all right,'
   j) 'I love ice-cream,'

2 a) *(that) she was leaving.*
   b) (that) he had seen the film on Monday.
   c) (that) she had missed the bus.
   d) (that) they lived in Marsden Street.
   e) (that) she would phone at 6.00.
   f) (that) she was having a good time.
   g) (that) they were arriving at 9.00.
   h) (that) he had forgotten to do his work.
   i) (that) he was wrong.
   j) (that) he had hurt his arm.

Grammar 65

1 a) *were stolen*
   b) has decided
   c) was visited
   d) have not found
   e) are discovered
   f) is chosen
   g) will be held

2 a) *were arrested*
   b) has been found
   c) are planted
   d) will be sold
   e) were taken
   f) has been discovered

3 a) *The bridge was built in 1996.*
   b) My sandwich has been eaten by a dog.
   c) The letter will be delivered tomorrow.
   d) Our train has been cancelled.
   e) A window in the classroom was broken by one of the students.
   f) Millions of bars of chocolate are eaten every day!

Grammar 66

1 a) *was given a lift to school by a friend.*
   b) will be played by Tom Smooth.
   c) was opened with a screwdriver.
   d) are grown in by a lot of farmers in Greece.
   e) was broken by a ball.
   f) was bought by a Japanese millionaire.
   g) of Tutankhamun was discovered by Howard Carter in 1922.
   h) are enjoyed by millions of people.
   i) is caused by heavy traffic.

2 a) *Thousands of new homes are built every year.*
   b) The match will be played on Sunday.
   c) Nowadays many trees are cut down for no reason.
   d) Jim was asked to go to the police station.
   e) My bike has been stolen.
   f) Our new washing-machine was delivered yesterday.
   g) The bank manager was kidnapped.
   h) It was decided to have another meeting on Wednesday.

Grammar 67

1 (Suggested answers)
   a) *Turn off the light!*
   b) Come back!
   c) Open your books!
   d) Close the door!
   e) Sit down!
   f) Lend me a pen!
   g) Stop talking!
   h) Take the first left!

2 a) *Sit down!*
 b) Come here!
 c) Turn off the light!
 d) Stop work!
 e) Close the window!
 f) Wake up!
 g) Push the door!
 h) Get on the bus!

Grammar 68

1 a) *running*
 b) Taking
 c) collecting
 d) Eating
 e) playing
 f) Shouting
 g) sailing
 h) Crossing
 i) going
 j) Jogging
 k) driving
 l) Playing

2 a) *Studying late at night is tiring.*
 b) Getting up early is hard.
 c) Learning a language takes time.
 d) Parking here is forbidden.
 e) Visiting other countries is interesting.
 f) Talking is not allowed.
 g) Booking a table is not necessary.
 h) Copying other people is wrong.
 i) Listening to music is relaxing.
 j) Smoking is not allowed.

Grammar 69

1 a) *It is*
 b) I will
 c) What is
 d) Do not, will not
 e) cannot
 f) It has
 g) I would
 h) Jane has

2 a) *I won't be home early.*
 b) Who's coming to your party?
 c) We're interested in football.
 d) I wouldn't do that if I were you.
 e) Paula couldn't lift the chair.
 f) They've sent me a letter.
 g) Helen's got a dog.
 h) It's very cold today.

3 a) *It's time for the news.*
 b) I've decided to buy some boots.
 c) Whose books are these? Are they yours?
 d) Sue's borrowed my paints.
 e) This new boat's ours. It's got sails and oars.
 f) I think the dog's hurt one of its legs.
 g) These are my photos. I'd like to see yours.
 h) My name's Toby. What's yours?

4 a) *If you asked me, I wouldn't tell you.*
 b) I don't know where he's gone.
 c) You haven't done it yet.
 d) I'll see you when you're back.
 e) Jane hasn't finished her homework.
 f) We weren't ready so we couldn't begin.
 g) If you're nervous, don't worry.

Grammar 70

1 a) *(that) he would be late.*
 b) (that) Kate knew the answer.
 c) (that) Mary was leaving at 8.00.
 d) (that) he couldn't find the keys.
 e) (that) the bus was going to be late.
 f) (that) he'd lost his books.
 g) (that) she was ready.

2 a) *has been broken*
 b) will be played
 c) is published
 d) was filmed
 e) were found
 f) will be opened
 g) are often changed
 h) has been discovered

3 a) *by someone*
 b) (all necessary)
 c) by a writer
 d) (all necessary)
 e) by the police
 f) by someone
 g) by workers
 h) by people

4 a) *water is wasted.*
 b) has been introduced.
 c) new sports centre will be opened next week.
 d) were injured by a falling tree.
 e) has been stolen.
 f) will be met at the airport.
 g) is taught by a French person.

5 (Suggested answers)
 a) *sit*
 b) Reading
 c) go
 d) Lend
 e) Talking
 f) Writing
 g) Getting
 h) Don't

6 a) *They are*
   b) We have
   c) It is
   d) will not
   e) It has
   f) I would
   g) does not
   h) Mary has

Think about grammar!

a) False. Passive sentences stress the object.
b) False. Common words like *don't* and *can't* are often used in formal writing.
c) False. It is about the activity in general.

Grammar 71

1 a) *yours*
   b) her
   c) mine
   d) our
   e) Their
   f) your
   g) my
   h) hers
   i) Whose
   j) its

2 (Suggested answers)
   a) *Is that big house theirs?*
   b) Whose bike is this?
   c) These books are mine.
   d) Is that boat hers?
   e) Have you got a computer?
   f) Is that dog yours?
   g) These houses are ours.
   h) This seat is hers.
   i) This classroom is theirs.
   j) Whose CD is this?

Grammar 72

1 a) *Is that book yours or Sam's?*
   b) David's sister's cat's name is Syrup.
   c) Have you met Pat's brothers?
   d) Are those shoes hers?
   e) These are the girls' fathers.
   f) Those are the teachers' cars.
   g) These sandwiches are ours, not yours.
   h) My books are in my friend's bag.
   i) Whose gloves are these?
   j) That is Jack's father's bike.

2 a) *the shop window*
   b) the table leg
   c) the car door
   d) the school playground
   e) the bicycle wheel
   f) the door handle

3 a) *is Jim's desk.*
   b) hers.
   c) yours or his?
   d) is this ruler?
   e) empty seats theirs?
   f) house belongs to
   g) Joe and Ella's caravan.
   h) Sarah's teacher's

Grammar 73

1 a) *What's your teacher like?*
   b) What's the end of the film like?
   c) What are your parents like?
   d) What's the weather in your country like?
   e) What are your next door neighbours like?
   f) What's Helen's new boyfriend like?
   g) What's the city centre like?
   h) What are the desks in your classroom like?

2 (Suggested answers)
   a) *good*
   b) Swiss
   c) old
   d) ill
   e) Japanese
   f) rich
   g) Chinese
   h) funny

3 a) *too*
   b) too
   c) enough
   d) too
   e) too
   f) enough
   g) enough
   h) too

Grammar 74

1 a) *a lovely new cotton shirt*
   b) a large old wooden house
   c) two beautiful large green apples
   d) an interesting new science-fiction film
   e) a beautiful old green vase
   f) a short red plastic coat
   g) a beautiful old blue carpet
   h) a sweet little black puppy

2 a) *a football boot*
   b) a running shoe
   c) a country road
   d) an athletics stadium
   e) a swimming costume
   f) a mountain village
   g) a university student
   h) a school bus

3 a) *boring*
   b) interesting
   c) tired
   d) exciting
   e) worried
   f) interested
   g) bored
   h) complicated

4
a) *tired*
b) shocked
c) amazing
d) disappointed
e) confusing
f) tiring
g) worried
h) amusing

Grammar 75

1
a) *The girl is taller than the boy.*
b) The woman is younger than the man.
c) The large box is more expensive than the small one.
d) The boy's hair is shorter than the girl's.
e) The girl's ice-cream is smaller than the boy's.
f) The girl's bike is bigger than the boy's.

2
a) *bigger*
b) happier
c) more beautiful
d) angrier/more angry
e) worse
f) more important
g) drier
h) better
i) hotter
j) more expensive

3
a) *than*
b) as
c) less
d) than
e) more
f) than
g) as
h) than

4
a) *younger than Tim*
b) smaller than ours
c) shorter than David
d) are better than Jack's
e) as expensive as this one
f) is faster than yours

5
a) *is bigger than*
b) is smaller than
c) is not as large as
d) is not as small as
e) is hotter than
f) is not as cold as
g) is not as rainy as
h) is rainier than

Grammar 76

1
a) *the longest*
b) the fittest
c) the funniest
d) the most terrible
e) the best
f) the widest
g) the nastiest
h) the strangest

2
a) *best*
b) oldest
c) more
d) worst
e) richest
f) happier
g) more

3
a) *Dave is the tallest.*
b) Tom is the shortest.
c) Jim is the eldest.
d) Tom is the youngest.
e) Tom is the heaviest.
f) Jim is the lightest.

Grammar 77

1
a) *belong*
b) the
c) enough
d) than
e) got
f) as
g) Whose
h) better

2 (Suggested answers)
a) *This is my pen./This pen is mine*.
b) Those are their bags./Those bags are theirs.
c) That is Tom's house./That house belongs to Tom.
d) That's their baby./That baby is theirs.
e) Who does this farm belong to?/Whose is this farm?
f) Is that your bike?/Is that bike yours?
g) That boat is Oscar and Cathy's./That is their boat.

3
a) *B*
b) A
c) C
d) A
e) B
f) B

4 (Suggested answers)
a) *My tea is too cold.*
b) What a great film!
c) You aren't old enough to see this film.
d) What's your brother like?
e) This piece of string isn't long enough.
f) I'm not interested in sport.

Think about grammar!
a) False. They come before the noun.
b) False. Comparatives compare two things. Superlatives compare one of many.
c) False. It follows the *s*.

Grammar 78

1
a) *quickly*
b) fast
c) wonderfully
d) happily
e) badly
f) specially
g) well
h) slowly
i) beautifully
j) sadly

2
a) *freshly*
b) sincerely
c) greatly
d) well
e) beautifully
f) specially
g) completely
h) frequently

3
a) *Jim works well.*
b) Ann dances wonderfully.
c) Carol writes accurately.
d) Tina sings badly.
e) Sam smokes secretly.
f) Ruth runs fast.
g) Pablo drives carefully.
h) Liz reads quickly.

Grammar 79

1
a) *there*
b) It's
c) their
d) It's
e) There
f) it's
g) they're
h) its
i) their
j) it's

2
a) *They're*
b) its
c) It's
d) It
e) There
f) their
g) It's
h) They're
i) There
j) It's

3
a) *It*
b) there
c) there
d) their
e) It
f) there
g) It
h) its
i) there
j) It

Grammar 80

1
a) *Has Jane got a new car?*
b) I haven't got a stamp.
c) Did Jim have a cold last week?
d) Have we got a problem?
e) You don't have a test today.
f) Has Paul got a sister?

2
a) *I had a cat.*
b) Did you have a bike?
c) Jim didn't have any time.
d) David had an exam.
e) We didn't have a house.
f) Did Tina have a cold?

3
a) *earn*
b) receive
c) buy
d) become
e) collect
f) arrive in

Grammar 81

1
a) *doing*
b) make
c) does
d) made
e) make
f) made
g) do
h) done

2
a) *went*
b) go/come
c) came
d) goes
e) go
f) going
g) went
h) going/coming

3
a) *6*
b) 2
c) 1
d) 7
e) 4
f) 5
g) 8
h) 3

Grammar 82

1
a) *walking*
b) going
c) about
d) to
e) cooking
f) in
g) to go
h) for
i) doing
j) for

2 (Suggested answers)
a) *for*
b) fancy
c) know
d) like/want
e) believe
f) doing
g) refused
h) to
i) to
j) for

3 a) *manage*
b) can't stand
c) refuse
d) apologize
e) wait
f) listen
g) enjoy
h) know
i) lend
j) choose

4 a) *to pay for my ticket.*
b) stand playing football.
c) you explain this to
d) to wait.
e) about you last night.
f) to go to the cinema tonight.
g) going to the park.
h) this pencil belong to you?
i) to finish the race in three minutes.
j) the chocolate cake/one.

5 a) *Do you fancy going swimming tomorrow?*
b) Can you lend me your phone, please?
c) We managed to sail home despite the storm.
d) She apologized for stealing the money.
e) Tim paid for the meal.
f) I want to visit the museum this afternoon.
g) They don't know very much about British history.
h) Sue doesn't enjoy watching television.

6 1) *A*
2) C
3) A
4) B
5) C
6) B
7) A
8) C
9) A
10) B

Grammar 83

1 a) *for*
b) at
c) from
d) of
e) with
f) about
g) on
h) for
i) with
j) in

2 a) *ready*
b) angry
c) full
d) tired/bored
e) good
f) to
g) right
h) afraid/scared
i) keen
j) pleased

3 a) *George was late for school.*
b) I'm bored with staying at home.
c) Ann is married to Chris.
d) I'm sorry about my behaviour.
e) Joaquim is very good at cycling.
f) Are you interested in history?

Grammar 84

1 a) *B*
b) A
c) B
d) C
e) C
f) A
g) B
h) B

2 (Suggested answers)
a) *well*
b) hard
c) carelessly
d) secretly
e) quickly
f) politely
g) loudly
h) badly

3 a) *refused*
b) listens
c) believe
d) pleased
e) found
f) good
g) interested

4 (Suggested answers)
a) *Ann is frightened of birds.*
b) Tina was late for school yesterday.
c) I apologize for missing you.
d) Harry is bored with his lessons.
e) I can't stand getting up early.
f) The cinema is full of people.
g) Ricardo is very bad at football.

5 a) *went*
    b) up
    c) getting
    d) forward
    e) in
    f) run
    g) made
    h) going

Think about grammar!
a) True.
b) True.
c) True.

Grammar 85

1 a) *3*
    b) 2
    c) 3
    d) 1
    e) 2
    f) 1
    g) 3
    h) 2
    i) 2
    j) 3

2 a) *It's six o'clock. It's time for the news.*
    b) I've decided to buy Jim's old boots.
    c) Whose books are these? Are they yours?
    d) Sue's borrowed Carol's paints.
    e) This new boat's ours. It's got sails and oars.
    f) My sisters are going to Jane's party.
    g) I think the dog's hurt one of its legs.
    h) Where's Helen's brother's bike?

3 a) *What's the matter with Mrs Smith's dog?*
    b) Carol's got two brothers, a sister and three cousins.
    c) That's not yours. It's mine.
    d) I bought some bananas, two apples and some sandwiches.
    e) Don't worry. The boys will borrow their friends' bikes.
    f) There's something wrong with Ann's car.
    g) Have you seen the swimming pool? It's fantastic.
    h) It's eight o'clock. It's time for the bus.

4 a) There was a big, red bus.
    b) We had meat, potatoes and vegetables for lunch.
    c) He was an angry, old man.
    d) We took a book, a pen and a ruler.
    e) My brother, sister and mother were there.
    f) We watched an old, scary film.
    g) The teacher shouted, screamed and ran out of the class.
    h) I got a new, blue jumper.

5 Dear Miss Green,
I'm writing to you to tell you that Steven isn't coming to school today because he's not feeling very well. He'll be in class again on Friday morning. If you'd like to talk to me, you can call me at home.
When is the last day of term?
Best wishes,
John Roberts

Grammar 86

1 a) *swimming*
    b) writing
    c) beginning
    d) deciding
    e) beautiful
    f) successful
    g) wonderful
    h) carefully

2 a) *chocolate*
    b) beautiful
    c) answered
    d) address
    e) accommodation
    f) beginning
    g) almost
    h) disappointed

3 a) *believe*
    b) diary
    c) biscuit
    d) cupboard
    e) changing
    f) different
    g) deeper
    h) blood

4 a) *disappeared*
    b) believe
    c) angry
    d) advertisement
    e) different
    f) apple
    g) coming
    h) arrives

5 Students' own answers.

Grammar 87

1 a) *February*
b) friends
c) eight
d) hundred
e) discussed
f) half
g) favourite
h) immediately

2 a) *forty*
b) foreign
c) fruit
d) fortunately
e) hungry
f) hospital
g) guess
h) enjoyed
i) dirty
j) family

3 a) *won*
b) meat
c) son
d) weak
e) were
f) know
g) steal
h) write
i) Whose
j) passed

4 Students' own answers.

Grammar 88

1 a) *library*
b) Wednesday
c) necessary
d) uncomfortable
e) scientist
f) Which
g) tomorrow
h) neighbours

2 a) *should*
b) swimming
c) programme
d) written
e) successful
f) writing
g) Where
h) putting

3 a) *letters, written*
b) leaving, alarm
c) going, holiday
d) remember, science
e) choosing, brought
f) writing, penfriend
g) wonderful, journey
h) successfully, landed

Grammar 89

1 a) *im* b) un c) im d) dis
e) un f) re g) un h) dis

2 a) *ous* b) ful c) er d) ing
e) ed f) ly g) ance h) able

3 a) *6*
b) 7
c) 8
d) 9
e) 4
f) 3
g) 10
h) 2
i) 1
j) 5

4 a) *in*
b) at
c) between
d) from
e) on
f) on
g) in
h) to

5 a) *bathroom*
b) raincoat
c) homework
d) suitcase
e) seaside
f) bookshop
g) underline
h) motorbike

6 a) *A*
b) B
c) B
d) A
e) B
f) C
g) B
h) B
i) C
j) A
k) C

Grammar 90

1 a) *C*
b) A
c) B
d) A
e) C
f) A
g) C
h) B
i) B
j) C

2 a) *lovely, beach*
b) successful, again
c) advertisement, accommodation
d) right, different
e) February, village
f) advice, your

3
a) *I was very disappointed when I couldn't answer the questions.*
b) A climbing holiday is different, but it's a bit dangerous.
c) Fortunately, all Helen's friends remembered her birthday.
d) Peter tries to learn a new foreign language every year.
e) Are you coming with us to the cinema tomorrow?
f) Do you believe that people can travel through time?
g) Jim has just written two letters to his uncle.
h) Oh bother! I've forgotten my keys. I'll have to go back.
i) Carol likes walking in the country and seeing wild animals.
j) Which is your favourite advertisement on television?

4
a) *on*
b) up
c) forward
d) up
e) up
f) off
g) for
h) on

5
a) *underline*
b) enjoyable
c) interesting
d) dishonest
e) helpful
f) seaside
g) unhappy
h) impatient
i) bookshop
j) dangerous

6
a) *A*
b) B
c) C
d) C
e) A
f) C
g) B
h) C

7
1) *A*
2) C
3) A
4) B
5) C
6) A
7) B
8) C

Think about grammar!
a) False. A full stop ends a sentence; a question mark ends a question.
b) False. A dictionary can help you check your spelling.
c) True and False. Something is only difficult if you think it is.

Vocabulary answers

Vocabulary 1

1
a) *What's your name?*
b) old
c) live
d) address
e) come
f) birth
g) stay
h) job

2
1 *d*
2 g
3 b
4 c
5 h
6 e
7 a
8 f

3
a) *woman*
b) friend
c) boy
d) children
e) family
f) girl
g) teenager
h) foreigner

4
a) *B*
b) C
c) A
d) A
e) B
f) B
g) C
h) B
i) B
j) C
k) B
l) B
m) C

Vocabulary 2

1
a) *Tom, Bill and Sue*
b) Jack and Jane
c) Tom and Bill
d) Sue
e) Bill
f) Sue
g) David
h) Jane
i) David
j) Jack
k) Sue
l) Jane

2
a) *to*
b) relatives
c) person
d) old
e) stranger
f) met
g) twins
h) eldest

3
1 *husband*
2 sister
3 daughter
4 father
5 son
6 brother
7 parents
8 mother
9 wife
10 grandfather

4
a) *daughter*
b) wife
c) son
d) twins
e) sister
f) children
g) husband
h) brother

Vocabulary 3

1
a) *6*
b) 1
c) 5
d) 7
e) 2
f) 3
g) 8
h) 4

2
a) *in*
b) favourite
c) join
d) spends
e) hobby
f) spare
g) member
h) to the cinema

3
1) *C*
2) A
3) C
4) D
5) D
6) A
7) D
8) B

4
a) *C*
b) B
c) B
d) A
e) A
f) C

Vocabulary 4

1
a) *ceiling*
b) door
c) floor
d) wall
e) light
f) chair
g) window
h) radiator

2 a) *bedroom*
  b) study
  c) living-room
  d) kitchen
  e) bathroom
  f) dining-room

3 a) *turn off*
  b) shut
  c) have
  d) doing
  e) knocking
  f) put
  g) turn on
  h) staying

4 a) *upstairs*
  b) ceiling
  c) desk
  d) furniture
  e) window
  f) floor
  g) bathroom
  h) armchair

5 1) *B*
  2) A
  3) D
  4) D
  5) B
  6) A
  7) C
  8) D
  9) C
  10) A

Vocabulary 5

1 a) *greengrocer's*
  b) bank
  c) market
  d) chemist's
  e) baker's
  f) butcher's
  g) post office
  h) newsagent's

2 a) *place*
  b) country
  c) capital
  d) centre
  e) village
  f) country
  g) town
  h) world

3 a) *B*
  b) B
  c) C
  d) A
  e) C
  f) A
  g) B
  h) A

4 a) *police station*
  b) hotel
  c) library
  d) cinema
  e) station
  f) theatre
  g) block of flats
  h) restaurant

Vocabulary 6

1 a) *company*
  b) typist
  c) dentist's
  d) electrician
  e) cook
  f) teacher
  g) were
  h) job

2 a) *7*
  b) 5
  c) 3
  d) 2
  e) 8
  f) 1
  g) 6
  h) 4

3 a) *architect*
  b) lawyer
  c) soldier
  d) nurse
  e) electrician
  f) gardener
  g) musician
  h) scientist
  i) actor
  j) sailor

4 a) *teacher*
  b) doctor
  c) actor
  d) shop assistant
  e) student
  f) writer
  g) dentist
  h) builder

5 1) *A*
  2) C
  3) B
  4) C
  5) A
  6) B
  7) A
  8) B
  9) B
  10) A

Vocabulary 7

1 a) *curtain*
  b) poster
  c) shelf
  d) wardrobe
  e) bed
  f) lamp
  g) carpet
  h) table

2 a) *cooker/fridge*
  b) blanket/wardrobe/pillow
  c) armchair/carpet/table
  d) mirror/shower
  e) desk/bookshelf
  f) table/chair

3 a) *A*
  b) A
  c) C
  d) B
  e) B
  f) C
  g) A
  h) C

Vocabulary 8

1 a) *some spaghetti*
  b) some biscuits
  c) some chips
  d) a salad
  e) a sausage
  f) a chicken
  g) some fruit
  h) some bread

2 a) *snack*
  b) menu
  c) breakfast
  d) meal
  e) lunch
  f) Dinner
  g) food
  h) picnic
  i) take-away
  j) course

3 a) *Boil*
  b) fry
  c) bill
  d) frozen
  e) vegetarian
  f) the food
  g) done
  h) bread
  i) cook
  j) chicken

4 a) *spoon*
  b) straw
  c) plate
  d) tray
  e) knife
  f) cup
  g) fork
  h) jug

Vocabulary 9

1 a) *horse*
  b) dog
  c) cat
  d) bird
  e) fish
  f) chicken
  g) monkey
  h) lizard

2 a) *take*
  b) pet
  c) barks
  d) fly
  e) wild
  f) ride
  g) climbing
  h) feeds
  i) deep
  j) tail

3 a) *bite*
  b) jump
  c) live
  d) make
  e) like
  f) sing
  g) hunt
  h) catch
  i) ride
  j) feed

4 a) *9*
  b) 6
  c) 7
  d) 10
  e) 5
  f) 1
  g) 2
  h) 3
  i) 4
  j) 8

Vocabulary 10

1 a) *Mrs Green*
  b) Mr Davis
  c) Paula
  d) Rick
  e) Paula
  f) Mr Davis
  g) Mrs Green
  h) Mr Davis

2 a) *sock*
  b) overcoat
  c) hat
  d) belt
  e) earring
  f) glove
  g) costume
  h) underwear

3 a) *A*
  b) C
  c) A
  d) B
  e) C
  f) A
  g) B
  h) A
  i) C
  j) B

4 a) *sale*
  b) size
  c) counter
  d) label
  e) shoplifter
  f) bargain
  g) customer
  h) assistant

Vocabulary 11

1 a) *4*
  b) 6
  c) 5
  d) 1
  e) 3
  f) 2

2 a) *clouds*
   b) thunder
   c) frozen
   d) shower
   e) blows
   f) sunshine
   g) wet
   h) lightning

3 a) *raining*
   b) sunny
   c) lightning
   d) freezing
   e) windy
   f) rain
   g) snowing

4 1) *B*
   2) A
   3) B
   4) C
   5) A
   6) B
   7) B
   8) C
   9) A
   10) B

Vocabulary 12

1 a) *hair*
   b) eye
   c) mouth
   d) arm
   e) hand
   f) foot
   g) leg
   h) finger
   i) nose
   j) ear

2 a) *legs*
   b) hand
   c) back
   d) hair
   e) nose
   f) fingers
   g) toes
   h) neck

3 a) *leg*
   b) hand
   c) foot
   d) eye
   e) arm
   f) waist
   g) head
   h) ear

4 a) *C*
   b) B
   c) A
   d) C
   e) B
   f) A

Vocabulary 13

1 a) *eye*
   b) soap
   c) have
   d) feet
   e) a cold
   f) have
   g) ill
   h) wash

2 a) *B*
   b) A
   c) C
   d) A
   e) B
   f) B
   g) A
   h) C
   i) C
   j) B

3 a) *healthy*
   b) well
   c) broken
   d) dangerous
   e) bleeding
   f) fit
   g) sore
   h) injured

4 a) *back ache*
   b) fever
   c) dizzy
   d) broken arm
   e) headache
   f) stomach ache
   g) cold
   h) sore throat

Vocabulary 14

1 a) *hill*
   b) tree
   c) lake
   d) fence
   e) field
   f) bush
   g) stream
   h) flower

2 a) *hill*
   b) river
   c) fields
   d) island
   e) lake
   f) beach
   g) country
   h) coast

3 a) *on*
   b) at
   c) in
   d) under
   e) at
   f) in
   g) on
   h) in

4 a) *river*
   b) field
   c) sea
   d) mountain
   e) forest
   f) island
   g) hill
   h) beach

Vocabulary 15

1 a) *stop*
   b) into
   c) trip
   d) on
   e) return
   f) home
   g) leave
   h) miss

2 a) *C*
   b) B
   c) B
   d) A
   e) B
   f) B
   g) C
   h) A
   i) B
   j) A

3 a) *bus*
   b) plane
   c) bike
   d) train
   e) car
   f) boat
   g) ship
   h) taxi

4 a) *plane*
   b) car
   c) ship
   d) bike
   e) bus
   f) boat
   g) train
   h) taxi

Vocabulary 16

1 a) *calculator*
   b) mobile phone
   c) camera
   d) dishwasher
   e) personal stereo
   f) video recorder
   g) kettle
   h) tin opener

2 a) *video recorder*
   b) tin opener
   c) camera
   d) mobile phone
   e) dishwasher
   f) calculator
   g) personal stereo
   h) kettle

3 a) *pencil*
   b) scissors
   c) locked
   d) went out
   e) washing
   f) tissues
   g) ruler
   h) clock

4 a) *C*
   b) A
   c) B
   d) C
   e) A
   f) C

Vocabulary 17

1 a) *passport*
   b) foreign
   c) continents
   d) map
   e) singing
   f) abroad
   g) dish
   h) trip
   i) takes off
   j) ranges

2 a) *to*
   b) in
   c) at
   d) in
   e) in
   f) to
   g) in
   h) at

3 a) *Italian*
   b) Spanish
   c) German
   d) French
   e) Greek
   f) Brazilian
   g) Swiss
   h) Turkish
   i) Polish
   j) Argentinian

4 a) *4*
   b) 1
   c) 6
   d) 8
   e) 3
   f) 2
   g) 5
   h) 7

5 a) *A*
   b) B
   c) C
   d) C
   e) C
   f) B
   g) A
   h) C

6 □ □   *Holland*
           England
           Poland

   □ □   Brazil
           Japan
           Iraq

   □ □ □   Malaysia
             New Zealand
             Morocco

   □ □ □   Singapore
             Bangladesh
             Pakistan

   □ □ □   Austria
             Germany
             Mexico

Vocabulary 18

1. a) *study*
    b) look it up
    c) homework
    d) teaches
    e) bookshelf
    f) hard
    g) absent
    h) failed

2. a) C
    b) A
    c) B
    d) C
    e) B
    f) A
    g) C
    h) B
    i) C
    j) B

3. a) *share*
    b) fail
    c) take
    d) copy
    e) explain
    f) mean
    g) have
    h) underline
    i) practise
    j) make

4. a) *lesson*
    b) term
    c) notes
    d) class
    e) attendance
    f) timetable
    g) break
    h) uniform
    i) subject
    j) project

Vocabulary 19

1. a) *record*
    b) swimming
    c) singers
    d) like
    e) to the cinema
    f) classical
    g) cartoon
    h) beat
    i) for a walk
    j) made an excuse

2. 1) B
    2) D
    3) C
    4) B
    5) C
    6) A
    7) A
    8) D
    9) B
    10) C

3. a) *health club*
    b) football club/stadium
    c) tennis club/court
    d) running club/track
    e) swimming club/pool
    f) playing field

4. (Suggested answers)
    a) *health club*
    b) swimming pool
    c) running track
    d) playing field
    e) football stadium
    f) tennis court

Vocabulary 20

1. a) *size*
    b) buy
    c) receipt
    d) money
    e) try
    f) closes
    g) loaf
    h) sign
    i) bag
    j) costs

2. a) 8
    b) 5
    c) 10
    d) 1
    e) 9
    f) 3
    g) 6
    h) 4
    i) 7
    j) 2

3. a) *At the newsagent's*
    b) At the post office
    c) At the chemist's
    d) At the butcher's
    e) A the grocer's
    f) At the travel agent's
    g) At the baker's
    h) At the café

4. a) A
    b) A
    c) C
    d) B
    e) A
    f) A
    g) B
    h) B

5. 1) D
    2) B
    3) A
    4) C
    5) B
    6) D
    7) D
    8) A
    9) C
    10) B